VOLUME 518

NOVEMBER 1991

THE ANNALS

of The American Academy *of* Political
and Social Science

RICHARD D. LAMBERT, *Editor*
ALAN W. HESTON, *Associate Editor*

RESOLVING REGIONAL CONFLICTS:

INTERNATIONAL PERSPECTIVES

Special Editor of this Volume

I. WILLIAM ZARTMAN

School of Advanced International Studies
Johns Hopkins University
Washington, D.C.

Ⓢ SAGE PUBLICATIONS   *NEWBURY PARK   LONDON   NEW DELHI*

THE ANNALS

© 1991 *by* The American Academy *of* Political *and* Social Science

Editorial Office: 3937 Chestnut Street, Philadelphia, PA 19104.

For information about membership* (individuals only) and subscriptions (institutions), address:

SAGE PUBLICATIONS, INC.
2455 Teller Road
Newbury Park, CA 91320

From India and South Asia,
write to:
SAGE PUBLICATIONS INDIA Pvt. Ltd.
P.O. Box 4215
New Delhi 110 048
INDIA

From the UK, Europe, the Middle
East and Africa, write to:
SAGE PUBLICATIONS LTD
6 Bonhill Street
London EC2A 4PU
UNITED KINGDOM

SAGE Production Staff: LINDA GRAY, LIANN LECH, and JANELLE LeMASTER
*Please note that members of The Academy receive THE ANNALS with their membership.
Library of Congress Catalog Card Number 90-63944
International Standard Serial Number ISSN 0002-7162
International Standard Book Number ISBN 0-8039-4252-4 (Vol. 518, 1991 paper)
International Standard Book Number ISBN 0-8039-4251-6 (Vol. 518, 1991 cloth)
Manufactured in the United States of America. First printing, November 1991.

The articles appearing in THE ANNALS are indexed in *Book Review Index, Public Affairs Information Service Bulletin, Social Sciences Index, Current Contents, General Periodicals Index, Academic Index, Pro-Views,* and *Combined Retrospective Index Sets.* They are also abstracted and indexed in *ABC Pol Sci, Historical Abstracts, Human Resources Abstracts, Social Sciences Citation Index, United States Political Science Documents, Social Work Research & Abstracts, Sage Urban Studies Abstracts, International Political Science Abstracts, America: History and Life, Sociological Abstracts, Managing Abstracts, Social Planning/Policy & Development Abstracts, Automatic Subject Citation Alert, Book Review Digest, Work Related Abstracts,* and/or *Family Resources Database,* and are available on microfilm from University Microfilms, Ann Arbor, Michigan.

Information about membership rates, institutional subscriptions, and back issue prices may be found on the facing page.

Advertising. Current rates and specifications may be obtained by writing to THE ANNALS Advertising and Promotion Manager at the Newbury Park office (address above).

Claims. Claims for undelivered copies must be made no later than three months following month of publication. The publisher will supply missing copies when losses have been sustained in transit and when the reserve stock will permit.

Change of Address. Six weeks' advance notice must be given when notifying of change of address to ensure proper identification. Please specify name of journal. Send address changes to: THE ANNALS, c/o Sage Publications, Inc., 2455 Teller Road, Newbury Park, CA 91320.

The American Academy of Political and Social Science

3937 Chestnut Street   Philadelphia, Pennsylvania 19104

Origin and Purpose. The Academy was organized December 14, 1889, to promote the progress of political and social science, especially through publications and meetings. The Academy does not take sides in controverted questions, but seeks to gather and present reliable information to assist the public in forming an intelligent and accurate judgment.

Meetings. The Academy holds an annual meeting in the spring extending over two days.

Publications. THE ANNALS is the bimonthly publication of The Academy. Each issue contains articles on some prominent social or political problem, written at the invitation of the editors. Also, monographs are published from time to time, numbers of which are distributed to pertinent professional organizations. These volumes constitute important reference works on the topics with which they deal, and they are extensively cited by authorities throughout the United States and abroad. The papers presented at the meetings of The Academy are included in THE ANNALS.

Membership. Each member of The Academy receives THE ANNALS and may attend the meetings of The Academy. Membership is open only to individuals. Annual dues: $39.00 for the regular paperbound edition (clothbound, $54.00). California residents must add 7.25% sales tax on all orders ($41.82 paperbound; $57.91 clothbound). Add $9.00 per year for membership outside the U.S.A. Members may also purchase single issues of THE ANNALS for $12.00 each (clothbound, $17.00). California residents: $12.87 paperbound, $18.23 clothbound. Add $1.50 for shipping and handling on all prepaid orders.

Subscriptions. THE ANNALS (ISSN 0002-7162) is published six times annually—in January, March, May, July, September, and November. Institutions may subscribe to THE ANNALS at the annual rate: $120.00 (clothbound, $144.00). California institutions: $128.70 paperbound, $155.44 clothbound. Add $9.00 per year for subscriptions outside the U.S.A. Institutional rates for single issues: $23.00 each (clothbound, $28.00). California institutions: $24.66 paperbound, $30.03 clothbound.

Second class postage paid at Thousand Oaks, California, and at additional mailing offices.

Single issues of THE ANNALS may be obtained by individuals who are not members of The Academy for $15.95 each (clothbound, $25.00). California residents: $17.10 paperbound, $26.81 clothbound. Add $1.50 for shipping and handling on all prepaid orders. Single issues of THE ANNALS have proven to be excellent supplementary texts for classroom use. Direct inquiries regarding adoptions to THE ANNALS c/o Sage Publications (address below).

All correspondence concerning membership in The Academy, dues renewals, inquiries about membership status, and/or purchase of single issues of THE ANNALS should be sent to THE ANNALS c/o Sage Publications, Inc., 2455 Teller Road, Newbury Park, CA 91320. Telephone: (805) 499-0721; FAX/Order line: (805) 499-0871. *Please note that orders under $30 must be prepaid.* Sage affiliates in London and India will assist institutional subscribers abroad with regard to orders, claims, and inquiries for both subscriptions and single issues.

THE ANNALS

of The American Academy *of* Political *and* Social Science

RICHARD D. LAMBERT, *Editor*
ALAN W. HESTON, *Associate Editor*

———————————— FORTHCOMING ————————————

CHINA'S FOREIGN RELATIONS
Special Editor: Allen S. Whiting
Volume 519   January 1992

WORLD LITERACY IN THE YEAR 2000
Special Editors: Daniel A. Wagner and Laurel D. Puchner
Volume 520   March 1992

DRUG ABUSE: LINKING POLICY AND RESEARCH
Special Editor: Eric Wish
Volume 521   May 1992

See page 3 for information on Academy membership and
purchase of single volumes of **The Annals.**

CONTENTS

BOOK DEPARTMENT CONTENTS

PREFACE

The Persian Gulf war has thrust regional conflict onto the consciousness of the post-Cold War world. For those used to seeing the Third World as a playground only for East-West rivalries, the conflict was a surprise. The rivalries were gone but the war was worse than ever. Rather than the end of history, the withdrawal of world communism from the global fray seemed to signal a new international disorder, where even the restraints and conventions of the bipolar system melted away before unbridled local rapacity. Whereas formerly, superpowers and their allies would restrain their clients or would help their clients restrain the clients of their rivals, the successive Iraqi adventures were undertaken in the belief that the aggressor could get away with them because the object of the attack—Khomeini's Iran, al-Sabah's Kuwait—could no longer call in superpower reinforcements. The counterpoint had to be made, lengthily and ambiguously in the first case, brutally in the second.

Both aspects of those experiences call for further discussion. How can we understand regional conflict in the Third World—where the stakes appear quite different from the historic clash of values behind the Cold War—in such a way that the conflicts can be reduced? What agencies, including cooperation between the former Cold War rivals, can promote peaceful management and settlement of such conflict? This collection of articles addresses those questions. It does so through specific discussions of causes and resolution, and of mechanisms for management, with a section in between that examines six different instances of regional conflict from different points of analysis, to provide a case base for the discussion.

The discussion is not only multiple in its approaches to the complex subject; it also seeks to provide the maximum diversity by involving analysts from many different national perspectives. Many of the chapters are written by Americans, but others are prepared by Soviets, and in addition there are British, Israeli, Lebanese, Egyptian, and Afghan authors. Some of the analysts are or have been practitioners of foreign policy. Analysis cannot be contained within national boundaries, but neither can it avoid reflecting the location and experience of the author. The outcome of having a mix of nationalities can only be a richer discussion. The articles presented here are the result of two international research projects centered at the Nitze School of Advanced International Studies of the Johns Hopkins University, one on conflict reduction in regional conflict, supported by the Carnegie Corporation, and the other on negotiating internal conflict, supported by the MacArthur Foundation.

THE ARGUMENT

Regional conflicts can be viewed in many different ways, with the differences suggesting different ways of reducing and managing them. Resolution is usually beyond the grasp of human hands, needing time to heal the wounds of conflict. But a reduction of the means of conflict and a conversion of the conflict from violent to normal political and diplomatic means are the goals of conflict management. If conflicts are regarded as a clash of wills, management involves finding a formula that turns a zero-sum (win-lose) perception of the situation into a positive-sum (win-win) potentiality. If conflict is seen as a confrontation of cost-benefit calculations, then management depends on finding or creating a ripe moment from a mutually hurting stalemate. If conflict is seen as an event in regime change, then management means easing the transition from a collapsing regime to a stable replacement. If conflict takes the form of a mutual standoff based on a sustainable but asymmetrical struggle, as is typically the case in internal conflicts that often lie at the heart of regional disputes, then management requires a use of that power asymmetry to find corresponding reformulations of the outcomes. All of these general notions for deductive use are explored in the first two articles in this collection.

A second approach to the subject is provided by an inductive look at some important regional conflicts that have undergone attempts at management but that still remain alive in one form or another. In all cases, a formerly stable arrangement or regime collapsed as expectations and power relations shifted, requiring a new settlement between newly empowered parties. In Angola, major elements of the decolonization conflict were resolved in the paired agreement on Cuban withdrawal from Angola and South African withdrawal from Namibia, but national reconciliation in Angola itself between the warring factions of the national liberation movement remained for other negotiation. In Afghanistan, too, the conflict exists on two levels; the one on the international level brought on by the Soviet invasion was resolved by superpower agreement, whereas the internal conflict continues despite desultory efforts at negotiation. In Eritrea, a conflict over decolonization once thought to be resolved with the Ethiopian federation reemerged when the federation was unilaterally abolished; the ensuing thirty-year war of the Eritreans threatens to bring down the entire Ethiopian state. In Lebanon, the power-sharing regime between confessional groups collapsed into civil war, Syrian invasion, and, finally, a Syrian-dominated truce that sharply illustrates the distinction between management and resolution. In Cyprus, the decolonizing formula over power sharing between Greek and Turkish Cypriots never held, and a whole binational history of conflict needs to be de-escalated as part of a management process preceding a new resolving formula. Similarly, the decolonization of Palestine, thought to be have been resolved in 1947 through partition, has evolved into interstate, regional, and even global proportions, requiring some creative thinking about trade-offs in order to get a management process started again. All of these cases in the second section of this volume tell their story of conflict and the requirement for management and resolution, illustrating elements in the articles of the first section.

The end of the Cold War has signaled a new interest in Soviet-American cooperation in managing regional conflict, since Soviet-American rivalry was held responsible for exacerbating, if not creating, such conflicts in the past. The mechanisms for helping to manage such conflicts are numerous, even if none has clear jurisdiction or uncontested power. The development of regional organizations as little United Nations organizations within a part of the globe that shares a common identification parallels the growth of regional conflicts. Some of these organizations are balance-of-power alliances against an endemic aggressor, whereas others are collective security organizations that try to handle conflict within their own midst. Codes of conduct and rules for cooperation were tried in the détente of the 1970s and more informally in specific functions and areas, but the post-Cold War era probably lends itself more to the more gradual evolution of such codes than to their specific negotiation. The establishment of rules and codes is also paralleled by the increasing use of organizations, above all the United Nations, in the institutionalization of superpower cooperation. It also requires a clear but informal understanding of the nature of power and leverage available to the superpowers—in regional conflicts where, the Persian Gulf notwithstanding, their power is not always super—and also of the balance involvement and distribution of interests that cooperation requires. On the other hand, realistic appreciation of the potentialities for such cooperation also requires an appreciation of the unequal nature of the two former rivals and the limits on their parallel action, stemming from different commitments to democracy and limited ability to control third parties. In some regional conflicts, holding off may be a preferable strategy for the superpowers to weighing in. The end of the Cold War does not guarantee the end of the local dimension to conflict. These arguments run through the third part of the collection, and return the argument to its starting point. Whatever the size, shape, or name of a Russia/USSR, consideration of this topic will long remain relevant.

I. WILLIAM ZARTMAN

ANNALS, *AAPSS,* **518,** November 1991

Conflict and Resolution:
Contest, Cost, and Change

By I. WILLIAM ZARTMAN

ABSTRACT: Regional conflicts can be thought of in three different ways, each suggesting a different approach to their resolution. One is as a clash of conflicting unilateral solutions, which then require a formula for a joint or multilateral outcome satisfactory to both parties. A second is as a succession of opposing policies based on cost-benefit calculations, which then require a ripe moment—comprising specific components of mutually hurting stalemate, impending catastrophe, and a formula for a way out—for resolution. A third is as an event in a process of change, requiring the negotiation of a new regime to replace an old one that previously embodied certain expectations and behaviors. These different notions are illustrated with many examples of regional conflicts and their attempted—and sometimes successful—resolution.

I. William Zartman is Jacob Blaustein Professor of International Organization and Conflict Resolution at the Nitze School of Advanced International Studies of the Johns Hopkins University in Washington, D.C. His doctorate in international relations is from Yale, and he has a diploma from the University of Copenhagen. His latest publication is Negotiating Internal Conflict *(1991).*

NOTE: An expanded version of this article will appear as chapter 20 in *International Negotiation: Analysis, Approaches, Issues,* ed. Victor Kremenyuk (San Francisco: Jossey-Bass, 1991).

REGIONAL conflicts present a real challenge for the maintenance of world order and the resolution and management of international political issues. Such conflicts often involve basic values of territorial integrity and political independence as well as the domestic political consolidation and international rivalries of recently independent countries in the Third World. As such they are not trivial. Their stakes are often typical of the high political values that have characterized state building in more established states and have animated the growth of the world political system. Furthermore, they frequently involve external powers, and sometimes superpowers themselves, called in to lend strength to the parties to the conflict or inserting themselves because of their own perceived interests in the parties or the outcomes. Since regional conflicts involve serious stakes for the parties and carry with them the danger of transcending the original actors and becoming no longer merely regional, they deserve serious attention.

An understanding of the mechanisms and possibilities of regional conflict reduction can be gained by linking management and resolution to theories of conflict itself.[1] A very basic notion sees conflict as a simple contest of parties each trying to impose a unilateral solution to a problem. In this view, conflict management and resolution mean finding a multilateral solution to the problem

that replaces the attempt of each to impose its will. The second notion sees conflict as an exercise in which parties will do what they want as long as the cost-benefit ratio stays below a certain level. Rather than contending with others as a source of conflict, parties contend with themselves. Conflict management and resolution then become a matter of comparing costs and benefits by calculating the opportunities offered by circumstances as viewed from each side. In this view, as opposed to the first, conflict, and its resolution, is not just a matter of contending wills but of the costs and advantages inherent in the context at any given time.

The third notion of conflict is both more complex and more benign. It sees conflict as the result of changes in patterns of world order or regimes and not just of contending wills or more or less costly contexts. Accepted patterns of action are continually challenged, but at some point, they begin to break down, the requirements of the new situation have to be identified, and a new order has to be established. The process is both lengthy and uncertain, and yet neither resolution nor even management of specific conflicts takes on meaning and durability only as part of regime testing and formation. Conflict and conflict reduction become part of an evolutionary process.

Each of the views of conflict and the measures of conflict reduction that they suggest fit into the following approach, providing a nest of concepts by which to analyze situations and appropriate responses.

1. Cf. Dean Pruitt and Jeffrey Rubin, *Social Conflict* (New York: Random House, 1986), pp. 89-96, 109.

FORMULAS FOR MULTILATERAL SOLUTIONS

Since cooperation requires compromise over ends and means, people prefer to accomplish their objectives by themselves whenever possible. The desire to act alone may sound out of place in an interdependent world, but it is basic to the egotistical nature of rational actors. In Namibia, Vietnam, Algeria, the Falklands, Palestine, Kuwait, Afghanistan, the Western Sahara, the Horn of Africa, and elsewhere, the party in possession at any time has wanted to be able to solve the problem unilaterally, by holding on and denying the claims or even the existence of the challenging party. The latter, in turn, feeling itself driven to desperation, wants to resolve the problem in its own unilateral fashion. When the two attempts at unilateral resolution run up against each other, there is conflict, and either one side can prevail or the conflict must be resolved by negotiation.

Seen in these terms, conflict management and resolution become an effort to make multilateral outcomes more attractive than unilateral ones. The usual concept of negotiation, as a process of exchanging concessions or reaching below the bottom line, makes negotiation sound like half a defeat and does not provide guidelines for making multilateral outcomes enticing. It is no surprise that negotiations conducted primarily as a mutual-concession process often come to naught, as seen in Cyprus and the Falklands. Conflict resolution involves finding a formula for agreement, conceived as a common definition of the problem and a principle of justice or terms of trade that can frame a solution.[2] Backing up these positive measures, but insufficient in themselves, are negative pressures to make multilateral solutions more attractive. The negative pressures lower parties' expectations and security points, outcomes obtained without negotiation.

Parties turn to multilateral solutions when unilateral solutions are out of reach. Unilateral solutions become impossible because of inadequate unilateral resources, because of effective counteraction by another party, or because of the innate impossibility of carrying out the action—like a handshake—alone. Often an adversary may prefer to forgo the outcome if the other party cannot be kept from sharing in it—the adversary refuses to have a handshake if it means recognition, for example. This is a particularly frequent perception when the outcome is to be a newly created good and therefore one that the party has lived without all along anyhow. Unresolved border disputes at a low level of hostilities—such as Morocco-Algeria, Ethiopia-Sudan, but even Iran-Iraq, where the level was not low—are an example. Palestine, the Falklands, and Cyprus are excellent examples of continuing conflicts in which parties cling to the vain hope of resolving the issue by themselves and refuse to do it jointly

2. The notion of formula is developed in I. William Zartman and Maureen Berman, *The Practical Negotiator* (New Haven, CT: Yale University Press, 1982); I. William Zartman, ed., *The Negotiation Process* (Beverly Hills, CA: Sage, 1978).

with the other party, who has a veto on its ultimate settlement.

The party that wants the multilateral solution must show the unilateralist that there is a solution available that will leave the other better off, not just through the end of a costly conflict but through a multilateral outcome that is attractive for the other party, and that it is willing and able to grant the other side a solution in exchange for recognition of its own place as part of the problem. The examples are not as frequent as one might like; however, Somalia can serve as one. Somalia's management of its conflict with Djibouti has come through its renunciation of its territorial claim in exchange for Ethiopian renunciation of a counterclaim, leaving Djibouti independent and the Djibouti Somalis a dominant force in the independent political system. Similar trade-offs were discussed in the 1986-88 conflict management arrangements with Ethiopia, a conflict still awaiting its resolution.[3]

A salient case of regional conflict management that has been treated as a search for a formula capable of enticing the parties away from competing attempts at imposing a unilateral solution is the Israeli-Palestinian conflict.[4] The first two decades of

3. I. William Zartman, *Ripe for Resolution: Conflict and Intervention in Africa*, 2d ed. (New York: Oxford University Press, 1989), chap. 3.

4. See Jeffrey Rubin, ed., *The Dynamics of Third Party Intervention* (New York: Praeger, 1981); S. Aronson, *Conflict and Bargaining in the Middle East* (Baltimore, MD: Johns Hopkins University Press, 1978); Saadia Touval, *The Peace Brokers* (Princeton, NJ: Princeton University Press, 1982); William B. Quandt, *Camp David: Peacemaking and Politics* (Washington, DC: Brookings Institution, 1986); Ga-

the conflict were punctuated by wars and other vain attempts to make division palatable. But the third decade was opened by the articulation of a formula—"territory for security"—in U.N. Security Council Resolution 242 and its implementation along the Syrian and, above all, the Egyptian borders. Unfortunately, the fourth decade was wasted in trying to apply the formula to the Lebanese and Jordanian borders, where it did not fit because territory and security were not the predominant ingredients of the situation. A new formula is needed, which also takes into account population and juridical entity, in order to apply to the Palestinian part of the conflict. Nonetheless, "territory for security" stands as a particularly concise example of a trade-off formula, serving as the basis for general formula notions such as normalization around established boundaries, an overarching definition of a goal designed to make a multilateral solution possible and more attractive than mutually frustrating attempts at imposing a unilateral solution.

In the same vein, the trade-offs proposed in the article in this *Annals* issue by Zviagelskaia as a basis for a formula for a solution to the Palestinian problem, where the Palestinian right to return is acknowledged in exchange for the Israeli right to remain, translates a large sense of impartial justice—equivalent exchanges—and also a broader sense of a future bistate situation in which two populations coexist, juxtaposed and intermingled. Although obviously not yet a reality, this

briel Ben Dor and David Dewitt, eds., *Conflict Management in the Middle East* (Lexington, MA: D. C. Heath, 1987).

formula could represent a goal at which to aim.

The Panama Canal dispute is another case of regional conflict that has been resolved through the search for appropriate formulas.[5] It took Panama a decade after the flag riots of 1964 to impress the United States with the fact that contested unilateral operation based on the 1903 treaty would be so costly as to be impossible. Thereupon, the two states turned to an effort, beginning with the Tack principles in 1973, to set up a formula that would combine elements that were important to each of the parties. The resulting formula, "use in exchange for sovereignty, with paired defense," served as a set of guidelines for the subsequent details of the treaty.

The conflict over Namibian independence was ended through a search based on successive formulas for a just, balanced outcome.[6] However, the formula that underlay the first attempt—"one-person-one-vote elections under UN and South African auspices"—while just in terms of current international law, did not contain equivalent trade-offs for both sides and so was not sufficient to entice all of the parties away from their

efforts to impose a unilateral solution. Originally formulated as U.N. Security Council Resolution 435, it provided a way to independence for Namibia but no compensations for South Africa that would make the outcome in any way attractive. But when Namibia was linked with Angola, and the formula was extended to a trade-off providing mutual military withdrawal from both territories, the framework for an agreement attractive to both sides was available. It would have taken a fully paired set of trade-offs, providing not just mutual military withdrawal but also paired one-person-one-vote elections, to cover all the issues of the two conflicts—not only Namibian independence and Cuban troops but also Angolan national reconciliation. Such a comprehensive settlement did not come about until two and a half years later, in June 1991.

Formula alone, however, does not explain the entire process of managing or resolving regional conflicts. Potential formulas and trade-offs are lying around for the taking, and often the final resolving package for a dispute is found in the archives of the early discussions of the problem. "NIBMAR"—"No Independence before Majority African Rule"—was launched as a slogan as early as the time of the unilateral declaration of independence of Rhodesia to bar attempts at compromise; when real independence finally came 14 years later, it was based on the NIBMAR formula.[7] Regional autonomy and a trade-off of economic cooperation for

5. William Jorden, *Panama Odyssey* (Austin: University of Texas Press, 1984); W. Mark Habeeb, *Power and Tactics in International Negotiation* (Baltimore, MD: Johns Hopkins University Press, 1988); W. Mark Habeeb and I. William Zartman, *The Panama Canal Negotiations* (Washington, DC: Johns Hopkins University, Nitze School of Advanced International Studies, 1986); Diane Bendahman and John McDonald, eds., *Perspectives on Negotiation* (Washington, DC: Department of State, Foreign Service Institute, 1986).

6. Zartman, *Ripe for Resolution*, chap. 5.

7. Steven Stedman, *Peacemaking in Civil War: International Mediation in Zimbabwe* (Boulder, CO: Lynne Rienner, 1991).

a confirming referendum have been mooted as a fair formula for resolving the Western Sahara conflict involving Morocco and Algeria ever since its beginning in the mid-1970s, but it was not scheduled to be implemented until 1991.[8] Something more than mere enticements to a positive-sum solution on a multilateral track is clearly needed.

RIPE MOMENTS FOR
CONFLICT RESOLUTION

A more time-oriented view of conflict goes beyond the notion of absolute incompatibilities of will and solutions and posits the idea that at any moment policies are chosen from among many desirable goals on the basis of comparative costs and benefits. Since these can be altered by both the external context and the parties' interactions, some moments are better than others for managing and resolving conflict. Thus the course of the conflict itself can be an effective influence on its management, and an evaluation of when and how to use carrots and sticks is important to an assessment of the possibilities for resolution. In this approach, the life cycle of the conflict, including its intensification, escalation, turning points, and crises, is as important in determining the chances of settlement as are the various outcomes.

The basic component of a ripe moment is a deadlock that keeps both parties from achieving their goals.[9]

But deadlock alone is not enough; it must be a particular kind of stalemate that hurts both parties enough to make them feel uncomfortable and unable to break out by an escalation with acceptable costs. But a mutually hurting stalemate is not enough either; in order to be effective, it generally needs to be riveted to the parties' perception through a recent or looming catastrophe that acts as a deadline or is remembered as a warning and that threatens to impose additional and unacceptable costs of a higher magnitude. But even this is not enough; it is not helpful to be painted into a corner, even a stifling one, if there is no way out. Finally, there must be not only a formula for a way out but an indication that the parties are willing in principle to choose it if it is attractive enough and that they will respond positively to the other's moves in that direction—a trait that can be termed "requitement."

It is a message of utmost importance, particularly in the light of the Persian Gulf crisis of 1990-91, that carrots or sticks alone will not get a party to the bargaining table. The two are required, as the model for the ripe moment suggests: the stalemate must be tight and hurting, reinforced by additional sticks if necessary, but there must also be inducements to choose the negotiated way out rather than make vain stabs at escalation. Furthermore, there is a particular characteristic to the laying on of

---

8. Zartman, *Ripe for Resolution*, chap. 2.

9. Ibid., chap. 6; George Modelski, "International Settlement of Internal War," in *International Aspects of Civil Strife*, ed. James

Rosenau (Princeton, NJ: Princeton University Press, 1964); Elmer Jackson, *Meeting of the Minds* (New York: McGraw Hill, 1952); Oran Young, *The Intermediaries* (Princeton, NJ: Princeton University Press, 1967).

sticks and escalation that produces the beginnings of movement. One party often seeks to escalate its way out of the stalemate only to be caught in an overly costly, unsuccessful attempt that it cannot maintain; the other party can contribute to the final ripening of the moment through an "escalation to raise," pointedly indicating its intent merely to produce a stalemate and pointedly refraining from escalating so far as to invite counterescalation.[10]

A number of regional conflicts have been handled in these terms. The war in the Western Sahara was waged on the basis of cost-benefit calculations, with the Polisario fighting on in the expectation that the burdens of the war would topple the Moroccan monarchy.[11] Instead, a stalemate was produced, but the threat of a catastrophe was largely removed by repeated Moroccan-Algerian agreements not to fight each other directly. Only when a number of external events weighed in, such as the fall of oil prices and the impending loss of European markets, and Morocco's defensive wall in the desert plus superpower disinterest blocked further chances of escalation, did the mutually hurting stalemate evolve, and even then it took the U.N. secretary-general and Saudi Arabia to provide parts of a way out in order for the possibilities of management leading toward resolution to appear. Yet the

absence of a real looming catastrophe and the uncertainty of requitement made it a real challenge to make that possibility a reality before the end of the secretary-general's term in 1992, the deadline that he had set for himself.

Cost-benefit analysis also explains why a settlement in Namibia and its neighbor, Angola, appeared when it did. Characterized initially as conflict management without conflict, the Namibian struggle for independence did not develop the possibilities for a mutually hurting stalemate or for a balanced formula attractive to both sides until the early 1980s, when explicit linkage brought in the Angolan problem as well, providing both a countervailing benefit and a gradually increasing cost for South Africa. Even then it was not until 1987 that the fully ripe moment appeared, based on a worsening economic situation for both sides and formed by a sudden escalation to call by the movement of a vastly increased number of Cuban troops to the Namibian border, providing both the hurting stalemate, the impending catastrophe, and a desire for a way out. The latter was crystallized by a formula provided both by the compound mediator and by the U.N. Secretariat.

The Zimbabwean conflict has been the subject of a serious debate over the question of a hurting stalemate, with some claims that the final agreement was snatched from the jaws of victory and defeat rather than from a mutually hurting stalemate.[12] Yet the

---

10. I. William Zartman, "Power Strategies in Deescalation," in *Timing and Deescalation*, ed. Louis Kriesberg (Syracuse, NY: Syracuse University Press, forthcoming).

11. Zartman, *Ripe for Resolution*, chap. 2; John Damis, *Conflict in Northwest Africa* (Stanford, CA: Hoover Institution Press, 1983).

12. Stedman, *Peacemaking in Civil War*; Robert Matthews, "From Rhodesia to Zimbabwe," in *Managing Regional Conflict*, ed.

debate may well be less sharp than would appear, since the case is an example of a hurting stalemate in a more dynamic sense; Zimbabwe is a case where stalemate was born of asymmetry, where a previously stronger side was weakening and a previously weaker side growing stronger, yet with victory still out of the short-term reach of the latter and the capacity to do damage still available to the former. The dynamic stalemate was dramatically exemplified in the situation after the war of October 1973 in the Middle East, where again the comeuppance to the formerly dominant power and the momentary surge of the reputedly weaker power, coupled with the mutual encirclement of the two armies on the banks of the Suez Canal, produced a mutually hurting stalemate in both symmetrical and dynamic terms. Costs and benefits were key to the calculations of the parties and to the tactics of the mediator.

The Iran-Iraq war was resolved on the basis of a cost-benefit analysis and a sense of the ripe moment. The stalemate grew out of the collapse of Iranian arms sources after both sides had been worn out by nine years of brutal war; the catastrophe was seen in the possibility of an Iraqi chemical missile raid on Tehran. Requitement was shown in Iraq's earlier acceptance of U.N. cease-fire plans in 1982 and 1987, contingent on Iranian acceptance, which was finally obtained through Iraqi escalation to call at the

Fen Osler Hampson and Brian Mandell, *International Journal* 45(2) (Spring 1990); Jeffrey Davidow, *A Peace in Southern Africa* (Boulder, CO: Westview Press, 1984); Bendahman and McDonald, eds., *Perspectives on Negotiation*.

end of 1987 and early 1988. Again, the U.N. secretary-general provided the formula for an agreement, finally enacted in 1991, when the regional agenda changed and Iraq needed Iran more as an ally than as an enemy.

The cost-benefit notion of conflict leads to a clearer understanding of the conditions of management and resolution and of the relation between the two. It also raises some of the important dilemmas of the business: Is conflict the only way to get to resolution? Must relations be pushed to war and costly encounters before obvious formulas in the public domain can be adopted? Once the means of carrying out the conflict have been managed, what is the incentive for resolution? Analysts and practitioners are still looking for ways through these dilemmas.

CONFLICT AS REGIME CHANGE

In the third approach, conflict and resolution are two sides of the same coin. As in the previous approaches, this one includes the others in its broader coverage. It sees conflict as an earthquake, a shifting of structures and relations that produces strains to the point where a specific restructuring is required. The structure can be thought of by using the current notion of regimes, the rules and routines that govern behavior around specific issues in international—or other sociopolitical—relations.[13] Regimes are not only pat-

13. Stephen Krasner, ed., *International Regimes* (Ithaca, NY: Cornell University Press, 1983); Oran Young, *International Cooperation: Building Regimes for Natural Resources and*

terns of behavior; they reflect power structures and regulate them at the same time. The broadest regimes are actually structures of world order, such as the colonial system or regional hegemonies.

Regimes are continually under challenge and are reaffirmed when they successfully overcome those challenges and reassert their structures and habits. But at times the challenges accumulate and begin to represent growing structural shifts, new issues, or an exhaustion of old answers. Forces favored by the existent regime exert their usual efforts to repel the challenges, with less and less success. An interregnum appears, in which new alternatives are proposed, debated, tried, discarded, and defended. During this process, structural relations continue to shift, until gradually the basis of a new regime is formed. Negotiation is necessary to create the replacement regime and have it accepted since there is no authority or decision rule in international relations to formalize a new order.

An understanding of the management and resolution of regional conflict within this ripening context brings in a number of crucial elements that the other approaches to conflict do not use or analyze. Conflicts are not resolved if the resolutions do not take into account the power relations between the parties, and they are unlikely to be durable if they are isolated from general routines, rules, and behaviors associated

the Environment (Ithaca, NY: Cornell University Press, 1989); idem, "The Politics of International Regime Formation," International Organization, 43(3):349-75 (May 1989).

with other, similar conflicts. Placing negotiations in an evolving context of regime change also helps explain why the search for a resolution takes so long. A shift from an old regime to a new one is an evolutionary process based on changes in reality that themselves take time, and it incorporates necessarily slow, incomplete, debated, and resisted changes in perceptions instead of unambiguous realities.

In this process of regime change, regional conflicts are eruptions that mark the challenges and changes in regimes. The Zimbabwean conflict, which has served as an example of analysis for the preceding two approaches, can also be interpreted as a case of ripening conflict and regime transition. Rhodesia was one of the last holdouts to challenge the collapse of the colonial order and its replacement by a large number of interacting, juridically independent and equal states. The Rhodesian attempt at a unilateral declaration of independence was the last effort to preserve the old regime under a new uniform; the subsequent effort at an internal settlement was part of the process of eliminating prominent alternatives before negotiating a settlement within the new regime. The guerrilla struggle, led by the Patriotic Front and its armies, forced the parties after 1965 to recognize the need for a new regime but also imposed a readjustment of the power relations in the country. Conflict resolution at Lancaster House in 1979, then, did not take place in a vacuum; its success was not predetermined, but its outcome was, since the direction of the settlement was indicated by the evolution of the applicable regime.

The conflict in Cyprus, another special case in regime transition, began as an instance of decolonization in 1960 but then turned into a series of attempts at finding an appropriate institutional structure for a binational state.[14] Since the independence formula included Britain, Greece, and Turkey as guarantors, the possibilities of competitive intervention were always available to be invoked by local forces who wished to improve the formula in their favor. As a result, independence was repeatedly compromised; the colonial conflict was resolved by the negotiations for an independent regime, but the binational conflict was not, and attempts to try out alternatives and adjust new power relations destroyed the original independence formula. Rothman's article in this *Annals* issue examines the lengths to which parties must be taken at the present stage of the conflict to be able to restructure their perceptions and search for a new regime.

Central America is a different case, where the independence regime established at the beginning of the nineteenth century to replace the previous colonial regime was soon transformed into a hegemonic regime based on dominance by the United States in collaboration with national elites of the region.[15] The Panama Canal dispute concerned an instance of colonization within, not of, a country. An attempt to provide a new treaty in 1967 was, like the Rhodesian internal settlement, a flawed effort at a resolving formula; the alternative had to be eliminated and it failed because it simply did not address the outstanding issues. Beyond the first approach, a new regime was needed because the world notion of legitimate relations had changed and Panama now had the legitimate power to make the canal inoperable. The 1977 treaty reflected these changes.

The Honduran conflict of 1954 was an attempt to break the old hegemonic regime, but it failed. In the Central American conflicts of the 1980s, centered around the Nicaraguan revolution and responses to it, the Arias and Esquipulas plans were attempts to set up a new security regime for the region and are still being elaborated and tested.[16] The situation bears marks of a hurting stalemate, also a sign of changing power relations.

Even in the absence of full regime transition and conflict resolution, regional conflict management can focus on the use of secondary regimes. Confidence-building measures and small security regimes are arrangements that permit de-escalation when ac-

1987); Liisa North and Tin Draimin, "The Decay of the Security Regime in Latin America," in *Managing Regional Conflict*, ed. Hampson and Mandell.

    14. Bendahman and McDonald, eds., *Perspectives on Negotiation*.

    15. Morris Blachman et al., *Confronting Revolution: Security through Diplomacy in Central America* (New York: Pantheon, 1986); R. Fagen, *Forging Peace: The Challenge of Central America* (New York: Basil Blackwell,

    16. P. Terrence Hopmann, "Negotiating Peace in Central America," *Negotiation Journal*, 4(4):361-80 (Oct. 1988); Bruce Bagley and Juan Tokatlian, *Contadora: The Limits of Negotiation* (Washington, DC: Johns Hopkins University, Nitze School of Advanced International Studies, 1987).

tual resolution is not yet possible. Thus Ethiopia and Somalia provided for a set of rules of interstate behavior in the years 1986-88 to reduce the heat of the conflict and prepare for its subsequent resolution. The same thing happened in 1967, but when the de-escalation did not produce any further results a decade later, Somalia reescalated and went to war.[17] A more complicated security regime was established between Israel and Egypt in first a simple form in 1956, to be removed in 1967 and then restored in greater complexity in 1974 and 1975, leading to the basis of conflict resolution in 1979.[18]

The shape of the agreement is best analyzed through the concept of a formula that then determines the implementing details; the timing of the agreements is best seen through the notion of the ripe moment; but the evolving relationship is best seen as a security regime for changing alternatives and power relations between the two countries.[19]

CONCLUSION

The current Persian Gulf crisis rudely reminds us that it is possible to have a clear understanding of a conflict in all its forms without gaining much insight into appropriate ways of conflict resolution. Regional conflict in the gulf—and indeed even linked to include the Palestinian problem as well—can be understood as a clash of unilateral pursuits of incompatible goals, as a cost-benefit exercise awaiting a ripe moment, and as a search for new systems of world order or at least as an attempt to take advantage of a breakdown in an old system not yet replaced by a new one. Yet formulas, ripe moments, and benign processes of regime change do not easily exorcize the conflict. The missing element is a desire to use the available ways of doing so, rather than taking advantage of an apparently ripe moment for escalating the conflict itself.

The situation recalls the distinction introduced in the classic work of Nicolson on diplomacy between the warrior and the shopkeeper.[20] The first was the leader who pursued conflict to victory alone, the second the leader who pursued conflict to a mutually satisfactory solution. In terms of modern game theory so helpful to thinking on conflict management and negotiation, the first sought zero-sum or win-lose situations and outcomes; the second, positive-sum or win-win results. Nicolson's warning, on the eve of World War II, was that a shopkeeper should not negotiate with a warrior. The nagging question, which he never answered, was, How to turn a warrior into a shopkeeper? There are indeed some conflicts, or some actors' views of conflict, that have moved beyond a search for solu-

17. Touval, *Peace Brokers*; Thomas J. Farer, *War Clouds on the Horn of Africa* (Washington, DC: Carnegie Endowment for International Peace, 1979).

18. Janice Stein, ed., *Peacemaking in the Middle East* (New York: Barnes & Noble, 1985); Nathan Pelcovitz, *Peacekeeping in the Sinai* (Lanham, MD: University Press of America, 1985).

19. Harold Saunders, *The Other Walls*, 2d ed. (Princeton, NJ: Princeton University Press, 1991).

20. Harold Nicolson, *Diplomacy* (New York: Oxford University Press, 1939).

tions and instead aim at the destruction of the other side, the ultimate zero-sum situation. Once a conflict has arrived at this point, in the reality of perception, it is hard to turn it back as long as the warriors are in control.

The answer to the question, then, is that positive-sum ways of perceiving conflict need to be propagated before escalation brings the warrior to the fore. Such thinking does not eliminate conflict and is not incompatible with it. It depends on conflict to trigger positive perceptions and creative conceptualization. As the gulf crisis indicates as well, the time for these various efforts to turn the conflict into reduction and resolution is to be sought before escalation, lest the parties—and the onlooking world—be required to wait for escalation to be played out in all its destructive potentialities.

ANNALS, *AAPSS*, **518**, November 1991

Classifying Conflicts:
Asymmetry and Resolution

By C. R. MITCHELL

ABSTRACT: It is suggested that one reason for the resistance of protracted, intranational conflicts to efforts at resolution arises from their asymmetric structure. The concept of asymmetry is examined and illustrated. The argument is made that asymmetry is a more complex conception than a simple matter of power imbalance. Various dimensions of asymmetry are outlined and some examination made of the implications of legal and structural asymmetries for conflict resolution. Finally, some suggestions are offered concerning the possible impact of asymmetric structure on feasible procedures for conflict resolution and the content of lasting solutions to protracted, intranational conflicts.

Christopher Mitchell is professor of international relations and conflict resolution at George Mason University, Virginia. He received his bachelor's degree and his doctorate from the University of London and taught international relations at the City University, London, for 15 years before coming to the United States. He is the author of The Structure of International Conflict *and* Peacemaking and the Consultant's Role *and is currently working on a study of conciliatory gestures in de-escalation.*

NOTE: This article arose from work undertaken as part of the Horn of Africa Project of the Center for Conflict Analysis and Resolution, George Mason University, supported by the United States Institute of Peace Grant SG 56-9, 1989-90.

THE phenomena under scrutiny in this article are intranational conflicts, occurring—and recurring—between human communities and involving organized physical violence as a strategy for pursuing interests and achieving goals.

Such conflicts are deep-rooted, in that they arise from values and needs —identity, security, recognition— that are difficult to satisfy in any final sense and that give rise to goals that, given conditions of scarcity, appear to be wholly irreconcilable with the goals of others. They are protracted in that they recur over long periods of time. They may, under certain circumstances, be ameliorated or suppressed so that they appear to have been finally resolved, only to emerge in slightly different forms when historical circumstances change. Protracted conflicts may thus pass through both dormant periods, when the issues appear to have been either settled or to have become irrelevant, and active periods, when issues emerge once more, adversaries organize to fulfill newly salient goals, and coercive tactics are contemplated and then, if conflict management strategies do not succeed, are used, often so as to pose serious threats to the stability and survival of the political system.

One major task for current research is to illuminate the circumstances under which existing sociopolitical structures cease to manage deep-rooted conflicts satisfactorily and the nature of triggers that give rise to the emergence of a protracted conflict from its dormant stage. An even more challenging problem is to discover whether it is possible to resolve such conflicts in any final sense, with root causes successfully removed so that the conflict does not recur.

THE NATURE OF PROTRACTED CONFLICT

Clearly, this introduction has two implications: (1) protracted, deep-rooted conflicts occur *within* the territorial and jurisdictional boundaries of polities, and (2) a common form of protracted conflict involves ethnolinguistic communities, or ethnonationalities, in contention with other such communities. Under these circumstances, one such community frequently controls the national decision-making and conflict-managing systems and is thus the political incumbent.

It is not necessarily the case, however, that all protracted conflicts fit neatly within the boundaries of a political system, a fact that reflects the often arbitrary manner in which political and jurisdictional boundaries were drawn in the past. Historians are familiar with "irredenta" problems, and many protracted conflicts take this form—or its neglected subvariant, irredentas within the same country, as exemplified by the 500,000 Serbs currently living within the borders of Croatia. Many such conflicts become internationalized, and further protracted, because one of the adversaries possesses an external government as patron, as do the Somalis in the Ogaden, the nationalists in Northern Ireland, and the Austrian community in South Tirol; because strong links exist to parts of a wider community outside the political system, as is true of the Oromo and the Kurds; or simply because outside political incumbents are likely to be drawn into an overt, protracted conflict as patrons of one side or the other.[1]

Even so, there is much evidence that many disputes in the 1990s and beyond will be protracted, intranational conflicts. Gurr recently noted that many of the 168 states in the modern world are "mosaics of distinct peoples whose identities may or may not be accepted by those who hold state power"[2] and where significant conflict over minority rights does or could exist. Recent events in the Horn of Africa, in Western and Eastern Europe, in Southwest Asia, and in the USSR reinforce the impression that many protracted conflicts over ethnic identity are emerging from the dormant to the active stage. It seems probable that the typical conflicts for the 1990s and beyond will be those arising from the existence of what Rupasinghe calls "unassimilable identity" within many multiethnic polities,[3] and from tardy efforts to find appropriate political structures and processes to accommodate such identities.[4] Such ethnonational con-

flicts, involving struggles to defend—and promote—identity on behalf of ethnolinguistic or ethnoreligious communities, contrast with internal regime wars, involving struggles over the control of a polity's state apparatus and the form of underlying economic and social systems.

In the past it has been the practice to treat these two types of protracted intranational conflict separately, emphasizing their distinctiveness. I would, however, like to use a major similarity between the two categories to explore the dynamics and resolution of both—namely, that, in both cases, the structure of the conflict system itself is highly asymmetric rather than symmetric. This may have a profound influence on the way in which such conflicts arise and become protracted.

This can be simply illustrated by noting that both internal regime wars and ethnonationalist conflicts take place between parties whose goals are quite different, one party being intent upon major change and the other favoring the defense of some status quo. Inevitably, this influences the interaction between the adversaries, the tactics that both use, the ideologies of the two sides, the manner in which they organize their internal as well as external support, and the nature of the bargaining, both tacit and formal, in which they engage. Positions on changing and maintaining the status quo are

1. C. R. Mitchell, "Civil Strife and the Involvement of External Parties," *International Studies Quarterly*, 14(2):164-94 (June 1970).

2. Ted Robert Gurr and James R. Scarritt, "Minorities Rights at Risk: A Global Survey," mimeographed (Washington, DC: U.S. Institute of Peace, 1989).

3. Kumar Rupasinghe, "Theories of Conflict Resolution and Their Applicability to Protracted Ethnic Conflict," *Bulletin of Peace Proposals*, 18(4):527-39 (1978).

4. Much U.S. analysis seems, to an outsider, to be dominated by an almost unconscious acceptance of the success of the melting-pot model or, at least, by a failure to distinguish between an ethnic group and ethnic nationalism. See Aftab A. Kazi, "Ethnic Nationalism and Superpowers in South Asia: Sindhis and Baluchis," *Journal of Asian and African Affairs*, 1(1):1-18 (July 1989).

merely one possible form of asymmetry, however. If other important forms exist, then the nature of the asymmetries making up the structure of the conflict system might be employed to categorize subtypes, thus revealing the nature, likely course, and probable outcome of the conflict.

The remainder of this article will concentrate upon forms of asymmetry likely to be important in classifying and helping to analyze ethnonationalist conflicts, but it should be borne in mind that similar arguments might apply equally to the importance of asymmetries in internal regime wars. In both cases, a key research question is, What effects will the asymmetric structure of such conflicts have upon their development and the range of possible outcomes? This issue forms the underlying theme of the remainder of this article. My initial thesis is that asymmetric structure is likely to exercise a strong influence on the behavior of the parties and the outcome of the conflicts.

ASYMMETRIC STRUCTURE ILLUSTRATED

A preliminary illustration of this thesis arises from Pruitt and Rubin's "dual concern" model of interpersonal conflict.[5] The two authors use this model to explain and predict the probable pattern of behavior of one party in a conflict. Behavior is classified as "inaction," "contending," "yielding," or "problem solving." The

5. Dean G. Pruitt and Jeffrey Z. Rubin, *Social Conflict* (New York: Random House, 1986).

variables chiefly determining the pattern of behavior selected by one party in conflict will be the level of concern of that party for its own goals and the level of concern within that party for the goals, concerns, and well-being of the other party in the conflict. Pruitt and Rubin illustrate their hypothesis by a simple model, outlined in Figure 1.

It should be noted that the model and its underlying theory are employed to explain the behavior of only one party to a conflict. Conflicts, by definition, involve at least two parties and also interactions, learning, and behavior change, all of which affect outcomes. If the Pruitt-Rubin model is applied to both parties in a dyadic conflict, then two structures are possible: (1) symmetric, where the two parties are equally concerned, or unconcerned, about their own and the other party's goals and welfare and thus employ similar strategies to achieve a satisfactory outcome to the conflict; and (2) asymmetric, where, for example, one party is unconcerned about its own goals but is highly concerned about the other's goals and welfare, and the second party is wholly unconcerned about the first's goals but highly concerned about its own; or where one party is highly concerned about both its own goals and its adversary's while the other is concerned only with its own goals. The model can exemplify other types of asymmetry, but I will concentrate on these for illustrative purposes.

Clearly, in the cases in the first category, the symmetric structure of the conflict system will lead to the employment, at least in an initial

FIGURE 1
THE PRUITT-RUBIN DUAL-CONCERN MODEL

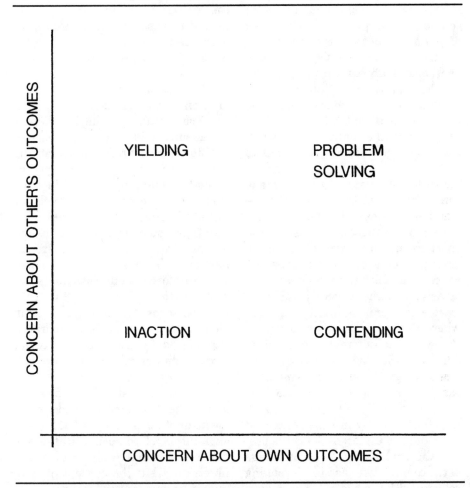

SOURCE: Dean G. Pruitt and Jeffrey Z. Rubin, *Social Conflict* (New York: Random House, 1986), p. 29. Reproduced by permission of McGraw-Hill, Inc.

phase of the conflict, of matching patterns of behavior or strategies. In the first example, if both parties are highly concerned about their own and the other's goals, the model suggests that both will, all other things being equal, employ problem-solving strategies, so that an innovative, win-win solution to their conflict might be found. In another symmetric case, where both parties possess highly salient goals but low concern for each other, both will adopt highly coercive strategies, and an escalatory pattern of interaction will develop as a prelude to some win-lose or lose-lose settlement. In a third symmetric case, should both parties have high concern for the other and low concern for their own goals, the model implies that a pattern of mutual yielding should develop, which seems highly improbable in most ethnonationalist conflicts but a quite normal pattern of behavior between friends, colleagues, and groups that hold one another in high regard.

Likely patterns of interaction in asymmetric cases are less clear. The model implies that, at least in the first stage of the conflict, parties will each use very different strategies to end the conflict and that this asymmetry of behavior is likely to make the achievement of a solution—whether win-lose, lose-lose, or win-win—more difficult, at least in the short and medium term. Consider an asymmetric case where one party's concern for both its own and its adversary's salient goals leads it toward a problem-solving strategy, but where the other party's concern for its own goals but indifference to its adversary's leads it to pursue a coercive strategy.[6] In such an asymmetric case, it seems likely that the first party, finding its own problem-solving efforts met by intransigence and coercion, will undergo a learning process that, at least by the second stage of the conflict, will lead to a lessening concern with the goals and welfare of the other party and to some modification of its own strategies toward what

6. It should be emphasized that other important dimensions in Pruitt and Rubin's theory about the selection of strategies in interpersonal and intergroup conflicts involve such variables as the anticipated effectiveness of the chosen strategy, which may also be asymmetric! The present concentration upon the dual-concern aspect of their work runs a danger of distorting the subtlety of their overall argument.

it will perceive as reactive and defensive coercion. By the third stage of the conflict, both parties seem likely to find themselves locked into a familiar escalatory pattern, heading in the direction of a win-lose or lose-lose outcome.

The interesting question that arises from these minor extensions of the Pruitt-Rubin model is whether all asymmetric-concern structures lead toward a learning and adapting pattern of interaction that promotes a further malign spiral of interaction—asymmetric cases involving initial yielding and problem-solving strategies suggest that this is not necessarily so—or whether there are particular patterns of asymmetry that reinforce tendencies for some conflicts to produce, at least for a time, patterns of mutual coercion and violence that can only be temporarily suppressed by the use of superior force or temporarily settled by a half-satisfactory compromise.

Further analysis of this problem and of the dual-concern model must await another article, but this brief exploration of some implications of the Pruitt-Rubin model has neatly illustrated that the concept of symmetric or asymmetric structure of a conflict can be important, both theoretically and taxonomically. This latter point reemphasizes the arguments: (1) that there are likely to be a number of ways in which conflicts can be considered asymmetric, and (2) that it is necessary to consider important ways in which conflicts might be asymmetrically structured as a preliminary to forming a helpful taxonomy for systematic theorizing about asymmetric conflicts.

The next section, therefore, focuses on the question, What important forms of asymmetry exist in protracted intranational disputes, particularly in ethnonationalist conflicts?[7]

KEY DIMENSIONS OF ASYMMETRY

Parties actually involved in protracted and deep-rooted conflict have no difficulty with the conception that conflicts are asymmetric. To them, it would be obvious that, in any intractable intranational conflict, a group of political protestants or insurgents —perhaps representing an ethnolinguistic community—must be different in nature from their adversary, the political incumbents representing another ethnolinguistic group. To many of those involved in a conflict, it often appears perverse that conflict analysts insist upon applying some symmetric analytical approach to both parties in conflict, asking similar questions about their structure and behavior, comparing their strategies as though they were alike, and attempting to argue that both may, for example, share very similar perceptions or be subject to similar behavioral dynamics.[8]

7. Another important, and related, question involves whether these salient forms of asymmetry can help us to discriminate between separate cases of protracted ethnonational conflict and different stages or cycles of the same case.

8. Apart from this assumption of asymmetry, which distinguishes conflict participants from conflict analysts, the former share a strong assumption of uniqueness and become indignant when it is suggested that their conflict can be fruitfully compared with others and lessons can be learned about causes, dynamics, and outcomes.

To some extent, this reaction is justified. There has been a marked tendency in conflict analysis to treat all conflicts as symmetric and to make statements about, for example, tacit bargaining behavior as though both sides were similar and could best be understood by assuming that both followed similar bargaining strategies. There is a tendency to generalize about misperceptions, as though both parties would experience similar patterns of stereotyping or attribution processes, irrespective of major differences in their internal structure and dynamics, past histories, and relationship with one another. These tendencies can be explained by the habit of taking the party in conflict, rather than the conflict system itself, as the unit of analysis. Undoubtedly, this is a necessary way of forming preliminary generalizations about phenomena in a relatively new field. Such a tendency, however, leads to an underplaying of the commonsensical notion that parties in conflict are also likely to behave differently depending upon their own structure and processes relative to those of their adversary and the overall structure of the system within which their conflict takes place. In other words, interaction and outcome vary according to the symmetry or asymmetry of the parties on key attribute dimensions.

What are such key dimensions? While it is undoubtedly the case that the parties involved in any conflict are likely to have clear ideas about key asymmetries, it may be that dimensions salient to the parties are neither the only ones on which the parties are, in fact, asymmetric nor those that are important in explaining behavior and predicting likely outcomes.

At this present stage of speculation, it is possible only to raise this issue of dimensional salience in asymmetric conflict structures and to begin outlining types of asymmetry that might, after future investigation, turn out to be important. I suggest that there are at least five different categories of asymmetry likely to affect the course and outcome of any conflict, but particularly protracted ethnonationalist conflicts: legal, structural, moral, relational, and behavioral asymmetries. I will take the first two of these to illustrate a general argument.

Legal asymmetry

It is a truism that conflicts between legally equal and legally unequal parties will take quite different courses and produce different outcomes. One has only to compare two individual citizens in mutual dispute with a single citizen in dispute with his or her government, or two governments in an international conflict with a government in dispute with a small, nationally based business enterprise. There are at least three major ways in which legal asymmetries might affect the course, conduct, and likely outcomes of an ethnonationalist conflict: (1) in the manner in which the conflict is perceived and defined by the rival parties, (2) in the strategies available to the rival parties, and (3) in the effects on available settlement processes.

The effects of legal asymmetries seem particularly marked in that many protracted conflicts—particularly those that involve the strong possibility of the breakup of an existing political system—come to involve issues of acceptance or denial of one party's status and rights even to participate in the conflict. The protracted struggle between the Eritrean movement and the Ethiopian state has been carried out by one party, the government in Addis Ababa, which, being the political incumbent, takes the legal position that a rebellion of a minority in one of its provinces exists. The conflict, from this viewpoint, is defined as being between a legitimate government and a set of rebels. The view of Eritrean nationalists, in contrast, is that the key issues involve the legitimacy of Ethiopian rule over Eritrea, imposed by force and accepted by a political minority in 1962. These issues also concern the nationalists' own status as true representatives of the Eritrean people—at least on the issue of continued Ethiopian rule. The Eritrean position is that they are not illegal rebels; Ethiopian rule is itself an illegal imposition.

A second major effect of legal asymmetry is that it has an impact on the manner in which the adversaries can prosecute the conflict. The legality of legal governments presents incumbents with a wide range of advantages denied insurgents. Incumbents are legally entitled to impose embargoes, to take action against insurgents' patrons and supporters in other countries, to import arms and counterinsurgency equipment, to institute conscription, to levy increased taxes, to seek support for their positions and policies in international forums, to declare states of siege, to introduce and enforce emergency legislation of all types, and to behave in any manner consonant with the conception of internal sovereignty. Insurgents are not.

The fact that the conflict is asymmetrically structured on a legal dimension means that, as the preservation or destruction of that asymmetry becomes a leading issue in the conflict, any peacemaking efforts that seek to treat the parties as legally the same are likely to be unsuccessful. Such initiatives may be supported by the insurgents, seeking to establish legal symmetry, but are likely to be rejected by incumbents seeking to preserve an advantageous legal asymmetry.

Third parties will usually find incumbents willing to engage in even the most informal range of discussions about a limited range of topics set only within assumptions of insurgent illegitimacy and a need to return to legitimacy—to an end to violence, surrender of arms, return to civilian life. They will find insurgents willing to engage in discussions only if issues deemed substantive—those that call into question the legitimacy of existing political structures and processes and of the incumbents themselves— are included on the agenda. Any third party is likely to find these demands mutually exclusive, at least up to the point where exhaustion may make one side willing, at least temporarily, to give in to the prenegotiation demands of the other and begin a dialogue. A temporary settlement may be reached, but it is likely to prove only temporary.

Structural asymmetry

The second type of influential asymmetry refers to key differences in the internal structure, conditions, and processes of the adversaries. Systematic evidence about what are, in fact, influential structural asymmetries is sparse. Hence all that I will attempt is to outline a number of structural asymmetries likely to affect conflict processes and outcomes. These involve asymmetries in access, salience of goals, survivability, internal cohesion, and leadership security.

Access. Access involves the ability of different parties within a political system to have their concerns and goals put onto the political agenda for action, particularly the ability to have goals and concerns noticed, considered, and acted upon by political incumbents. In the early stages of protracted intranational conflicts, adversaries are likely to have both differential access to national decision-making circles and differential capability for organizing campaigns to put forward demands and inform the national political community about goals and aspirations.

In a polity containing one or more dominated minority communities, unless the political incumbents are particularly sensitive to the need for considering minority views—and this is unlikely once a situation of protracted conflict has moved from a latent to an overt stage and minorities consistently become sources of what are perceived as disruption and disloyal behavior—adversaries are likely to have very different abilities to voice their concerns and to have them dealt with. In Northern Ireland, for example, the concerns of the nationalist community were virtually ignored by the dominant unionists for over forty years until a major protest and civil rights movement developed in the mid-1960s. Demands may be perceived as evidence of further disaffection, and the dominant community may react by suppression through the state apparatus. In turn, this may lead to a violent reaction from the dominated minority as a way of obtaining attention and action, so that the conflict cycles into a malign spiral once again.

Salience of goals. Another important way in which parties in protracted conflicts are likely to be highly asymmetric, especially in the early stages of any cycle of conflict, is in the importance that the adversaries attach to the issues in the conflict. For political incumbents it is often initially the case that dealing with the concerns of a dominated minority is only one of a multiplicity of problems they face. Frequently, it is nowhere near the top of their agenda of concerns. Even in later stages of the conflict or in its latest cycle, the dispute remains merely one of a number of important issues, and this is likely to continue to be the case until the conflict has reached a critical stage at which the survival of the incumbents in office or of national unity is genuinely threatened. For the revolutionary Marxist government in Addis Ababa in 1975, the Eritrean conflict was only one of a series of major problems it had to confront. Similarly, for the British government in 1921, dealing with the Irish Ques-tion, while important, was not the most important item on its political agenda; it is not the most important in 1991.

For Eritreans and Northern Irish, however, their goals and aspirations remain central. The same is invariably true of other dominated communities in divided polities. The issues in ethnonationalist conflict are the issues that dominate their activities and that come to overwhelm all others, especially if the conflict cycles into organized violence and counterviolence and a protesting community become political dissidents.

In many ways, this differential salience can work either to shorten or to prolong the conflict. If the political incumbents make timely concessions on issues that are, initially at least, not salient—in that they do not threaten the unity of the polity or the survivability of the regime—then the conflict might be settled. If, however, the conflict escalates so that the insurgents' goals and demands change from greater participation or limited autonomy to separation or secession, then the issues will become highly salient for the incumbents. Sadly, this new symmetry of salience is likely to lead to the willingness of both sides to make major sacrifices in prosecuting the conflict. Nonetheless, as many writers have pointed out,[9] there will remain an asymmetry between incumbents and dissidents who may become insurgents. The latter's resistance increases because of the importance of the issues to

9. See Andrew J. R. Mack, "Why Big Nations Lose Small Wars: The Politics of Asymmetric Conflict," *World Politics*, 27(2):175-200 (Jan. 1975).

them. The conflict will be only temporarily suppressed even if the incumbents' coercion succeeds in achieving overwhelming military dominance.

Survivability. Linked to a probable asymmetry in the salience of issues to incumbents and insurgents is another crucial asymmetry, namely, survivability. Clearly, there are likely to be major differences between a conflict in which, whatever the outcome, both parties will remain in being and a conflict in which the very existence of one or both is in question.

Equally clearly, the influence of this asymmetry will depend upon the precise meaning of "existence" and whose existence is involved. In internal regime wars, the continued existence of the political incumbents as incumbents is obviously in question. This is what is at issue in ethnonationalist conflicts, when it is frequently the case that the continued existence of a unified national polity is under attack, given that insurgents in such struggles aim for separation and independence. In contrast, it seems rare that the continued existence of an entire community appears genuinely threatened, although such a perception clearly occurs in some conflicts and makes them more than usually intractable and resistant to any long-term solution. Some such perception has obviously existed for many decades for the Oromo in Ethiopia, for the Afrikaner *volk* in South Africa, for the Israelis in the Middle East, and for the Kurds in Iraq.[10] This

perception of the imminent destruction of an entire community, or a way of life, is obviously more easily rationalized in the case of a threatened minority—either dominated or dominant—and seems likely to prove an important asymmetry.

Intraparty cohesion. Another important form of asymmetry may arise from the internal structure of the adversaries. In general, it seems likely that political incumbents will be more cohesive and better organized than dissidents and insurgents, if only due to the fact that they control the state apparatus and have opportunities to organize and mobilize that are not encouraged in a protesting, dominated community and are not open to political insurgents. Moreover, it is often the case that there are rival organizations contending for the allegiance of disaffected communities, or that several disaffected communities are in conflict with the political incumbents and are searching for unity—or, at least, coordination—between themselves. The first model can be exemplified by the

10. In some protracted conflicts, the issue of survivability is obviously associated with perceptions about the finality or reversibility of any settlement of a cycle in the dispute. In Israeli eyes, Arab success in forcing a solution on Israel might result not merely in the final destruction of Israel as the Jewish state but in that of the Jewish ethnonational community in Israel through genocide. There could be no reversal of either outcome; moreover, both would involve a double level of destruction—of state and community. In the case of the unionist community in Northern Ireland, there exists a strong perception that, should a nationalist majority for a politically united Ireland somehow come into being, there would be no possibility of their reversing either the decision about political unity or the—admittedly gradual—process of destruction of their own community and identity, a destruction that they perceive as having occurred with the Protestant community in the south.

Zimbabwean struggle against the Rhodesian government—and white minority community—from 1965 to 1980, and the second by the first Sudanese civil war, from 1956 to 1972, which ended only when the disparate southern Sudanese insurgent organizations managed to form themselves into a—temporary—coalition to make peace.

This dominant model of cohesive political incumbents facing a disunited or loosely united opposition, consisting of a number of dissident groups, needs to be treated with some caution, however. For one thing, it is rarely the case that political incumbents are not themselves internally divided on issues of goals and appropriate means for dealing with protestants or insurgents. Sometimes these divisions can produce significant splits and overt conflict within a government that is facing separatist communities. The early and violent divisions within the Ethiopian Derg over the issue of how to deal with the Eritrean secessionist movement contributed to the violent overthrow of one, pro-negotiation faction within the Ethiopian military and its replacement by another. Incumbents can suffer from lack of internal cohesion just as insurgents can achieve a high level of unity.

Moreover, it is often the case that incumbents, if the conflict reaches the stage of a major threat to their survival and the survival of a unified polity, will call in the assistance of external patrons to help them prosecute the conflict and prevent insurgents from winning.[11] In many such

cases, external patrons enter the conflict with their own agenda of objectives, which differ from those of the internal incumbents. Hence serious divisions can develop within this incumbent-patron coalition, just as they can within an insurgent or insurgent-patron coalition. Divisions between the Ethiopian Derg and their Soviet and Cuban patrons over Eritrea are well documented. It cannot be argued that the relationship between the United States and the government in Saigon was entirely free from division. In many such cases of patron intervention, the resultant structure produces continued conflict between two internally divided coalitions, a structure that is made more complex should the insurgents themselves achieve the aid of external patrons through a process of counterintervention.

Bearing these arguments in mind, an asymmetric-cohesion model can be either inappropriate—both adversaries can be cohesive or both can be divided—or misleading—incumbents can be divided and insurgents cohesive. Each conflict needs to be examined to see which version of the model is appropriate. Only then can analysis begin of the effects of symmetric or asymmetric cohesion on the course and outcome of that conflict.

Leadership insecurity. Closely linked to the concept of internal cohesion is that of leadership insecurity—the existence of a threat to the continued power of leaderships among incumbents and insurgents. This is both an important asymmetry and a major influence on the course and outcome of the conflict.

---

11. See Mitchell, "Civil Strife."

The issue concerns how secure the leaderships of the two sides are likely to be and what effect symmetric or asymmetric levels of insecurity might have on the conflict, particularly on any termination process. A number of different situations can be envisaged. First is an asymmetric one, where the leadership of one of the adversaries is highly insecure and vulnerable to intraparty rivals, while the other adversary faces no serious intraparty threats. The second is a symmetric one, in which both leaderships are reasonably secure and face only a low level of containable opposition within their own ranks. The third is an alternative symmetric structure in which both leaderships are insecure and face a major potential challenge to their leadership positions, part of which is likely to involve the issue of the continued prosecution of the conflict.

ASYMMETRIC STRUCTURE AND THE SEARCH FOR SOLUTIONS

There is little agreement about the nature of structural effects or their relation to particular dimensions of asymmetry. Therefore there is room for some tentative ideas about possible effects of asymmetry, first, on the process of terminating the conflict and, then, on the likely form and content of solutions, including the structure of future relations between asymmetric parties to a protracted conflict.

The resolution of asymmetric conflict: Process

It is a truism that most protracted conflicts do not end in a negotiated settlement but in victory for the incumbents, as with Nigeria and Biafra, or for the insurgents, as in East Pakistan. Part of the reason for this is the difficulty of starting and continuing successful negotiations between parties involved in an asymmetric structure that works against starting negotiations and concluding compromise settlements in a number of ways.[12]

First, relational asymmetries make it difficult for many protracted conflicts to achieve a mutually hurting stalemate, which many writers argue is a precondition for negotiations to be contemplated by embattled leaders. Many protracted intranational conflicts seem to achieve, for long periods, conditions of mutual standoff, with insurgents unable to force incumbents toward concessions by inflicting unacceptable costs, and incumbents unable to do more than contain insurgency within reasonable limits. As John Darby has argued with respect to Northern Ireland, some asymmetric conflicts can be "contained" in the sense that their damaging effects can be confined to limited geographical areas or social strata and thus become routinized and bearable.[13]

In such situations, other changes might bring about a desire for a negotiated settlement on the part of one set of leaders. Kriesberg suggests

12. Enough conflicts—or conflict cycles—do end in negotiated solutions—for example the Anglo-Irish conflict of 1916-21 or the First Sudanese Civil War of 1956-72—to indicate that such endings, while difficult to achieve, are not impossible.

13. John Darby, *Intimidation and the Control of Conflict in Northern Ireland* (Syracuse, NY: Syracuse University Press, 1987).

that one such factor might be a major change in other conflicts in which one party—usually the incumbent—is simultaneously involved,[14] while major switches in fortune—short of final triumph or disaster—also raise the possibility of negotiation for one side. While such factors may be influential in the decision-making process of one party to an asymmetric conflict, however, that asymmetry ensures that the other side is unlikely to be similarly affected. As Holsti pointed out succinctly over twenty years ago, it is necessary for both sides to come simultaneously to the conclusion that negotiations are worthwhile for negotiations to have any chance of beginning, let alone succeeding.[15]

A second obstacle to starting a process of dialogue is the asymmetric price likely to be demanded by the adversaries for opening talks. Truces and cease-fires have differential effects upon the forces of incumbents and insurgents, particularly as far as willingness to restart the fighting are concerned. Moreover, there are many ways in which the opening of talks renders the insurgents more vulnerable than it does the incumbents. Revelation of the form and structure of leadership and elites is likely to affect insurgent groups detrimentally to a far greater degree than incumbents. Insurgents are also likely to pay a heavier cost in moral—and

morale—terms for being seen to negotiate with the very incumbents they are ostensibly committed to overthrow or secede from, although governments who have vowed never to talk with those whom they have classified as murderers or assassins also open themselves to charges of undermining law and order if they indicate that they might be willing to negotiate with rebels as a reward for rebelling. All such differential costs have to be considered by parties to an asymmetric conflict and form obstacles to the commencement of serious negotiation, thus militating for the continuance of the conflict to some coerced solution.

A further obstacle to the successful opening of discussions arises from structural asymmetries, particularly in cases where an integrated party confronts an adversary that is far less cohesive and that sometimes is utterly incoherent. For a start, there is a strong temptation for the integrated party to try to take advantage of the divisions within its rival in order to split and weaken it still further in the hope of being able to impose a favored solution. A salient aim becomes the detaching of some key faction from the adversary by judicious—strictly limited—concessions.

On the other hand, if the integrated party wishes to begin discussions leading to an agreeable and, it is hoped, stable long-term solution with its adversary, the problem arises of finding a negotiating partner that can bargain in any meaningful way, coherently represent the other side, and deliver and guarantee any agreement that might be reached. The experience of the British government in

14. Louis Kriesberg, "Interlocking Conflicts in the Middle East," in *Research on Conflict, Social Movements and Change*, ed. Louis Kriesberg (Greenwich, CT: JAI Press, 1980), 3:99-119.

15. Kalevi J. Holsti, "Resolving Conflicts Internationally: A Taxonomy and Some Figures," *Journal of Conflict Resolution*, 10(3): 272-96 (Sept. 1966).

1921 in negotiating a treaty with the representatives of Sinn Féin, only to have the latter movement split over accepting the agreement, with the intransigents fighting another war aimed at repudiation, is only an extreme example of the dilemma created by such structural asymmetry.

Finally, it is also important to recall the fact that asymmetric conflicts tend to draw in outsiders as patrons and supporters of one or of both sides in the struggle. Inevitably, this creates a two-tier problem, if and when participants decide the time has come to seek a solution, as opposed to a victory. Processes have to be devised to deal initially with the mode of the withdrawal of the patrons, who inevitably have developed their own interests in and agenda for the conflict, and then to deal with the issues in the core conflict itself. Examples of conflicts where one tier of the process has been accomplished but not the other—the war in Afghanistan is merely one of the most recent examples—indicate the difficulty of dealing with such complex, asymmetric structures.

*The resolution of asymmetric
  conflict: Form and content*

A second set of ideas linking asymmetric conflict structure to the process of achieving a solution to that conflict concentrates on the relationship of asymmetries to the content of solutions. Many of these ideas focus on the asymmetry of the objectives of the adversaries and the impossibility of reconciling pro-change with pro-status quo goals, particularly when these are concerned with the survival or unity of an existing polity. What might the content of a solution to an asymmetric conflict be, other than preservation of the status quo or major change, usually involving separation?

In many conflicts it is true that the parties' definitions of goals and objectives preclude any possibility of a solution. If one side aims at the preservation of a political system and the other at its division, what room for alternatives exists? What concessions might one party be able to offer the other—and accept in exchange—given this imbalance of goals? One answer might be for the parties to analyze whether, in fact, they do face a wholly zero-sum situation and whether their definition of the options facing them —often as simple dichotomies—is the only one possible.

In such an approach, the asymmetric nature of the adversaries and their deep-rooted interests may become an advantage rather than the obstacle it is conventionally held to be. It is not necessarily the case that the content of any agreed-upon settlement has to involve the reproduction of one of the adversaries, in the sense that a solution results in the insurgent group's becoming structurally similar to the incumbents—an independent political system in its own right. Recall that the key asymmetry of goals in ethnonationalist conflicts often involves the preservation of an existing political system on one hand and the protection of threatened identity on the other.[16] If this is the case, then a solution can be

16. It could be argued that the preservation of the existing political system for incum-

sought by exploring the possibilities of asymmetric exchange between the adversaries, so that the incumbents provide some desired good for the insurgents in exchange for some desired—but different—incumbent good. This sounds complex, but it is only so if goods such as independence are regarded as unidimensional and indivisible and if the defense of such values as community identity is perceived as only being attainable through a strictly limited set of means—for example, the establishment of a new and independent political system. If it is not the case that one can be only either independent or dominated, or that community identity can be preserved only through separation and a new polity, then discussions between parties with asymmetric goals can occur about what means might exist by which both could achieve their objectives not at the expense of the other.

In other words, the content of a variable-sum solution to an asymmetric conflict may be easier to devise, at least in principle, than a similar solution to a symmetric conflict, where the adversaries want the same or very similar things.[17] If the pro-change party in an asymmetric conflict wishes to preserve and protect its community identity through becoming independent, then discussion

might begin with an inquiry about how many types of independence and autonomy there are, which are key and which peripheral to protecting community identity, and how many of these might be arranged that would preserve some degree of unity for the overall polity. Analysis of the content of such a solution might then lead to consideration of all future relationships between the adversaries and structures that might be established to protect and enhance independent identities, preserve the overall unity of the political system, institutionalize and manage the continuation of residual conflicts between the adversaries, and cope with other conflicts that might arise in future.

The argument here is the basically simple one that the very asymmetric structure of a conflict might, in itself, provide unexpected opportunities for solutions, arising from the fact that the parties to such conflicts are indeed different and possess different underlying goals. In this sense, asymmetry becomes a factor for achieving positive-sum solutions rather than being, as it is usually portrayed, a major obstacle to such outcomes. The problem of achieving a positive-sum solution, if these tentative arguments are correct, arises less from any fundamental problem of principle than from tactical problems of conducting a dialogue to search for a positive-sum outcome in circumstances where the asymmetric structure of the conflict presents major obstacles to such a search.

bents is, in fact, a means of defending the latter's own identity.

17. This may turn out, upon further analysis, to be a major difference between protracted internal regime wars and protracted ethnonationalist conflicts.

ANNALS, *AAPSS,* 518, November 1991

Great- and Medium-Power Mediations: Angola

By DONALD ROTHCHILD and CAROLINE HARTZELL

ABSTRACT: Two types of conflict situations existed concurrently in Angola: conflict in the interstate realm and conflict in the intrastate realm. In this article, the conflict management processes are analyzed by dealing separately with these two realms of mediatory activity. After an examination of the origins of interstate and intrastate tensions, the different mediation processes and their apparent consequences are compared and contrasted. The great- and medium-power mediators are differentiated in terms of their status, determination, and the resources they were able to bring to bear on the various disputing parties. The Zairian and Portuguese mediation processes are then analyzed in terms of the change over time in the incentives influencing the preferences of the various actors. In the concluding section, an attempt is made to link the shift in actor incentives and the mediators' resources, abilities, and motivations to moves toward a settlement of each conflict situation.

Donald Rothchild is professor of political science at the University of California, Davis. He is author of Racial Bargaining in Independent Kenya *and coauthor of* Scarcity, Choice, and Public Policy in Middle Africa *and* Politics and Society in Contemporary Africa.

Caroline Hartzell, a Ph.D. candidate at the University of California, Davis, is currently a Fulbright scholar in Colombia.

I N Angola, two types of conflict situations existed concurrently: conflict in the interstate realm and conflict in the intrastate—that is, the interethnic/interregional—realm. As a consequence of U.S. Assistant Secretary of State Chester A. Crocker's determined mediation efforts, backed by the Soviet Union, the interstate dimension of the conflict was ultimately settled in the December 1988 tripartite agreement, providing, *inter alia*, for Namibia's movement by stages to independence and for the redeployment and disengagement of Cuban troops from the country. Meanwhile, the internal war between the state, led by the Popular Movement for the Liberation of Angola (MPLA), and the insurgent movement, the National Union for the Total Independence of Angola (UNITA), continued until 1991, when a Portuguese-mediated effort, actively supported by the United States and the Soviet Union, resulted in the Estoril accord.

In this article, the conflict and conflict management processes will be analyzed by dealing separately with these two realms of mediatory activity. After examining the origins of interstate and intrastate tensions, the two different mediation processes and their apparent consequences will be compared and contrasted. The great-power and Zairian and Portuguese mediators will be differentiated in terms of their status, determination, and the resources they were able to bring to bear on the various disputing parties. The mediation processes will then be analyzed in terms of the change over time in the incentives influencing the preferences of

the various actors. In our concluding section, we will attempt to link the shift in actor incentives and the mediators' resources, abilities, and motivations to movement toward a settlement of each conflict situation.

THE PRE-INDEPENDENCE CONTEXT

What began as a struggle by Angolan nationalist movements in the early 1960s against the colonial power, Portugal, had become, by the time of Angola's independence in 1975, a war characterized by conflict on both the interstate and intrastate dimensions. The three leading nationalist movements, the MPLA, the National Front for the Liberation of Angola (FNLA), and UNITA, although sharing the goal of liberating Angola from Portuguese colonial rule, had distinct ethnic roots, varying ideological inclinations, and different ties to external actors. All of these variables proved to be key factors influencing the course of the interstate conflict in Angola over a period of one and a half decades.

Although they fought for a number of years, the three nationalist movements were unable to achieve any major military successes against the Portuguese. The road to Angola's independence was cleared by the Movement of the Armed Forces' coup in Portugal in April of 1974. Then, on 15 January 1975, Holden Roberto, Agostinho Neto, and Jonas Savimbi, the respective leaders of the FNLA, MPLA, and UNITA, met with the Portuguese to sign the Alvor accord. This accord provided for a transitional government and Angolan independence, beginning on 11 November 1975. Renewed fighting broke out among the three nationalist movements, however, contributing to the undermining of the Alvor accord. The fighting for Luanda, the capital of Angola, became intense, and on 10 November—the day Portugal withdrew from Angola—the MPLA, assisted by Cuban troops, decisively defeated the FNLA's forces. This military victory left the MPLA free to proclaim an independent People's Republic of Angola on 11 November 1975. From that moment forward, the conflict in Angola ceased to be a colonial one and became a civil war with an important international dimension. In this situation, the nationalist movements had linkages with external powers, foremost among them the United States and the USSR as indirect intervenors, which made commitments of economic and military assistance to their local nationalist allies without sending combat troops to the area, and Cuba and South Africa as direct intervenors, which deployed their regular combat troops in Angola.

THE POST-INDEPENDENCE CONFLICTS

In the period after Angola's independence, the Popular Armed Forces for the Liberation of Angola (FAPLA), bolstered by Cuban forces and Soviet-supplied military equipment, began the process of consolidating its control. In doing so, FAPLA faced two major antagonists. Internal opposition consisted of UNITA, the government's main internal opponent, which was linked to a powerful exter-

nal opponent, the South African Defense Forces (SADF). Clashes beween these forces proved inconclusive and by the mid-1980s a stalemate had developed. In this situation a relatively well-trained and well-equipped FAPLA army controlled the major cities and the oil-producing areas of the country, but it lacked the ability to inflict a decisive defeat on the South Africa-backed UNITA insurgents.

If they were to overcome the stalemate on the ground, two basic choices faced the Angolan government and the Cubans and South Africans: either they could fight on and hope to attain a military victory, or they could seek a political settlement through negotiations. Although some proposals were being floated on the diplomatic front, movement toward a negotiated settlement could not progress far as long as the two sides still believed in the possibility of a military victory. An armed engagement remained inevitable prior to serious talks leading up to a negotiated settlement.

The summer and fall of 1987 saw FAPLA become involved in two major military encounters against UNITA and South African ground forces in the towns of Mavinga and Cuito Cuanavale. Although in neither case was FAPLA able to defeat those forces decisively, its emergence at this time as an effective fighting force able to stand up to the SADF on its own ground signaled an important change in the correlation of military forces in the region.

By spring 1988, the newly enlarged Cuban force went on the offensive in southern Angola, concentrating its attack on the SADF contingents there. Cuban troops clashed with the South Africans on 26 June near the hydroelectric dam at Calueque. In an air raid, Cuban-piloted MiG-23s reportedly bombed South African positions as well as the dam itself. At least 12 white South Africans were killed, the largest number in any one battle throughout the war. According to Gillian Gunn, a change in the balance of forces in the area best explains why an SADF counterattack never materialized. "The Angolan-Cuban forces," Gunn writes, "now had a significant edge in the air war and could give the SADF a good run for its money on the ground."[1] For the South Africans, as well as for the MPLA regime and the other intervenors, a point had now been reached at which the costs of the war exceeded its anticipated benefits. This contributed to a change of perceptions on all sides that resulted in raising a negotiated peace to the status of a preferred option.

THE INTERSTATE MEDIATION PROCESS

The battle of Cuito Cuanavale and the encounter at the Calueque Dam represented a turning point in two respects. First, as noted previously, they indicated an important change in the balance of strategic forces. Cuban air superiority undermined South African pretensions to military invincibility in the region, and the

1. Gillian Gunn, "A Guide to the Intricacies of the Angola-Namibia Negotiations," *CSIS Africa Notes*, 8 Sept. 1988, no. 90, p. 12; also see Howard Wolpe, "Seizing Southern African Opportunities," *Foreign Policy*, Winter 1988-89, no. 73, p. 61.

ability of the FAPLA to hold on to the town and airfield at Cuito Cuanavale showed them to be worthy opponents in their own territory. Second, the heavy costs of the struggle had contributed to a sense of war weariness on the part of the MPLA regime and the direct and indirect intervenors. When these two factors became linked to a third—increasing pragmatism in the relations between the superpowers—movement toward mutual disengagement on the part of the direct intervenors became a serious possibility. The two indirect intervenors—the United States and the USSR, which gave military and economic assistance to their allies—conscious that the New Thinking in the Soviet Union had created unforeseen opportunities for tacit cooperation on regional conflict issues, were prepared to explore initiatives aimed at peacemaking. As these three factors converged in the summer of 1988, the perceptions of the various parties changed and a move from a military deadlock toward a negotiated settlement became a realizable objective.

The critical negotiations to end the stalemate and bring about a regional settlement stretched across an eight-month period, from the prenegotiation talks in London in May 1988 to the signing of two accords on Namibia's independence and the withdrawal of Cuban troops on 22 December 1988. The process proceeded through a number of rounds in accordance with well-established principles of third-party mediation. After some encouraging discussions with representatives of the Angolan government and the two direct intervenors in early 1988, Crocker and his American team began the formal process of mediation. This formal process started with exploratory talks between representatives of the Angolan, Cuban, and South African governments in London and, following an arduous set of talks between the South Africans and Angolans in Brazzaville, went on to examine the positions taken by the Angolans and the two direct intervenors at the follow-up rounds in Cairo. The process then moved ahead in the following stages: the setting out of the principles for a peace settlement in New York, the announcement of a ceasefire at Geneva and work on the modalities for this at Ruacana, Namibia, an attempt to narrow the difference between the parties at meetings in Brazzaville, tentative acceptance of a timetable for Cuban troop withdrawal in New York, the reaching of a preliminary agreement in Geneva on the withdrawal of Cuban troops from Angola and SADF from Namibia, examination of the verification issue in Brazzaville, the approval of a provisional agreement at Brazzaville accepting the terms for a political settlement, and, finally, the signing of a formal agreement in New York providing for Namibian independence and the withdrawal of Cuban forces. Clearly, once all sides had come to recognize the military stalemate and the costs of continuing the status quo, they were able to advance at a steady pace toward a peaceful settlement of some of their important differences, most notably, the problem of Cuban troop withdrawal from Angola and a South African pullout from Namibia.

CHANGED ACTOR INCENTIVES

Certainly there were some continuities between 1975 and 1988 in the incentives that the United States, the USSR, South Africa, and Cuba had for being engaged in the Angolan conflict. Despite some important differences, the incentives of the 1975 intervenors, as well as their perceptions of one another, tended to have a common denominator in the confrontation between East and West. The superpowers sought to gain or maintain their position in southern Africa in order to deny the area to their rival; the South Africans shared the U.S. perceptions of the destabilizing implications of an Afro-Marxist regime in their region; and the Cubans united with the Soviets in their determination to challenge South African apartheid as well as America's overarching hegemony on the continent.

By 1988, as the Cold War waned, the totalist perceptions that the East and West had of one another had eased, and pragmatic views gradually gained ascendancy in Moscow and Washington. For Reagan, the "evil empire" became a state with national interests, and Gorbachev's New Thinking encouraged Soviet leaders to reassess the costs of a substantial involvement on the side of the MPLA in Angola. This made the Soviets more prepared to experiment with joint problem-solving efforts aimed at dealing with regional conflicts. The direct intervenors, Cuba and South Africa, were slower to adjust to the new détente, but in time, changing regional and global imperatives left them with little alternative. The upshot was a settlement enabling the Angolan government and the direct and indirect intervenors to achieve some of their major objectives: the Angolan government brought about an end to the internationalized dimensions of a very destructive conflict; the Cubans emerged as champions of Third World causes; the South Africans secured a formal agreement on Cuban troop withdrawal and an informal agreement on the closing of African National Congress training camps in Angola; the Soviets showed themselves to be supportive of African purposes at a critical juncture; and, with the agreement on the Cuban withdrawal, the United States promoted its larger security objectives for the region, as well as raising U.S. prestige through its role as peacemaker.

It is important to take account of the changes taking place in Angolan government circles. The authorities in Luanda, who had experienced decades of warfare against a colonial power and internal rivals and external intervenors, had every reason to look positively on an end to the military struggle. The continued war against the insurgent movements and South African interventions was costly, not only in terms of funding and supplying an army and air force but also in terms of social and economic development. To deal with economic and social deterioration, Angolan government authorities came to view it as necessary to take steps to overcome the military stalemate and to begin the process of normalizing regional and extraregional relations.

Of the direct intervenors, Cuba was the most determined proponent of a confrontationist stance, increasing its military combat forces significantly following the siege of Cuito Cuanavale and going on to strike a telling blow against SADF units during the Calueque Dam incident. The overall effect was to alter the correlation of forces in Angola in favor of Luanda; this enabled Castro to claim a victory and, therefore, to negotiate on disengagement without loss of face. Having displayed "a strong internationalist spirit" and effectively championed the Marxist-Leninist revolutionary cause in Angola, the Cubans could rest content and avoid becoming further enmeshed in an extended war of attrition;[2] hence they were in a position to accept a negotiated settlement, especially one favored by their Soviet mentors.[3] Moreover, the alternatives would likely have proved potentially burdensome in terms of health hazards—particularly acquired immune deficiency syndrome—increasing battle casualties and, with Angola unable to cover the full costs of Cuban military activities because of the drop in world oil prices, financial outlays.

The other direct intervenor, South Africa, gradually altered its assessment of the external and internal situations in 1987-88. Internationally, the Soviets came to appear less adventurous and less inclined toward an expansion of their influence in southern Africa. Moreover, the Americans seemed more determined than ever to press Pretoria to change its policies on Namibian independence

2. Interview with Fidel Castro, *Granma Weekly Review*, 13 Mar. 1988, p. 7.
3. Chas. W. Freeman, Jr., "The Angola/Namibia Accords," *Foreign Affairs*, 68(3):133 (Summer 1989).

and apartheid, enacting sanctions legislation and threatening to tighten these laws if necessary. In the region, the easy military dominance that SADF units had displayed in the cross-border raids of the early 1980s now gave way to a difficult and costly war of attrition with well-armed Cuban and Angolan government forces. At home, the seemingly endless war involvement in Angola was beginning to have psychological and economic costs. The loss of military superiority held out the prospect of increasing white casualties and a lengthy military commitment with uncertain benefits. Moreover, the economy, averaging a growth rate of under 2 percent, seemed stagnant, mired in heavy foreign debts, rising inflation, and a lack of investment capital. To reduce the diplomatic and economic pressures on their country and to regain legitimacy in the eyes of the world community, South African leaders reassessed their priorities and began to view a negotiated solution to be in their long-term interests.

As the two indirect intervenors had been careful to avoid sending their own nationals into combat in Angola, it was less difficult for them to alter their priorities and to disengage than was the case with the direct intervenors. For the Reagan administration, initial U.S. goals with respect to the Angola-Namibia negotiations were clear: "to restore and advance U.S. influence in the region; to expand [U.S.] cooperative relations with African states; and to deny to the Soviet Union the opportunity to use its influence to exacerbate already dangerous situations in Angola, South Africa, and the other countries of the area."[4] Subsequently, the issue of Cuban troop withdrawals and an Angolan national reconciliation that included UNITA in the ruling coalition became important aims.

If U.S. incentives for becoming involved in the Angolan conflict remained reasonably constant between 1975 and 1988—the persistence of these incentives explaining, in part, the United States' decision to resume military assistance to UNITA in 1985 and afterwards—the same cannot be said of the Soviet Union. Certainly, Soviet strategic and economic interests in Angola were limited. Soviet policymakers decided to become involved in Angola out of a sense of ideological association with the MPLA; a desire to deny the territory to its superpower rival, the United States, and its ideological rival, China; and a feeling of hostility toward apartheid and the dominant regime in South Africa. With the emergence of Mikhail Gorbachev as general secretary in the mid-1980s, there was a growing recognition of the costs to the Soviets of continuing superpower rivalries in Third World conflicts.

Although the Cubans, South Africans, and Angolans all displayed a degree of war weariness, particularly after confrontations such as those at Cuito Cuanavale and Calueque Dam, all had the will and capacity to continue to fight unless some face-saving alternative surfaced. Such an alternative emerged most decisively dur-

4. Chester A. Crocker, *The U.S. and Angola, a Statement before the Senate Committee on Foreign Relations, February 18, 1986,* Current Policy no. 796 (Washington, DC: Department of State, Bureau of Public Affairs, 1986), p. 1.

ing the 1988 negotiations in the form of tacit cooperation on the part of the two superpowers. As indirect intervenors for whom the conflict was less salient, the United States and the USSR were able to exert leverage over the Angolan government and the two direct intervenors through the manipulation of incentives.

Clearly, it would be an overstatement to contend that the two indirect intervenors controlled the Angolan government or the two direct intervenors. Because the Angolans, Cubans, and South Africans were partially autonomous state actors, the two indirect intervenors could only achieve their purposes through the use of quiet pressures or positive and negative incentives. Castro, who received some $5 billion a year in economic subsidies, as well as logistical support and matériel from the Soviets for his African campaign, was described as "highly vulnerable to Soviet politico-economic coercion."[5] Similarly, the MPLA regime was in no position to reject Soviet preferences, having received billions of dollars in military assistance from Moscow over the years. The result was to give the Soviets considerable, but not unlimited, influence over the decision processes of these two allies.

In a like manner, the Reagan administration exerted some leverage over the South African government, despite all the efforts of the latter to insulate itself from American pressures. Determined to achieve a Namibian settlement prior to leaving of-

fice, Crocker increasingly acted to affect South African affairs, implementing the sanctions legislation mandated by Congress and bypassing the South African government to give support to anti-apartheid groups on the scene. In addition, he "repackaged" the linkage proposal, formerly the object of scorn on the part of the Front Line States, so that Namibia would gain its independence before the full withdrawal of Cuban troops from Angola.[6]

THE GBADOLITE PROCESS

With the signing of the Angola-Namibia accords in December 1988 and the beginning of the redeployment and disengagement of Cuban and South African forces, the stage was set for a concerted effort to resolve the long and destructive Angolan civil war. The conflict in the country's southeast had proved unwinnable, even when external forces had been involved in a major way. Now the internal opponents were being left increasingly to their own devices, and a continuing struggle offered them little prospect of significant benefits. Even so, the problem following the international settlement was how to overcome the political stalemate and begin the search for a peaceful solution. President Mobutu Sese Seko of Zaire stepped into this situation resolutely.

Harsh rhetoric notwithstanding, a perceptible softening of government and insurgent positions on the issue of a political solution to their differ-

5. Jiri Valenta, "Comment: The Soviet-Cuban Alliance in Africa and Future Prospects in the Third World," *Cuban Studies*, 10(2):34 (July 1980).

6. Pauline Baker, "The American Challenge in Southern Africa," *Current History*, 88(538):245 (May 1989).

ences became apparent in early 1989. Low-level talks between the two sides took place in January, limited to a discussion of a government offer of amnesty for UNITA troops who laid down their arms. This proposal was rejected by UNITA's spokesmen; however, at the request of Côte d'Ivoire leader Houphouet-Boigny, who was acting as an intermediary between the adversaries, guerrilla leader Jonas Savimbi did call off UNITA's planned rainy-season offensive. In March, Savimbi extended this moratorium on offensive action and announced the release of MPLA prisoners, declared a willingness to reopen the Benguela Railway to non-military traffic, and indicated a preparedness not to participate in a transitional government that would lead the country to free elections. The MPLA responded with its own peace platform, essentially consisting of its program of amnesty for the rank and file of UNITA soldiers.

For Mobutu, the Gbadolite agreement "was not achieved in haste" but was the culmination of an extended process.[7] It began, he asserted, with the informal gathering of heads of state at Tokyo on 22 February 1989, the conference of regional leaders in Luanda on 16 May, and separate meetings that the Zairian president held on two occasions with Savimbi and Angolan President Eduardo dos Santos. The Luanda conference was highly significant, as it identified national reconciliation as an objective and recognized Mobutu's legitimacy as mediator. At Luanda, the eight

African heads of state—from Zaire, Congo, Gabon, Zimbabwe, Mozambique, Zambia, Sao Tomé and Principe, and Angola—endorsed a seven-point Angolan government peace plan. The peace plan, which emphasized a peace zone along the Benguela railroad, an end to foreign interference, the cessation of support to UNITA, and the application of an amnesty by the government, made only limited concessions to the insurgent movement.

Prior to the Gbadolite summit, then, the Angolan government made few concessions to UNITA's demands for power sharing and an autonomous existence. It insisted upon Savimbi's temporary exile and the integration of UNITA's civilian and military components into the MPLA-led one-party state. Savimbi, on his side, called for multiparty elections and the possibility of coalition government. He denied seeking absolute power for himself, only the enactment of the 1975 Alvor accord principles on a transition government of the MPLA, UNITA, and FNLA prior to the holding of open elections.[8] The gap between adversaries remained wide. Even so, as Savimbi observed, 14 years of war had shown that neither side was capable of a military victory.

With the war proving costly and unwinnable and with some signs of conciliation in evidence, external facilitators found themselves at a favorable position to take the next step —the summit meeting at Mobutu's country residence in Gbadolite, Zaire.

7. BBC Monitoring Service, ME/0532, 11 Aug. 1989, p. B/6.

8. BBC Monitoring Service, ME/0491, 24 June 1989; p. B/1.

This necessarily involved a meeting between the two main antagonists—dos Santos and Savimbi—something not easy to arrange. Reportedly, when dos Santos received a phone call from Mobutu just prior to his departure from Luanda informing him that Savimbi might be present at Gbadolite, dos Santos reacted angrily and sought to cancel his travel plans. At this point it appears that various African heads of state interceded and persuaded him to reconsider and to attend the summit meeting.[9] Through the seven-hour, closed-door summit meeting, the two adversaries were kept apart, with Savimbi placed in a room adjacent to the main conference hall. During the day, Mobutu met with first one and then the other, cajoling and pressuring them in order to extract agreement on the summit declaration.

In an attempt to use the opportunity provided by the meeting to put pressure on the adversaries to reach an agreement, Mobutu assembled an impressive array of African leaders in Gbadolite. In all, some 20 countries were represented at the summit, 18 of them by their heads of state. Included in this gathering were General Moussa Traoré, the current chairman of the Organization of African Unity and president of Mali, President Kenneth Kaunda of Zambia, President Paul Biya of Cameroon, King Hassan II of Morocco, President Ibrahim Babangida of Nigeria, and President Robert Mugabe of

9. On the pressures used on dos Santos to encourage him to attend the summit, see *Africa Confidential*, 7 July 1989, p. 8; BBC Monitoring Service, ME/0491, 24 June 1989, p. B/1.

Zimbabwe. Clearly Mobutu intended to use this impressive array of leaders to pressure the adversaries into negotiating in earnest.

What emerged from this effort was not a carefully worked-out peace agreement; rather the summit at Gbadolite on 22 June 1989 represented an advance in a larger negotiating process. The fact that Africans had taken the initiative and quickly produced results in the form of a communiqué setting out the principles of agreement was viewed as a heartening sign. The first direct encounter between dos Santos and Savimbi and a handshake between these adversaries signaled a willingness to search for national reconciliation by political means. In setting the framework in which this handshake could take place, Africa's leaders were facilitating Savimbi's emergence from the dim shadows of unrespectability.

At the substantive level, there was confusion on a number of unwritten understandings arising from the day's long and turbulent negotiating session, but at least three principles were put forth in the text of the final Gbadolite Declaration. These principles acknowledged a desire on the part of both sides to stop fighting and to move toward national reconciliation, a desire that was given some shape through the proclamation of a cease-fire, which was to become effective on 24 June 1989, and through the formation of a commission that was to plan for national reconciliation under the mediation of President Mobutu.

Clearly, Gbadolite left unresolved a number of issues important to the main adversaries. Over and above the fact that the points of agreement were not written down is the larger reality of profound differences of perceptions and interpretations between adversaries. Dos Santos and his supporters came away from Gbadolite convinced that Savimbi had agreed to a voluntary and temporary exile and that UNITA's civilian and military elements would be integrated into the MPLA's party, bureaucratic, and military units. Savimbi dismissed talk of his exile, refused the proposed offer of amnesty, rejected the integration of UNITA into MPLA institutions, and demanded the establishment of a multiparty system and free, open elections. Savimbi was determined to preserve UNITA's separate identity and to compete with the MPLA for power at the political center of the country. For him, democratic elections in Angola were not only possible but necessary.

In a situation of state softness; persistent party, ethnic, and regional conflict; and personal animosity, highly conflictive negotiations such as those at Gbadolite are likely to have symbolic rather than substantive results. Dos Santos felt compelled to go to the summit meeting in order to demonstrate his party's commitment to peace. Savimbi, for his part, was distrustful of the process from its inception and appeared to participate only to the extent it advanced his interests. A highly personalistic leader, he looked upon himself as indistinguishable from UNITA, making somewhat academic the claims that he had agreed to his exile and the integration of UNITA into the MPLA-dominated state structure.[10] "If I leave Angola," he asked, "who is going to lead UNITA into this process of national reconciliation?"[11] Each leader sought peace, but only on his own terms.

Although the parties at Gbadolite had agreed in principle upon a cease-fire to become effective on 24 June, they failed to give this meaning by establishing a mechanism to determine the rules of permissible behavior or to resolve violations. Not surprisingly, therefore, the cease-fire never really took hold. At first, the hostilities between the MPLA and UNITA forces were limited and strategic in nature; soon, however, they increased in intensity, culminating in heavy fighting around Mavinga in late December 1989 and early 1990. Despite the continuing military engagements in the field, Mobutu pushed ahead resolutely with his mediatory initiative. Following the Gbadolite summit, a series of four inconclusive meetings were held in Kinshasa to work out a cease-fire agreement. Then, on 22 August a second regional summit was held, attended by the leaders of eight African states: Angola, Congo, Gabon, Mozambique, Sao Tomé and Principe, Zaire, Zambia, and Zimbabwe. The summit took place in Harare to review the situation since Gbadolite and to make recommendations on questions not dealt with at the earlier summit. Quite significantly, UNITA was not

10. On this, see the interview with Herman J. Cohen, the U.S. Assistant Secretary of State for African Affairs, in *Africa Report*, 34(5):16 (Sept.-Oct. 1989).

11. BBC Monitoring Service, ME/0494, 28 June 1989, p. B/1.

represented at Harare, no invitation having been issued to Savimbi.

The five-hour meeting reportedly brought sharp differences into the open. The more radical frontline leaders were highly critical of the conservative Mobutu and his failure to secure agreement on the peace terms from dos Santos and Savimbi in writing. The final Harare communiqué, reflecting the frontline presidents' mood of dissatisfaction with Savimbi's behavior since Gbadolite, was specific in encouraging Savimbi's temporary and voluntary retirement from Angola and the integration of UNITA into the MPLA and its state institutions. As anticipated, Savimbi "violently" rejected the communiqué, and Radio UNITA warned darkly "about the plot being prepared against [UNITA] as an organization, its leader, and peace in Angola."[12]

On 18 September, eight regional heads of state met at Kinshasa for another summit. In this case Savimbi was invited to attend, but, despite pressures from U.S. Assistant Secretary of State for African Affairs Herman J. Cohen and others, he declined to join the gathering. Under these circumstances, the conferees at Kinshasa could do little more than reaffirm their support for the Gbadolite agreement and call upon Savimbi to sign a new draft statement on the implementation process. Savimbi refused and countered with his own plan, which proposed the creation of a multinational force to verify and guarantee the cease-fire and called for open elections.

As the memories of Gbadolite dimmed, the adversaries appeared to become more preoccupied with the issues dividing them than with the urgent need to negotiate over outstanding issues.[13] Savimbi, the highly personalistic and charismatic leader of UNITA, ruled out significant concessions on the issues of his own exile and the integration of UNITA into MPLA structures, which he refused, and of multiparty elections and power sharing, which he demanded. For his part, dos Santos appeared equally unwavering on the reverse of these points. In addition, as time wore on, factionalism seemed to increase among MPLA officials, making new conciliatory gestures even more difficult than before. One Zairian diplomat reported that dos Santos was under "tremendous pressure from hard-liners in the Government." Feeling "burned" by Savimbi in the past, these hard-liners reportedly saw little to gain from a new cease-fire agreement at this point and argued instead for a military solution to the problem of insurgency.[14] What started at Gbadolite was being complicated by a combination of historical memories, personal antagonisms, developing schisms within one of the bargaining parties—the MPLA —and the character of the stakes involved in the conflict. Taken together, such variables placed severe constraints on what the African heads of state could achieve as facilitators in Angola.

12. BBC Monitoring Service, ME/0544, 25 Aug. 1989, p. B/1.

13. Interview, Herman J. Cohen, *Africa Report*, 34(5):17.

14. Kenneth B. Noble, "Rebel Head Agrees to Angolan Truce," *New York Times*, 4 Dec. 1989.

The mediator as source of opportunity and constraint

In a sense, Mobutu's credentials to act as a mediator were the source of his weakness. The Zairian government, which had recognized the Luanda regime and at the same time had friendly relations with UNITA—even acting as a transshipment point for U.S. military supplies—was in a favorable position to communicate with both sides. Not surprisingly, therefore, the eight heads of state at Luanda authorized Mobutu to begin a peace initiative in May 1989. If the African heads of state held a dim view of Mobutu personally, they nonetheless had little choice but to sponsor him as a mediator in this conflict situation. Therefore, despite their irritation over his failure to secure an agreement in writing at Gbadolite and the renewal of fighting, the heads of state assembled at the Harare summit reaffirmed their "total confidence" in the mediator.[15]

At various points in the negotiations, Mobutu's past seemed to stand in the way of his peacemaking venture. The frustrations on all sides of the continuing civil war were placed largely on the mediator's shoulders, for his failure to secure a written and binding agreement on the modalities of the cease-fire and the terms of the peace agreement were deemed responsible for the breakdown that followed. As Mobutu tried to respond to these charges, holding dos Santos to the accord while securing Savimbi's exile and UNITA's incorporation into the MPLA, he found himself unable

to satisfy either side. The MPLA leadership showed increasing signs of dividing into pragmatists and hardliners, and Savimbi not only rejected the Harare summit plan but questioned the impartiality of the mediator himself.[16] The mediator, in brief, had facilitated the negotiating process but had also emerged as part of the larger problem of peace in Angola. By March 1990, President dos Santos, determined to see the stalled peace talks renewed, told Parliament that he was keen to have Mobutu's role assumed by an alternate mediator.[17]

The roles of South Africa and the superpower rivals

In explaining the lack of movement toward a resolution of the Angolan conflict following the Gbadolite summit, it is also important to note the parts played—or not played—by the strongest military power in the region and the two superpowers. Under the terms of the Angola-Namibia accords of 1988, Cuban troops would be redeployed north of the fifteenth parallel by 1 August 1989 and north of the thirteenth parallel by 31 October 1989; all Cuban troops would be withdrawn from Angola by 1 July

16. Warren Clark, Jr., *National Reconciliation Efforts for Angola, a Statement before the Subcommittee on Africa of the House Foreign Affairs Committee, September 27, 1989*, Current Policy no. 1217 (Washington, DC: Department of State, Bureau of Public Affairs, 1989), p. 2; BBC Monitoring Service, ME/0565, 19 Sept. 1989, p. ii; ibid., ME/0574, 19 Sept. 1989, pp. B/2, B/3. In addition, Savimbi stated that the peace talks were not achieving their desired results "because they were not prepared properly." *Times* (London), 13 Sept. 1989.

17. *Africa Research Bulletin* (Political Series), 15 Apr. 1990, p. 9628.

15. BBC Monitoring Service, ME/0543, 24 Aug. 1989, p. B/3.

1991. In addition, South Africa would cease supplying UNITA with weapons and confine its troops to Walvis Bay. With Cuba and South Africa disengaging, the internal adversaries were to be left on their own, save for the continuing shipments of Soviet and U.S. military equipment to their respective clients and on a basis that substantially favored the MPLA.

Although the Cubans withdrew their troops from Angola as scheduled, the South Africans sent mixed signals regarding their intentions. On one hand, there was evidence of diplomatic initiatives by the South Africans in August and September 1989 to keep the Gbadolite peace process—and the Angola-Namibia accords—from foundering. Reportedly, pressure was to be put on both the MPLA and UNITA to abide by the cease-fire.[18] Even so, the question that remained to be answered was how much leverage the South Africans possessed and how much pressure they were prepared to bring to bear.

In the case of the two superpowers, both of whom had played such a significant role in cooperating tacitly to overcome the deadlock prior to the achievement of an Angola-Namibia settlement, the same question of leverage and willingness to exert pressure is relevant. Certainly, they both gave general support to the Gbadolite peace process. But what would these great powers be prepared to contribute to a successful outcome? The two superpowers contributed simultane-

ously to the arming of the combatants and to the process of conflict management. During the Angola-Namibia talks, there were frequent references to Soviet-Cuban pressures on the dos Santos government to negotiate with UNITA. Then, at the Gbadolite meetings in June 1989, various observers concluded that Soviet pressures were a significant factor in wringing concessions from a hesitant and reluctant dos Santos.[19] While important, these and other indications of a subtle behind-the-scenes role by Moscow were not intense enough to bring about a change of perceptions and incentives on the part of the Angolan government.

Similarly, U.S. involvement with and pressures on Savimbi's insurgent movement—as well as the MPLA—have not proved sufficient to bring about a major change in perceptions and incentives. In backing the African initiative at Gbadolite, the United States combined both negative and positive incentives to push the process ahead. Both nonrecognition of the Angolan government and continued military aid to the insurgents—the latter increased to an estimated $50 million in 1989—were viewed as means for changing MPLA preferences.[20] Washington also made use of positive incentives to promote cooperation, however. Not only did

18. Christopher S. Wren, "De Klerk in Zaire to Discuss Angola," *New York Times*, 26 Aug. 1989.

19. Lisa Hopkins, "Is Peace Finally in Store for Angola?" *Guardian* (New York), 5 July 1989; Kenneth B. Noble, "For Angola Rebel, New Respectability," *New York Times*, 26 June 1989.

20. U.S., Congress, Senate, Committee on Foreign Relations, *Hearings* [on the nomination of Herman J. Cohen to be assistant secretary of state for African affairs] 3 May 1989 (Washington, DC: Alderson Reporting, 1989), p. 26.

the Bush team hold out the prospect of normalizing relations with the Luanda regime once it had concluded an internal settlement with the insurgent movement, but it gave "tacit assurances" that with national reconciliation it would consider ending military aid to UNITA.[21] With respect to the mediation effort itself, the United States exerted pressure on Savimbi to attend the Gbadolite and subsequent summits. Despite these positive initiatives, however, Savimbi refused to attend the Kinshasa summit. Steadfast U.S. support of Savimbi gave the American team sufficient leverage to press for cooperation but not enough to assure movement toward a compromise agreement.

THE ESTORIL ACCORD

With the Gbadolite process deadlocked and Mobutu unable to bring sufficient political and economic resources to bear on the disputing parties to come to a settlement, a new approach became imperative. The two Angolan adversaries remained extremely wary and distrustful of one another. Nevertheless, neither the Angolan government nor the UNITA insurgents could muster sufficient military capacity to eliminate the opposition or force its capitulation. Moreover, the conditions for a sustained military effort were less and less encouraging. Not only were Angolans weary of the protracted civil

21. Martin Lowenkopf, "If the Cold War is Over in Africa, Will the United States Still Care?" *CSIS Africa Notes*, 30 May 1989, no. 98, p. 5; Robert Pear, "U.S. and Angola Discuss Forging Diplomatic Ties," *New York Times*, 27 Jan. 1989.

war, but their external supporters were disengaging. Cuban forces withdrew from Angola in advance of the schedule set out in the Angola-Namibia accords, and South African assistance, reportedly extended in a clandestine manner, was obviously diminutive in comparison with former levels. Most significant, the superpowers, having made the shift from adversarial to cautiously cooperative relations, were now quite anxious to reduce their involvement in the internal war in Angola and pursue new openings toward peace.

Recognizing that the Mobutu initiative had stalled and forthright about the need to regain momentum in the negotiations, President dos Santos called for the acceptance of a new third-party intermediary. Portugal, the former colonial power, rose to the occasion, and from mid-1990 onward chaired a series of talks between representatives of the Angolan government and UNITA. By December, the Portuguese-initiated talks were given an important boost when Secretary of State James A. Baker III met publicly with the Angolan foreign minister, and Foreign Minister Eduard Shevardnadze conferred openly with UNITA's Savimbi. Then the United States and the Soviet Union cosponsored a meeting in Washington, D.C., of the two Angolan rivals, the Portuguese intermediary, and the two great powers. With the Americans and the Soviets present, the two antagonists managed to work out what became known as the Washington Concepts Paper, the basic framework for the serious negotiation sessions to follow. Unlike Gbadolite, where the great powers gave general support to Mobutu's peace initiative but displayed little urgency over the proceedings, the United States and the USSR were now brought directly into the Portuguese negotiations as official observers. As Assistant Secretary Cohen commented on their active involvement in the negotiating process, "We both played a very important role in helping to bring about compromises under the overall jurisdiction of the Portuguese mediator."[22]

The Washington agreement on basic negotiating principles gave a new impetus to the flagging talks at Estoril. By the time the sixth round of talks took place on 4 April, most of the major points of disagreement had been resolved and the negotiators were able to focus their attention on the key remaining issues: the formation of a unified national army; the setting of dates for a cease-fire and the holding of multiparty elections; and the international monitoring of the cease-fire. The election date proved to be the most contentious point. Whereas UNITA proposed that elections be held between 9 and 12 months after the cease-fire, the Angolan government proposed a waiting period of three years. The Portuguese recommended a compromise of 18 months before the elections. Although the MPLA indicated a willingness to accept a reduction to 24 months, UNITA representatives continued to insist on a 12-month period.

This haggling over the major outstanding issues continued through the remainder of April when to the surprise of many, the conferees achieved a breakthrough to peace. On 1 May, Lopo do Nascimento, representing the Angolan government, and Jeremias Chitunda, of UNITA, initialed the various documents making up the peace accords. Under the terms of these preliminary agreements, a complex package of provisions was settled upon, including a cease-fire, to come into force on 15 May; UNITA's recognition of the Angolan government and President dos Santos until general elections are held; UNITA's right to take part in political activities in a multiparty democracy; free and fair elections under the supervision of international observers; the consultation of all Angolan political forces to determine the specific timetable for elections, tentatively set for late 1992; and, once the cease-fire comes into effect, the creation of a single national military force, made up of the current Angolan government air force and navy and an army evenly divided between government and UNITA troops.[23] Significantly, the great powers who had helped to overcome hurdles in the way of a negotiated settlement, now agreed to take part in the implementation process.

CONCLUSION

This article compared the processes of negotiation and mediation of intense international and internal conflicts in Angola since independence. It examined the successful conflict

22. Herman J. Cohen, "Ceasefire and Political Settlement in Angola," *U.S. Department of State Dispatch*, 6 May 1991, p. 328.

23. Foreign Broadcast Information Service, *Sub-Saharan Africa*, 91(086):7 (3 May 1991); ibid., 91(084):16 (1 May 1991).

management processes culminating in the Angola-Namibia accords, the lack of sustained momentum toward a cease-fire and political settlement during the Gbadolite initiative, and the breakthrough to peace in the Estoril mediation effort. Three important concepts were explored: the extent to which the incentives for state intervention changed over time; the roles of the mediators in facilitating the peace process; and the ability of the mediators to exert pressures and manipulate incentives effectively.

In the interstate negotiations, we examined movement by the four major external actors—the United States, the USSR, Cuba, and South Africa—from interventionist to disengagement behaviors between 1975 and 1988 and found the change to be explained primarily by shifts in each actor's incentive patterns. The late 1980s were the dawn of a new cooperative relationship between the superpowers. As the Soviets stepped back from their political, military, and ideological competition with the United States and increasingly emphasized their own domestic developmental objectives, possibilities for great-power collaboration were enhanced. The practical consequence in the Angolan case was an important behind-the-scenes cooperation in the mediation process, with the Soviets exerting pressure on the Angolan government and the Cubans at key points, and U.S. mediators seeking to influence South African preferences regarding Angola and Namibia. The internal negotiations at Gbadolite and Estoril, however, brought little fundamental change in the perceptions that the two adversaries had of

one another. Because the great powers displayed a greater involvement and sense of urgency during the Estoril mediation process than was the case with the Mobutu-led initiative, they were able to facilitate an agreement despite the evident distrust that continued to divide the adversaries. If such distrust between the MPLA and UNITA remains evident in the period ahead, it could come to represent a threat to the survival of the peace agreement.

With respect to the roles of the mediators in promoting constructive outcomes, the situations in which the third-party intermediaries found themselves differed in important ways. From the moment he took office, Crocker showed great resolve in his search for an internationally acceptable solution to the Namibian independence issue. At times, as with his initial suggestion of the idea of linkage, he may have complicated his task for some years—prior to the stalemate, while the diplomatic process remained fluid, linkage may well have made a peace settlement more difficult; once the military stalemate on the ground was recognized, however, linkage became a means for face-saving and for addressing the differences.[24] In any event, Crocker's relentless pursuit of every possible opening, coupled with the fact that he represented a global power—and as

24. For one participant in the mediation process, linkage was the "only available framework for a settlement." Freeman, "The Angola/Namibia Accord," p. 133. Also see Colin Legum, "Southern Africa: Analysis of the Peace Process," *Third World Reports*, 11 Jan. 1989, L.B/1, p. 6; G. R. Berridge, "Diplomacy and the Angola/Namibia Accords," *International Affairs* (London), 65(3):471 (Summer 1989).

such had enormous resources at his disposal, which he could employ to influence outcomes in a constructive direction—as well as with the change in the correlation of military forces and the shift in superpower perceptions, created new opportunities for decisive moves toward an Angolan settlement.

At the internal level, however, no comparable convergence of opportunities took place at Gbadolite. The Bush administration backed Mobutu's initiative but expressed reservations over the possibility of becoming a mediator in any formal sense. Lacking the skills and determination displayed by Crocker in the earlier negotiations and unable to bring the resources of a great power to bear on promoting an internationally acceptable settlement, Mobutu was not in a position to alter the perceptions and incentives of the MPLA and UNITA. Subsequently, Portuguese mediators made concerted efforts to involve the superpowers in the negotiating process, and with evident success. As a consequence, a medium-power mediator was backed during the final, critical weeks of the negotiations by the resources that the Soviet Union and the United States could exert on their allies. The importance of the superpower role in the mediation process was not lost on the rival Angolan leaders. Thus Savimbi noted, when expressing his appreciation for the Portuguese effort, "Without the Americans and Soviets on their side, Durao Barroso [the Portuguese mediator] would not have gotten anywhere."[25]

Finally, the mediators' credibility and capacity to mobilize resources had a direct bearing upon their ability to exert pressures and manipulate incentives. In the international negotiations on an Angola-Namibia agreement and in the internal mediation effort leading up to the Estoril accord, the successful outcomes depended substantially upon parallel American and Soviet pressures on their respective clients. At various points, Crocker pressed the South Africans to cease their military assistance to UNITA and to agree to an international settlement; in the 1991 internal negotiations, American officials reassured MPLA leaders as to their good intentions while at the same time pressing UNITA, which relied heavily upon the United States for sophisticated military equipment, to make concessions on such key issues as the timetable for elections. Similarly, the Soviets, who had provided the Angolan government forces with ideological support and extensive war matériel over the years, were at a favorable position to influence their MPLA allies. During the international negotiations, Soviet diplomats were well placed to clarify critical points of contention, to encourage Luanda's leaders to bargain in earnest, and to adopt a conciliatory position on such questions as the redeployment and withdrawal of Cuban forces. At Estoril, the Soviets played an active part in facilitating an agreement, meeting with Savimbi at the Soviet embassy in Washington,

---

25. Sergio Trefaut, "UNITA Embarks on Electoral Campaign," Semanario (Lisbon), as reproduced in Foreign Broadcast Information Service, Sub-Saharan Africa, 91(085):16 (2 May 1991).

helping to shape the Washington Concepts Paper, and pressing MPLA leaders to make concessions on important points of difference.

By contrast, Mobutu had no comparable pressures and incentives that he could bring to bear on the disputing parties during the Gbadolite process. Through a combination of persuasion and pressure he did manage to get the rivals to the summit at Gbadolite and to extract an agreement on certain broad principles from a reluctant dos Santos and Savimbi. But once the Gbadolite conferees dispersed, there was little influence that Mobutu could bring to bear to overcome the stalemate. To be sure, the United States sought to pressure Savimbi to attend the Kinshasa summit, and some African leaders gave general support to Mobutu's mediatory effort, but these initiatives were intermittent and lacking in firmness and conviction. Taken together, then, these factors show the structures of these three mediation processes to be quite distinct, accounting in part for the varying results from each peacemaking attempt.

Evolution of a Dual Negotiation Process: Afghanistan

By IMTIAZ H. BOKHARI

ABSTRACT: The negotiations in Afghanistan following the introduction of Soviet troops during a military coup in 1978 were pursued along two tracks. The first consisted of sporadic negotiations between the Soviet-supported Afghan government and several *mujahidin* resistance groups. To date, these talks have not reached fruition. The second track consisted of negotiations officially conducted between Pakistan and Afghanistan, but in reality between the United States and the Soviet Union over the withdrawal of Soviet troops. The negotiations were conducted in Geneva and in the region over a seven-year period under U.N. mediation. The result was the Geneva Accord of 14 April 1988; the agreement provided for the withdrawal of Soviet troops and the termination of arms supplies by the United States and the Soviet Union, which was dependent upon both sides' observation. The success in the international negotiations can be attributed to the existence of a ripe moment and the skill of the U.N. mediation, neither of which elements are present in the internal negotiations.

Imtiaz H. Bokhari is a retired officer from the Pakistani army and is currently senior research fellow at the Institute of Strategic Studies in Islamabad, Pakistan. He received his doctorate from the Johns Hopkins University. He is the author of a number of analyses of political events in the subcontinent.

THE signing of the Geneva Accords on 14 April 1988 under the auspices of the United Nations marked the successful culmination of difficult and protracted negotiations for the withdrawal of Soviet troops from Afghanistan. Spread over six years, nine shuttle missions to the region, and 11 rounds of indirect talks at Geneva, it represents a highly complex case of regional negotiations. Official parties to the proximity talks were Pakistan and Afghanistan, but —except on one occasion—Soviets were part of the Afghan delegation while Islamabad closely coordinated its position with Washington and consulted *mujahidin* leaders before and briefed them after each round of talks. The four instruments constituting component parts of a political settlement on Afghanistan were

- bilateral agreement between Pakistan and Afghanistan on the principle of mutual relations, in particular on noninterference and nonintervention;
- a declaration on international guarantees signed by the Soviet Union and the United States;
- bilateral agreement between Pakistan and Afghanistan on the voluntary return of refugees; and
- an agreement on interrelationships for the settlement of the situation relating to Afghanistan signed by Pakistan and Afghanistan and by the Soviet Union and the United States as guarantor-states. This instrument provided for a phased withdrawal of the foreign troops starting 15 May 1988.[1]

THE AFGHAN CRISIS: BACKGROUND

The immediate precipitant to the Afghan crisis, to which the Geneva proximity talks were seeking a solution, can be identified as the 1978 Saur revolution, which overthrew Sardar Daud Khan in a bloody coup and brought in Muhammad Taraki, leader of the People's Democratic Party of Afghanistan (PDPA), a Communist party with links to Moscow. There was serious and widespread mass opposition to this "Godless," Communist regime, and the religious tradition of the Afghan nation coupled with Afghan revulsion for alien ideas and foreign domination resulted in a near collapse of the Soviet-backed regime. In order to save this socialist regime, the Kremlin, under the Brezhnev doctrine, was left with no choice but to move into Afghanistan militarily.

The Soviet Union introduced its "limited military contingent" into Afghanistan on Christmas Eve in 1979. This was the first instance since World War II that the Soviet Union had intervened militarily in a Muslim and nonaligned state. This situation gave rise, on one hand, to the Afghan resistance, which constitutes one of the most determined

1. For the text of these accords and instruments, see *Pakistan Horizon*, 41(3) (July 1988); *Afghanistan Report*, May 1988, no. 49. *Afghanistan Report* is a monthly report published by the Institute of Strategic Studies, Islamabad.

guerrilla movements in modern times, and, on the other hand, to a very hostile and a strong international reaction, in which the United States played an important role.

The nucleus of the Afghan resistance was formed in opposition to the leftist-leaning government of Sardar Daud Khan, who had deposed King Zahir Shah in 1973 and declared Afghanistan a republic. This provided the core around which resistance forces gathered in opposition to the 1978 Communist coup. The *mujahidin* forces showed a rapid increase following the Soviet invasion, as did the number of Afghan refugees in Pakistan and Iran. The *mujahidin* forces can be identified by the three distinct areas from which they operate: Afghanistan; refugee bases and sanctuaries in Pakistan; and Iran. They are further divided by ideology, ethnic makeup, and personal rivalries.[2]

INTRA-AFGHAN NEGOTIATION PROCESS

Internal negotiation in Afghanistan differed markedly from classical

2. Richard P. Cronin and Francis T. Miko, "Afghanistan: Status, U.S. Role, and Implications of a Soviet Withdrawal" (Update, Congressional Research Service, Library of Congress, 2 Aug. 1989). For more details of the resistance forces and seven parties located in Pakistan, see Imtiaz H. Bokhari, "The Afghan War: A Study in Insurgency and Counter-Insurgency," *Strategic Studies* (Islamabad), 5(3) (Spring 1982). For more details on the evolution of resistance groups, see Bruce J. Amstutz, *Afghanistan: The First Five Years of Soviet Occupation* (Washington, DC: National Defense University Press, 1986), pp. 97-110; and for a tabulated listing, see Andre Brigot and Oliver Roy, *The War in Afghanistan* (London: Harvester Wheatsheaf, 1988), pp. 106-7.

cases in which the de jure government refuses to negotiate with insurgent leaders in order to deny them legitimacy. In the case of Afghanistan, the reverse was true. The regime in Kabul had lost its legitimacy domestically as well as internationally, and the *mujahidin* leaders were not willing to enter into negotiations with it lest it reclaim legitimacy.

Contact between a *mujahidin* military leader and the Soviets was reported as early as 1983. These negotiations between Ahmed Shah Massoud, a leading resistance military leader and commander of the Panjshir Valley, and the Soviets resulted in the February 1983 truce agreement. Ahmed Shah Massoud refused to enter into negotiations with Babrak Karmal's government, however. The cease-fire in the Panjshir Valley remained intact for the stipulated period of one year, but negotiations for its extension beyond February 1984 did not succeed. From the negotiation perspective, it is interesting to note the degree of autonomy exercised by major military leaders, their hesitancy to negotiate with the regime in Kabul, and the willingness of the Soviet Union to negotiate with the *mujahidin* over the head of the Kabul regime.

As the negotiations for the Geneva Accords were entering their final phase in early 1988, the intra-*mujahidin* and inter-Afghan negotiations also gained considerable momentum. In March 1988, eight parties based in Iran agreed to form the United Council of Afghan Mujahidin.[3] In Paki-

3. *Afghanistan Report*, Apr. 1988, no. 48, p. 49.

stan, after negotiations over a two-week period, the *mujahidin* leaders announced their decision to form an interim government.

Toward the end of 1988, as the deadline for the completion of the withdrawal of Soviet troops was drawing near, the *mujahidin* leaders were coming under increasing pressure to evolve a mechanism acceptable to the majority of the Afghans to replace Najibullah's government. With this end in mind, the *mujahidin* leaders in Afghanistan were engaged in negotiations with the Soviets as well as with Tehran-based *mujahidin* leaders. A *mujahidin* delegation under Burhanuddin Rabbani, leader of the Peshawar-based seven-party alliance, and the Soviet delegation, led by Yuli Vorontsov, Soviet ambassador in Kabul and first deputy foreign minister, met in Taif, Saudi Arabia, in the first week of December. For the *mujahidin* this meeting was their first high-level direct negotiations with the Soviets; the *mujahidin* had been demanding such negotiations, but the Soviets had been consistently rejecting them.

In December 1988, Burhanuddin Rabbani led a delegation to Tehran to discuss convening a *shoora* to elect an interim government once the Soviets had withdrawn. Earlier, both the seven-party Afghan Alliance and Ayatollah Mohsini, leader of the Iran-based *mujahidin*, had rejected the Cordovez plan for the establishment of a national government in Kabul for peace and reconstruction of Afghanistan.[4] After 14 days of heated discussions, the Afghan *mujahidin* based in

Pakistan succeeded in electing an interim government that was supposed to take power in Kabul after the fall of the Soviet-backed regime of Najibullah. The Iran-based eight-party alliance boycotted the *shoora* proceedings, as their demand for an increased number of seats was not accepted. Their leader, Karim Khalili, criticized the *shoora* and said that it was not comprehensive and did not represent the entire Afghan nation. This lack of intra-*mujahidin* negotiations has continued until today and has had an adverse effect on the course of events since the withdrawal of Soviet troops from Afghanistan.[5]

While *mujahidin* leaders of all parties were insistent on not dealing with the regime in Kabul, there is a strong possibility that covert inter-Afghan negotiations occurred between Najibullah and some of the *mujahidin* leaders. Reportedly these secret negotiations had been arranged by the Palestine Liberation Organization leader, Yasir Arafat, during 1989.

According to Arafat, four meetings were held between a four-member PDPA delegation and a three-member delegation from Gulbadin Hekmatyar's Hizb-i-Islami. These meetings were held in four different Arab capitals, including San'a, Baghdad, and Tunis—to avoid media attention. Another report says that the leader of Hizb-i-Islami, Hekmatyar, had established contact with the Kabul government before the USSR had withdrawn its troops. More recently, there were reports that Dr. Najibullah met the leader of the National Islamic Front, Syed Ahmad Gailani, and rep-

4. *Muslim*, 13 July 1988; ibid., 15 July 1988.

5. *Afghanistan Report*, Mar. 1989, no. 59, pp. 41-42.

resentatives of former King Zahir Shah in Geneva on 1 December 1990. During his stopover for refueling in Mashhad, Najibullah reportedly met with two more *mujahidin* leaders, possibly including the president of the Afghan interim government, Professor Sibghatullah Mujadeddi. Whether or not these covert contacts lead to any formal and open negotiations between the *mujahidin* and the Kabul regime is hard to predict, but these meetings constitute important links in internal negotiations.

EVOLUTION OF THE GENEVA NEGOTIATION PROCESS

The second United Nations General Assembly resolution of 20 November 1980 authorized the secretary-general to attempt to negotiate a political solution to the Afghan problem. The resolution listed four essential points to form the basis of a solution: (1) preservation of the sovereignty, territorial integrity, political independence, and nonaligned character of Afghanistan; (2) the right of the Afghan people to determine their own form of government and to choose their economic, political, and social system free from outside intervention, subversion, coercion, or constraint of any kind whatsoever; (3) immediate withdrawal of foreign troops from Afghanistan; and (4) creation of the necessary conditions that would enable the Afghan refugees to return voluntarily to their homes in safety and honor.[6] Pakistan urged the secretary-general to follow up on the resolution

and also suggested trilateral negotiations involving Pakistan, Iran, and the Kabul regime. Moscow's stand on the question of negotiations was one of ambivalence. While it supported a political settlement of the Afghan problem, it wanted only a minimal role for the United Nations and pressed for the recognition of the Kabul regime before negotiations could start. Pakistan refused to recognize the Kabul regime in accordance with the decision of the foreign ministers of the Organization of the Islamic Conference. In December 1980, however, Moscow, without mentioning the question of recognition, told Pakistan that Kabul was prepared to talk.[7]

On 11 February 1981, U.N. Secretary-General Kurt Waldheim appointed Javier Perez de Cuellar, then under secretary-general, to be his personal representative. On 24 August 1981, eight months after the Soviets lent their support for talks, the Kabul government indicated to Pakistan that it no longer insisted on bilateral talks, and the Afghan foreign minister, Shah Dost Mohammad, told Rajiv Gandhi in New Delhi that Kabul was "flexible" on procedural matters.[8]

In August, after two shuttle missions to Kabul and Islamabad, Perez

Talks: An Annotated Chronology and Analysis of the United Nations-Sponsored Negotiations (Washington, DC: Library of Congress, Congressional Research Service, 1988); Newspaper Clippings files on Afghanistan at the Institute of Strategic Studies, Islamabad; *Afghanistan Report*; and Rosanne Klass, "Afghanistan: The Accords," *Foreign Affairs*, 66(5) (Summer 1988).

7. *Far Eastern Economic Review*, 13 Feb. 1981.

8. *New York Times*, 8 Sept. 1981.

6. This part of this article is based on *Keesing's*; Richard P. Cronin, *Afghanistan Peace*

de Cuellar reported to the secretary-general that Pakistan and Afghanistan had agreed on the following four-point agenda: withdrawal of Soviet forces from Afghanistan; pledges by both countries to refrain from interfering in each other's internal affairs; international guarantees concerning noninterference; the return of the refugees.[9]

Following this breakthrough, the first indirect talks were held at U.N. headquarters at New York. At these talks, both parties hardened their positions. Afghanistan's foreign minister expressed readiness for bilateral or trilateral talks but stressed Kabul's insistence that they be direct government-to-government talks and that the question of a timetable for the withdrawal of the Soviet troops was a matter to be determined by agreement between Afghanistan and the Soviet Union. Pakistan also hardened its position, by refusing to talk directly to Kabul's delegation even as a representative of the PDPA.

For the third shuttle mission, in April 1982, the new U.N. representative, Diego Cordovez, visited Islamabad, Kabul, and Tehran—this was the first time that Tehran had received a U.N. negotiator. As a result of this shuttle mission, the first round of the Geneva negotiation process between Pakistan and Afghanistan began on 16 June 1982. Cordovez reported that both countries had made important concessions, but he gave no further details.

It was generally believed that Yuri Andropov, who became the secretary-general of the Communist Party of the Soviet Union after Brezhnev's death in December 1982 and had not supported the decision to intervene militarily in Afghanistan, would have a more flexible position on the question of the withdrawal of Soviet troops. There was a heightened sense of optimism when, at Brezhnev's funeral, Andropov reportedly told President Zia ul-Haq of Pakistan that the Soviet Union wanted to get out of Afghanistan and would withdraw quickly if Pakistan ceased its support of the resistance. Even Cordovez said that he saw a "window for diplomacy."[10]

Cordovez undertook his fourth shuttle mission to Tehran, Kabul, and Islamabad between 21 January and 7 February 1983, during which he presented a working draft of an agreement. On 25 March, Cordovez and Secretary-General Perez de Cuellar met with Andropov and Andrei Gromyko in Moscow and secured their support for the Geneva II talks, which were held from 8 to 22 April 1983. Indications were that considerable progress had been made on the working draft.

In May 1983, after meeting the U.S. ambassador to the United Nations, Jeane Kirkpatrick, and securing U.S. support for the talks, Cordovez reported that 95 percent of the text of the draft comprehensive settlement was ready and that "only blanks in a withdrawal time-table had to be filled in."[11] His optimism soon proved unfounded, however.

During the June round of the Geneva II, both sides hardened their

10. *Far Eastern Economic Review*, 24 Dec. 1982, p. 24.

11. Agha Shahi, "The Geneva Accords," *Pakistan Horizon*, 41(3):34 (July 1988); Klass, "Afghanistan."

9. *Far Eastern Economic Review*, 28 Aug. 1981, cited in Cronin, *Afghanistan Peace Talks.*

negotiating positions. Pakistan refused to accept any part of the agreement as final until all the other parts of the package were in place; it sought to reopen discussions on clauses concerning noninterference; and it raised the issue of devising a mechanism for consulting the refugees on the issue of their return to Afghanistan. In turn, the Soviets refused to discuss—through the Afghan representatives—a specific timetable for withdrawal of troops and concentrated on obtaining watertight commitments from Pakistan regarding noninterference clauses. The parties did agree, however, that Cordovez could initiate consultations with Moscow and Washington to seek their agreement to act as guarantors.

Chernenko and continuing impasse

After a 10-month break in the negotiation process, Cordovez resumed his efforts in his fifth shuttle mission and visited Tehran, Kabul, and Islamabad in April 1984. Soviet policy had hardened under Chernenko, who had taken over after Andropov's death, but Cordovez secured agreement to the format of the proximity talks, which would involve discussions alternately with the parties in adjacent rooms. Cordovez also changed the framework of the negotiations to include the following four instruments: noninterference, international guarantees, return of the Afghan refugees, and interrelationships. The question of the withdrawal of foreign forces, as was mentioned in the earlier draft, was to be covered under the instrument of interrela-

tionships,[12] as the Soviet Union insisted that withdrawal of troops was a matter between Kabul and Moscow.

The Geneva III talks, held from 24 to 30 August 1984, did not achieve any substantive results. For the first time since the inception of the Geneva talks, the Afghan delegation was without a Soviet adviser, and some observers saw this as an indication of a lack of any significant movement in the Afghan position.[13] Both Pakistan and Afghanistan expressed their satisfaction with the Geneva talks and agreed to continue their proximity talks.

Cordovez undertook a visit to the region—the sixth shuttle mission—from 25 to 31 May 1985. During this visit Afghanistan and Pakistan agreed that the settlement should consist of "a bilateral agreement on non-interference and non-intervention;" "a declaration (or declarations) on international guarantees;" "a bilateral agreement on the voluntary return of refugees;" and "an instrument that would set out the interrelationship between the aforementioned instruments and the solution of the question of the withdrawal of foreign troops in accordance with an agreement to be concluded between Afghanistan and the Union of Soviet Socialist Republics."[14]

At the end of the Geneva IV talks, held from 20 to 25 June, Cordovez spoke about the end of the "deadlock"

12. *Far Eastern Economic Review*, 12 Apr. 1984; ibid., 21 June 1984.
13. Cronin, *Afghanistan Peace Talks*, p. 17.
14. United Nations, Report, Oct. 1985, para. 9, pp. 2-3, cited in Cronin, *Afghanistan Peace Talks*, p. 18.

which had prevailed since 1983.[15] According to the secretary-general's report, the instruments of noninterference and nonintervention, international guarantees, and the return of refugees essentially had been settled. The instrument of interrelationships, which linked the withdrawal of Soviet troops to Pakistan's commitment to restrain the *mujahidin* from operating from its territory, had yet to be completed. At this stage, Afghanistan insisted on concurrent action on noninterference and international guarantees, whereas withdrawal of Soviet troops was to follow later at some unspecified time. Pakistan insisted that all aspects of the package must begin simultaneously, with a specific time frame for a Soviet withdrawal.[16]

In Geneva V, from 26 to 30 August 1985, Afghanistan made the most determined bid to force Pakistan to accept face-to-face negotiations. Pakistan refused to yield, and after two days of deadlock, Cordovez reverted to the previous format, in which he shuttled between separate rooms.[17] There was not much progress, and the basic impasse remained, preventing consideration of the interrelationship instrument.[18] In a letter presented to Cordovez on 10 December, the United States expressed its willingness to be a guarantor in the context of a comprehensive and balanced agreement in which the central issue of Soviet troop withdrawal and its interrelationship to the other instruments would be resolved.[19]

At Geneva VI, in December 1985, there was a continuing deadlock over the negotiating format as the Afghan side again insisted on face-to-face talks as a price for continuing the negotiations. The Afghans reportedly gave Cordovez a schedule for troop withdrawal that could be discussed if Pakistan agreed to negotiate directly. Pakistan refused on the ground that such negotiation represented recognition of the Soviet-installed regime.[20]

The seventh shuttle mission, in March 1986, took Cordovez to Moscow, Islamabad, and twice to Kabul. Cordovez announced that the Kabul government had given him a timetable for the withdrawal of Soviet troops, although there was a major gap between the positions of Afghanistan and Pakistan. The question of format, however, seemed to have been temporarily resolved, with Kabul agreeing to continue with indirect talks.

Gorbachev and gradual change

Following his accession to power in early 1985, Mikhail Gorbachev intensified Soviet military operations against both the Afghan resistance and the civilian population. He also escalated pressure on Pakistan through political means, military incidents, and increased terrorist acts.[21]

15. Lawrence Lifshultz, "Afghanistan: The Choice Ahead," *Muslim*, 5 Aug. 1985.

16. United Nations, Report, para. 10, p. 3, cited in Cronin, *Afghanistan Peace Talks*, pp. 19-20.

17. *Washington Post*, 31 Aug. 1985.

18. United Nations, Report, para. 12, p. 3, cited in Cronin, *Afghanistan Peace Talks*, p. 22.

19. *New York Times*, 14 Dec. 1985; Klass, "Afghanistan."

20. *Washington Post*, 3 Jan. 1986.

21. Klass, "Afghanistan."

Babrak Karmal was abruptly replaced as head of the PDPA by General Najibullah, the chief of Afghan secret police, on 4 May 1986, just on the eve of another round of the Geneva talks. Some observers interpreted this move as a concession while others thought it was designed to more effectively prosecute the war.

The Geneva VII talks, from 19 to 23 May 1986, were held against the background of intensified Soviet military pressure. As far as the negotiations were concerned, two important developments took place: first, Kabul rescinded its demand for direct negotiations; and, second, for the first time, the talks included consideration of the interrelationship instrument. The gap in the position of the two sides on withdrawal remained very wide; the Afghans were talking in terms of three to four years and Pakistan was speaking in terms of six months or less.[22] The two sides did agree on some points, however, including provisions that the final document would be legally binding, that it would be signed by the two foreign ministers, and that it would be enforced by an international monitoring team composed of representatives of mutually acceptable countries.[23]

The week-long talks of Geneva VII that began on 30 July failed to narrow the gap still between the two parties on two key issues, namely, the withdrawal time frame and measures for monitoring and verifying compliance with the agreement. Nonetheless, Cordovez said that "the process [was] very much alive and [would] continue."[24]

The eighth shuttle mission, in November 1986, took Cordovez to Islamabad, Tehran, and twice to Kabul. Cordovez obtained an agreement to restart the talks and to have an "effective implementation of the settlement."[25] On reaching New York, on 9 December, Cordovez said that the schedule for the withdrawal was the only matter left to be resolved.[26]

On 28 July 1986, however, Gorbachev had called for the formation in the near future of an Afghan government " 'with the participation in it of those political forces which found themselves outside the country'—a reference to exiled resistance leaders, refugees, and the former king."[27] After returning from Moscow, on 30 December 1986, Najibullah had announced the details of a proposal for national reconciliation. The initiative proved stillborn as the resistance responded unanimously in the negative.

In the round of the Geneva VII talks from 25 February to 9 March 1987, both Pakistan and the United States insisted that no solution to the Afghan crisis would be acceptable that did not involve political arrangements that would be acceptable to the Afghan *mujahidin* and would induce the refugees to return home. On the question of the time frame for a Soviet troop withdrawal, there was a narrowing of the gap between posi-

22. *Muslim*, 24 May 1986.

23. *Far Eastern Economic Review*, 3 July 1986.

24. *Muslim*, 6 July 1986.

25. Ibid., 4 Dec. 1986.

26. *New York Times*, 10 Dec. 1986.

27. Barnett R. Rubin, "Afghanistan: The Next Round," *Orbis*, Winter 1989, p. 61.

tions: Afghanistan offered 18 months and Pakistan insisted on 7. The round of Geneva VII talks from 7 to 10 September was held at the request of the Soviet and Afghan governments. Apparently, this round of talks did not achieve much. The Afghan side reduced its time frame for troop withdrawal slightly, from 18 to 16 months and Pakistan increased its own from 7 to 8.[28]

On the military front, the Kremlin gave the Afghan Communists a year to build a stable base of power with the help of Soviet troops. Withdrawal of Soviet troops would begin in early 1988, Gorbachev reportedly told Najibullah in Moscow in July 1987, saying, "I hope you are ready in twelve months because we will be leaving whether you are or not."[29]

In November 1987, Cordovez received signals that Moscow had decided to propose a short timetable for withdrawal without conditions about progress on the formation of a national government.[30] Starting with the December 1987 Reagan-Gorbachev summit, the Soviet position on an internal settlement began to crystallize. Under Secretary of State Richard Armacost was quoted as saying "that the Soviets do not link the withdrawal of their troops to prior resolution of issues of an interim government or transitional arrangements among Afghans."[31] Meanwhile, the U.S. policy to support the *mujahidin* indicated that the start of the Soviet pullback could coincide with the ab-

rogation of American assistance to the *mujahidin*.[32]

Cordovez, in his ninth shuttle mission, from 19 January to 9 February, visited Islamabad and Kabul. During this trip, he laid the groundwork for the agreement that was to be signed during the final round of negotiations in Geneva VIII. These negotiations started on 2 March 1988 and within two days, agreement was reached between Pakistan and the Kabul regime on a phased withdrawal of the Soviet forces commencing 15 May, the date on which the agreement was to come into force. The withdrawal was to be "front-end loaded," with one-half of the troops to be withdrawn by 15 August 1988 and the withdrawal to be completed within nine months.[33]

The negotiations were stalled, however, as there was new thinking on two issues by Pakistan and the United States. Pakistan insisted that, before they sign an agreement, Najibullah's government be replaced by an interim Afghan coalition government before the Soviets leave Afghanistan. This was a reversal of Pakistan's previously stated position. The United States demanded, under strong pressure from the Congress, that the Soviets agree to stop sending supplies to the Kabul regime simultaneously with a cutoff of U.S. arms deliveries to the *mujahidin*.

Pakistan's demand was not accepted by Cordovez on the grounds that a transitional government was not a part of the four instruments that formed the basis of the Geneva

28. *Washington Post*, 6 Sept. 1987.
29. Rubin, "Afghanistan," p. 61.
30. Ibid., p. 64.
31. *Far Eastern Economic Review*, 24 Dec. 1987.

32. *Washington Times*, 16 Dec. 1987.
33. Agha Shahi, "Geneva Accords," p. 25.

negotiations. Even Pakistan's scaled-down demand to finalize the modalities and procedures for the formation of a transitional regime were not acceptable to the Kabul side. The two superpowers resolved the issue by agreeing that Cordovez should provide his good offices in his personal capacity of facilitating agreement between different Afghan parties on the formation of a broad-based government. This formula provided Pakistan with a way out from an isolated position.

The Soviet Union rejected the U.S. proposal that called for a moratorium on military aid by both sides—positive symmetry—during the period of Soviet withdrawal. On 30 March 1988, George Shultz, the U.S. secretary of state, offered a compromise proposal under which the United States would reserve the right to supply military equipment to the *mujahidin* as long as the Soviet Union supplied the Najibullah regime—negative symmetry. This proposal was finally accepted by the Soviet Union and on 8 April Cordovez announced that the Geneva Accords were finalized and ready to be signed, as was done on 14 April 1988.

CONCLUSION

The Geneva Accords provide a highly complex but equally instructive study of regional conflict management and of its attendant problems. Officially, there were bilateral negotiations between Kabul and Islamabad, and, by excluding the *mujahidin*, they demonstrated the art of the possible. Successful negotiations between the Kabul regime and the *mujahidin* would have been almost impossible. Even if the two had come to an agreement in principle, the attempt at conflict resolution would have become the victim of its own contradictions—over twenty parties were trying to put up a joint negotiating position with the Kabul regime.

From Pakistan's point of view, the talks provided an opportunity to secure a political settlement to a problem that would have defied a military solution—and a military solution possibly would not have been in the interests of Pakistan. Pakistan succeeded in securing an agreement for the withdrawal of Soviet troops, but it did not manage to get an environment conducive enough to the return of the refugees to their homes.

The Geneva Accords are a case of negotiations in which the interests of the host state became entangled with the interests of the resistance forces, which sought and operated from sanctuaries provided by the host state. The Geneva Accords also provide an example of the role of the United Nations in situations where it can be a useful mediator. In situations where conflict becomes an East-West issue, with the two superpowers directly or indirectly involved, no party other than the United Nations has the *locus standi* for attempting mediation.

The negotiation process reviewed in this article illustrates the usefulness of the concept of ripeness as an analytical tool for both understanding and steering the negotiation process.

ANNALS, *AAPSS*, **518**, November 1991

Mediation in a Transitional Conflict: Eritrea

By MARINA OTTAWAY

ABSTRACT: After thirty years of war, the conflict between the Ethiopian government and the Eritrean nationalists was further than ever from a solution. Liberation movements had been organized in other areas of the country, most notably in Tigre, where the Tigrean People's Liberation Front had won major victories. What had started as a bilateral conflict between the government and the Eritrean nationalists thus entered a phase of transition to a multilateral conflict. This made the prospect of a negotiated solution more remote. By definition, many of the conditions necessary for successful negotiations are absent in transitional conflicts, most notably a mutually hurting stalemate and the existence of valid spokesmen.

Marina Ottaway received a Ph.D. in sociology from Columbia University. She has taught at Addis Ababa University and other African universities as well as at the American University and the Johns Hopkins School of Advanced International Studies in Washington, D.C. She has written many books and articles on the Horn of Africa, including Ethiopia: Empire in Revolution, *coauthored with David Ottaway (1978), and she has recently edited* The Political Economy of Ethiopia *(1990). She is currently doing research in South Africa.*

FOR almost thirty years, various liberation movements in Eritrea have been pitted against the Ethiopian government in an attempt to gain independence for the former Italian colony, which was reintegrated into Ethiopia in 1952. In late 1990, the Ethiopian government appeared close to defeat, with the army increasingly reluctant to fight. But this did not necessarily mean that the Eritrean People's Liberation Front (EPLF), at this time the most important of the Eritrean movements and the only one actually fighting, was close to victory. The nature of the conflict itself had changed. What had started in 1962 as a bilateral Eritrean-Ethiopian conflict had turned in the late 1980s into a conflict pitting the Ethiopian government against a very loose alliance of regional and ethnic liberation movements, in which the Tigrean People's Liberation Front (TPLF) had come to play a role almost as important as that of the EPLF. Relations among the members of the alliance were unclear enough to suggest that the collapse of the Ethiopian regime was more likely to lead to further strife between the various groups than to uncontested independence for Eritrea and a return to peace.

The transitional nature of the conflict made the prospects for negotiations extremely poor. An initiative by former President Jimmy Carter resulted in the opening of official talks between the two parties, in September 1989 in Atlanta and again in November in Nairobi. But the talks made very slow progress on form and none on substance, and they were finally called off by the EPLF in the spring of 1990. Subsequently, Assistant Secretary of State Herman Cohen took up the mediation attempt, with no further progress, and the government of Mengistu Haile Mariam fell to the TPLF in May 1991 without thereby resolving the Eritrean question.

The negotiations had started at an unpromising time, prompted not by favorable conditions but by the humanitarian concerns of the mediator. From a political point of view, the intervention came either too late or too early. By the time the talks started, it was too late to tackle the Eritrean conflict as a bilateral one. But the new, multilateral conflict was still too undefined, the relations between the parties too unclear, and, above all, the hopes for a military victory on the part of the TPLF too high for an attempt at mediation to be conceivable. The conflict was in a transitional stage, and as a result the prospects for negotiations were very poor.

This article will look at the changing nature of the conflict and at previous attempts to negotiate a solution. It will conclude with a discussion of the special problems of negotiations in a transitional conflict.

THE ERITREAN PROBLEM AND THE DISINTEGRATION OF THE EMPIRE

The problem of Eritrea was created by Italian colonialism. The territory became an Italian colony in 1890. Italian hopes of further expansion were dashed in 1896 by the Ethiopian victory at Adowa. That defeat gave Eritrea its present borders.

Past these basic points, which are too clearly recorded to leave room for controversy, the two sides' interpretations of the Eritrean problem diverge sharply.

For the Ethiopian side, the territory incorporated by Italy was an integral part of the Ethiopian empire. For the Eritrean side, it was a territory with a history separate from Ethiopia's since the end of the Axumite empire. Both positions are absurd. The Ethiopian empire never had fixed boundaries, and certainly many parts of Eritrea had only loose and intermittent connections with the center. It is not a forgone conclusion that, but for Italian intervention, the entire territory we know as Eritrea would have ended up within the boundaries of Ethiopia. But the Eritrean contention that ties between Ethiopia and Eritrea were severed many centuries ago is quickly belied by the language, religion, and other cultural traits shared by the highland population north and south of the Ethio-Eritrean boundary line.

The Ethiopian position on Eritrea has remained unchanged since the collapse of the Italian empire in 1941: Eritrea is part of Ethiopia. The Eritrean position has, if anything, hardened. The EPLF, which has always claimed the right of Eritrea to self-determination because it was a colony, is now also arguing that Eritrea in any case had nothing in common with Ethiopia.[1] In a continent where efforts to reconstruct the past—and occasionally to invent one of dubious authenticity—abound, Eritrea represents a paradoxical case of a country denying parts of its recorded history and culture because they do not fit present political requirements.

Both the Ethiopian government and the Eritrean nationalists have found it convenient to consider the problem of Eritrea unique. Indeed, when the war started in 1961, in the context of a seemingly stable empire, this was not an unrealistic point of view. But the overthrow of Emperor Haile Selassie in 1974 set in motion a process of change, focusing on the transformation of the socioeconomic system in the 1970s and, increasingly, on the relation of the component parts of the old empire in the 1980s. The "problem of the nationalities" flared up, but so did the historical competition for control over the empire between Amharas and Tigreans. By the end of the 1980s, the survival of an Ethiopian state coterminous with the twentieth-century empire could no longer be taken for granted. In this second period, the Eritrean problem appeared not unique but part of the overall process of remolding Ethiopia from empire into state.

THE OLD CONFLICT

The conflicting claims of the emperor and the Eritrean nationalists delayed a decision on the future of the colony until 1952. The United Nations, responsible for the former Ital-

---

1. For example, some Eritreans argue that Tigrinya should be written in the Latin alphabet, rather than in the alphabet it shares with Amharic. Also, the final communiqué of the Atlanta talks, issued on 19 Sept. 1989, did not mention Tigrinya as one of the negotiating languages but listed just Amharic, the language of the Ethiopian side; Arabic, the language of the Eritrean side; and English, the neutral language.

ian colonies, finally compromised by giving Eritrea to Ethiopia, but in a federal structure under which Eritrea had an elected parliament and executive. This did not fit at all with Haile Selassie's views, and in 1962 he succeeded in causing the Eritrean parliament to vote for the complete reintegration of Eritrea into Ethiopia. The vote did not reflect the real sentiment of the parliament—it was called in the absence of many representatives certain to oppose reintegration, but a strong unionist current existed in Eritrea at the time. This last point is important because it might affect the relations between EPLF and TPLF in the future.

An armed conflict started even before the dissolution of the federation, escalating slowly through the 1960s and much more rapidly after Haile Selassie's overthrow. Two major factors have sustained a conflict of such duration and prevented serious negotiations. First, the EPLF, like all liberation movements, can only survive by fighting. Second, the rapid political change in the rest of Ethiopia since 1974 has given hope to each party in turn that victory could be achieved.

Initially, the imperial government believed it could defeat the new nationalist movement easily. This conviction was strengthened by a schism in the Eritrean ranks, with the new EPLF splitting off from the original Eritrean Liberation Front (ELF).[2] The ELF was seen as rural-, lowland-, and Muslim-oriented. The EPLF had its roots originally among urban,

better-educated, and Christian highland Eritreans, the population from which the emperor had received some support in the past. In the short run, the split within nationalist ranks was good for the central government, for the two movements were soon fighting as much against each other as against the imperial army.

In the early years the Eritrean nationalists did not score major victories but could find encouragement in their growing ranks. After 1974, they suddenly began to see the possibility of a quick military victory. The crumbling of the imperial regime, and the apparent disarray of the Derg, the military committee that replaced Haile Selassie, led the Eritrean movements to the conclusion that it was time to strike. An attack on Asmara in January 1975 marked the beginning of a crescendo of military activity, which culminated in a near victory in 1977, at a time when the Ethiopian army was also fighting against Somalia in the Ogaden. The government was forced to abandon most garrisons—in the end it only controlled four towns—and the nationalists began to close in on Asmara, the Eritrean capital.[3] Victory appeared near, but in the end the insurgents failed. A major reason was the incapacity of the EPLF and the ELF to set aside their differences and make a final joint effort.

After 1978 it was the turn of the Ethiopian government to believe again in the possibility of a military

2. See John Markakis, *National and Class Conflict in the Horn of Africa* (New York: Cambridge University Press, 1987), esp. chap. 5.

3. In early 1978, only Asmara, Barentu, and the port cities of Massawa and Asab remained firmly in government hands. See ibid., p. 245.

victory. Large Soviet arms supplies allowed the government to increase the size and strength of the military.[4] Somalia had been defeated in 1978 after an initial success, and 15,000 Cuban troops were helping to protect that border.[5] Finally, the government was slowly making progress in reorganizing the country internally, creating a political party and thus establishing more effective control in most areas.

In 1982 the government was confident enough of its new position to launch the Red Star campaign in Eritrea. Initially conceived as a "multifaceted approach to the Eritrean problem, including recognition of the guerrilla movements, a search for a non-military solution, and attention to the economic and social problems of the region," the campaign eventually degenerated into a purely military exercise that failed to break the stalemate.[6]

Despite the 1982 failure, the government still believed that it could settle the Eritrean problem on its own terms through the new territorial arrangement created by the 1987 constitution.[7] Largely inspired by the Soviet model, the constitution envisaged the division of Ethiopia into regions and subregions, some of them autonomous. In particular, Eritrea was divided into two autonomous regions, named, respectively, Eritrea and Asab. The new Eritrea in turn was divided into three subregions. The government's ploy was simple enough. First, it hoped to separate from Eritrea most of the coast and especially the port of Asab, which serves Addis Ababa. The new Asab region corresponded roughly to the territory occupied by the Afars, and the government hoped they would welcome the creation of their own independent region and strive to keep the EPLF from operating there. The fact that there were apparently repeated contacts between the Ethiopian government and the ELF in the late 1980s suggests a plan to play the weaker and thus potentially more docile ELF against the stronger movement.

The government's hope that the constitution would provide a solution proved illusory. The EPLF, on the other hand, again started hoping that a military victory was possible. Inside Eritrea, the movement appeared to be well organized and strong, encountering little competition. The

4. Between 1977 and 1987, the Soviet Union delivered over $8 billion worth of military equipment to Ethiopia. See Arms Control and Disarmament Agency, *World Military Expenditure and Arms Transfers, 1988* (1991), pp. 84, 111.

5. Cuban troops never fought in Eritrea, theoretically refusing to take sides in an internal conflict and above all to go against the Eritrean nationalists they had supported in the days of Haile Selassie. Of course, the Cuban troops on the Ogaden front freed Ethiopian troops for Eritrea. Cuban troops withdrew completely from Ethiopia in 1989.

6. Dawit Wolde Giorgis, "The Power of Decision-Making in Post-Revolutionary Ethiopia," in *The Political Economy of Ethiopia*, ed. Marina Ottaway (New York: Praeger, 1990). Dawit does not explain what recognizing the liberation movements meant, or what kind of political solution the government had in mind.

7. On the constitution, see Edmond Keller, *Revolutionary Ethiopia: From Empire to Republic* (Bloomington: Indiana University Press, 1988), pp. 239ff.; Bereket Habte Selassie, "Empire and Constitutional Engineering: The PDRE in Historical Perspective," in *Political Economy of Ethiopia*, ed. Ottaway.

ELF still existed, and endless factional struggles were creating new splinter groups, but they did not have significant guerrilla forces. Outside Eritrea, an increasingly strong TPLF had the Ethiopian army tied down in combat even before it reached the northern region. Finally, there were signs of disarray inside the Ethiopian army. The strength of the Addis Ababa regime ultimately resided in its ability to keep the allegiance of the military—this was still true after the 1984 launching of a political party.[8]

The rise of the TPLF

The transformation of the TPLF during the 1980s from one of many liberation movements of marginal importance opposing the Addis Ababa regime into a major player in the politics of Ethiopia made it much more difficult to separate the Eritrean problem from that of the overall transformation of the Ethiopian empire.

The TPLF was formed after 1974, with the encouragement and direct support of the EPLF, which aimed at creating a buffer between Eritrea and the Ethiopian army. The ploy worked extremely well. There was no shortage of grievances in Tigre for the new movement to draw upon, because the region, historically part of the empire's core, had turned into an economic and political backwater. Tigre had enjoyed a brief period of renewed importance in the late nineteenth century, when "the revival of

commerce and arms trade in the Red Sea" gave Tigre enough of an advantage for a Tigrean to become emperor as Yohannes IV.[9] But his Amhara successor, Menelik II, embarked on a program of conquest that definitively moved the geographic and economic center of the empire to the south, leaving Tigre politically marginal. It was also an impoverished region, overpopulated, badly eroded, and extremely vulnerable to drought and famine. But Tigreans never quite accepted the authority of Addis Ababa, and Haile Selassie managed the problem only by allowing descendants of Yohannes to act as governors of the province.

The TPLF, like all other major opposition groups in the country, was led by young, educated, and extremely ideological and contentious individuals, who had honed their political skills in the struggles of the student movement.[10] The organization was characterized by a mixture of hard-line Marxist ideology and intense greater-Tigrean nationalism. While the TPLF in theory was a front representing a wide spectrum of ideological trends, its core was the League of Tigrean Communists, a faction that called itself pro-Albanian to show its ideological purity and its rejection of the revisionist trends evident both in China and in the Soviet Union.

8. On the Workers' Party of Ethiopia, see Christopher Clapham, *Transformation and Continuity in Revolutionary Ethiopia* (New York: Cambridge University Press, 1988), chap. 4.

9. Haggai Ehrlich, *Ethiopia and the Challenge of Independence* (Boulder, CO: Lynne Rienner, 1986), p. 19.

10. On the TPLF's link with the student movement, see broadcast of the Voice of Tigray Revolution, 21 Oct. 1989, in Federal Broadcast Information Service, *Sub-Saharan Africa*, 24 Oct. 1989.

But the TPLF was also intensely chauvinistic—its detractors said imperialistic. Maps of Tigre appearing on TPLF publications depicted a region with much enlarged boundaries, in fact extending all the way to the Sudanese border, strongly suggesting the existence of an element of Tigrean imperialism within the movement. Furthermore, the TPLF fought fiercely not only against the Ethiopian army but also against other movements operating in Tigre.[11] The TPLF grew slowly initially. It had its strongest impact in rural areas, but the towns and main roads of Tigre remained in Ethiopian hands, and feeding camps for famine victims continued to be operated in the region by foreign agencies in cooperation with the Ethiopian government.

All this changed suddenly in 1988, due to the collapse of the Ethiopian military. In April of that year, government troops suffered a major defeat at Afabet, in Eritrea, after an officers' mutiny and the subsequent purges left the garrison bereft of leadership.[12] The defeat at Afabet signaled the beginning of the army's disintegration. Purges followed the defeat, and more purges took place after an attempted coup d'état in May 1989. The morale and the fighting capability of the troops in Eritrea and Tigre diminished rapidly as a result.[13] Entire garrisons started surrendering.

The first beneficiary of the disintegration of the Ethiopian army was the TPLF. By late 1989 it had wrested virtually all Tigrean towns from Ethiopian control, and it had pushed well south into Welo province and even into northern Shewa. Fighting there was carried out not by the TPLF proper but by the Ethiopian People's Democratic Movement (EPDM), an organization closely associated with the TPLF—possibly totally controlled by it—but supposedly multiethnic.

Success affected the TPLF's goals.[14] The TPLF was not a secessionist movement, but it originally fought for regional autonomy. With success, however, came the ambition of replacing the central government with one in which the TPLF would play a major role.[15] This broader plan was manifested in the formation of the EPDM and later of the Ethiopian People's Revolutionary Democratic Front (EPRDF). The former was a non-Tigrean organization, operating mostly in Welo province, the latter an umbrella organization including both the TPLF and the EPDM. The TPLF controlled the other two organizations, however, allowing the TPLF to operate outside Tigre province with-

11. See Markakis, *National and Class Conflict*, pp. 254ff.

12. See *African Confidential*, 29 Apr. 1988.

13. On the coup, see ibid., 26 May 1989.

14. On the TPLF, see Markakis, *National and Class Conflict*, pp. 252ff.; Clapham, *Transformation and Continuity*, pp. 204ff.

15. A TPLF statement of 13 June 1989, issued in London, summarizes a TPLF peace proposal. The major point is "the establishment of a provisional government constituted from all political organizations, for a transitional period, until a constitution has been adopted by the people and a democratic government has been elected." Contrary to the EPLF, the TPLF seeks a role in the central government.

out creating resentment and opposition among non-Tigreans.[16]

The internal collapse of the Ethiopian army, coupled with the Tigrean offensive, undoubtedly broke the stalemate that had been developing during the 1980s. The possibility of a military victory became real once again. Yet, it is at this moment that the EPLF agreed to enter into negotiations with the government, with former President Jimmy Carter as mediator. The TPLF in turn rushed to set up its own process, opening talks with the government in Rome under Italian government auspices. This paradox can only be understood by taking into consideration the impact that the rise of the TPLF had on the conflict in Eritrea.

THE NEW CONFLICT

The establishment of the TPLF was encouraged by the EPLF, but the sudden success made the Tigrean movement threatening. Officially, the Eritreans denied that this was the case. The TPLF recognized the Eritrean right to self-determination, they argued. Far from being a problem, the success of the TPLF would hasten Eritrean independence.

There were reasons to doubt that the relation between the two movements was so simple. The TPLF was fighting either for a central role in a new government coalition or for control of an autonomous Tigre. In either case, the independence of Eritrea would limit its power. It would leave Ethiopia a much weakened and landlocked country, and it would thwart

16. On EPDM and EPRDF, see *Africa Confidential*, 3 Nov. 1989.

greater Tigrean nationalism by making many Tigrinya speakers into Eritrean citizens.

The TPLF's recognition of the Eritrean right to self-determination should not be given much weight until confirmed by events. The Ethiopian political culture is marked by a passion for duplicity and double meanings, "wax and gold" in the Ethiopian expression.[17] Since the beginning of the revolution, there has not been a genuine political alliance between any two movements in Ethiopia. In the mid-1970s the All-Ethiopian Socialist Movement (MEISON) supported the military council and tried to use the relation to build a political organization capable of overthrowing the military.[18] In 1978 an alliance of Marxist-Leninist organizations cooperated with the military council in trying to form a new party. This time the alliance collapsed because each movement was doing its Machiavellian best to undercut the others.[19] The EPLF and the ELF tried to negotiate a unification agreement in late 1975 and failed—in fact, a new splinter group was formed instead. The list could continue.

Another reason to question the sincerity of the EPLF-TPLF alliance

17. This cultural trait is analyzed at length in Donald Levine, *Wax and Gold* (Chicago: University of Chicago Press, 1965).

18. On the relationship between the Derg and the All-Ethiopian Socialist Movement, see David Ottaway and Marina Ottaway, *Ethiopia: Empire in Revolution* (New York: Africana, 1978), pp. 122-23, 187-89.

19. See Negussay Ayele, "The Ethiopian Revolution: Political Aspects of the Transition from PMAC to PDRE," in *The Political Economy of Ethiopia*, ed. Ottaway.

is the fact that in 1989 they entered into separate negotiations with the government. The EPLF participated in the Atlanta talks at a time when the TPLF was scoring significant military victories, suggesting that it was not confident that the ascendancy of the Tigreans guaranteed Eritrean independence. The Tigreans responded by immediately initiating a separate process. This suggests that the TPLF did not want a special solution for Eritrea and it did not trust the EPLF not to enter into an agreement with the government detrimental to itself.

Finally, the TPLF leadership admitted that relations among the various movements were difficult. In late 1989, the TPLF secretary-general declared that the opposition to the Ethiopian government was very divided and that "armed clashes" between the movements could not be excluded after the fall of the Mengistu regime.[20]

All these factors suggest that in 1990 the Eritrean conflict was no longer clearly a bilateral one between the Ethiopian government and the EPLF. At the same time, it was not a three-way conflict between government, EPLF, and TPLF either. Rather, it was a conflict pitting the government against a loose alliance of movements, of which EPLF and TPLF were by far the most important. With the collapse of the Mengistu regime, Tigrean and Eritrean nationalism could easily come into conflict with each other.

20. See Federal Broadcast Information Service, *Sub-Saharan Africa*, 28 Nov. 1989, p. 2.

PAST ATTEMPTS AT CONFLICT RESOLUTION

In the past thirty years, numerous attempts have been made to settle the Eritrean conflict, with and without the intervention of third parties. The first attempt by the military regime took place in September 1974. General Aman Michael Andom, then defense minister and later Derg chairman, led a delegation to Eritrea with the message that all problems would be solved in the new Ethiopia. As Derg chairman, he later opposed the sending of more troops to the region. Aman's position on Eritrea was one of the factors leading to his dismissal and his death while resisting arrest on 23 November. Troops were dispatched to the northern region within hours of his death.

In January 1975, the Derg sent envoys to Eritrea to open a dialogue with the ELF and EPLF through town elders. Like Aman, these envoys only had a vague message of goodwill, not specific proposals. The Eritrean nationalists responded with a major attack on Asmara.

The pattern established in this early stage was never modified. Numerous contacts took place in the following years, always without an agenda or concrete proposals. The Nine-Point Policy of April 1976, to which the Derg still subscribed in 1990, was a paragon of vagueness and ambiguity. It recognized "the right of any nationality existing in Ethiopia to self-determination," but it also defended "the unity of Ethiopian nationalities . . . based on the common struggle against feudalism, bureaucratic capitalism, imperialism and reactionary forces." In any case, the Derg stated, Eritrea was not a nationality. Finally, the military committee offered to negotiate with "any progressive groups and organizations in Eritrea which are not in collusion with feudalists, reactionary forces in the neighborhood, and imperialists," but it also stated that the purpose of the negotiations was to "promote the unity of the oppressed classes of Ethiopia."[21] At this time, the Derg was hoping to make a deal with the EPLF, the progressive Marxist-Leninist movement, excluding the ELF and thus weakening the ranks of the Eritrean nationalists. Not surprisingly, contacts with the nationalists in the months following the issuing of the policy achieved nothing.

Third-party attempts did not add concreteness to the discussion either. In March 1977 the Soviets and Cubans came in with a grand scheme to solve all conflicts in the Horn of Africa at one stroke, suggesting the formation of a federation including Ethiopia, Eritrea, Somalia, and the People's Democratic Republic of Yemen. The proposal was immediately rejected by all sides.

After the acute phase of the war was over in 1978, East Germany offered its services as a mediator, but the EPLF became convinced that the East German representatives were simply supporting the Ethiopian position. The Italian Communist Party tried to facilitate talks between the government and the ELF, even after it had ceased to be a fighting force

within Eritrea. In the meantime, bilateral contacts between the government and the EPLF continued—according to the Eritreans there were 10 encounters between 1982 and 1985—as desultorily as ever.

Against this background of peacemaking without concrete proposals, the Atlanta talks of September 1989 and the Nairobi talks of November 1989 represented a real turning point. The two parties admitted that they were talking, and they worked toward the establishment of an agenda with the help of an impartial and experienced mediator. Indeed, had the Eritrean conflict still been the old one, there might have been a chance of success. But the situation was in transition, and the conditions for progress toward solving the new conflict were not even remotely present.

NEGOTIATING A TRANSITIONAL CONFLICT

Zartman has singled out four major factors that create favorable conditions for negotiations: a mutually hurting stalemate, a deadline, valid spokesmen, and a vision of an acceptable compromise.[22] We will consider the four factors in turn.

A mutually hurting stalemate existed less in 1989 than two or three years earlier, when the old, bilateral Ethio-Eritrean conflict had reached a dead end. Both sides had tried repeatedly to launch major, decisive offensives, and in the end both had failed to break the stalemate. The

21. See Ethiopian Herald, 21 Apr 1976. See also Ottaway and Ottaway, Ethiopia, p. 158.

22. I. William Zartman, "Negotiations in South Africa," Washington Quarterly, 11(4): 141-58.

level of fighting remained high even between major offensives, with severe casualties, significant loss of matériel, and increasing impoverishment of the civilian population. But the new conflict, in which the TPLF figured prominently, could not be considered stalemated. On the contrary, the government was losing the war.

There was no deadline that gave all parties to either the old conflict or the new one a sense of urgency. The TPLF was a relatively new movement, and time appeared to be on its side. The government faced a deadline—the arms-supply agreement with the Soviet Union was expiring at the end of 1990, and Moscow had stated officially that it would not renew it on the same generous terms. However, it was unclear whether in 1989 the government took Moscow's threat seriously. While undoubtedly there were frictions between Moscow and Addis Ababa, the Soviets' behavior in Afghanistan and Angola suggested that they remained extremely reluctant to abandon their clients.[23]

The EPLF had reasons to hasten into an agreement with the government but also to postpone negotiations. The growing power of the TPLF suggested that it might be better to reach an agreement with the weakened Mengistu regime soon rather than with a strong TPLF later. On the other hand, even in early 1990 the government appeared so close to collapse as to make negotiations point-

less. This seems to be the conclusion reached by the EPLF leaders when they suspended the talks in the spring of 1990, and also their attitude in the talks under Secretary Cohen.

In conclusion, there was no clear deadline concerning either the old or the new conflict. There were some time pressures, particularly for the parties to the old conflict, but they were both ambiguous and asymmetrical, thus not likely to facilitate negotiations.

The existence of valid spokesmen was not a problem in the old conflict. The EPLF was a formally constituted organization, with a structure remarkably similar to that of the Ethiopian government.[24] In the preparation of the Atlanta conference, there was no argument concerning who had the right to represent either side. While the government still maintained contacts with the ELF, they were more an irritant than a real obstacle to the negotiations.

In the case of the new conflict, the situation was very different. Who would negotiate with the government and the Eritreans? The EPLF, the TPLF, and the Oromo Liberation Front were preparing talks with the government under Secretary Cohen. In the event, it was the EPRDF that took over the capital as an umbrella for the Tigreans but separate from the EPLF. But the alliance was loose, the goals uncertain, and many of the organizations too divided or too shadowy for common spokesmen to be accepted easily by all.

23. Weapon deliveries to Ethiopia increased substantially in January 1990. This may have simply been a long-scheduled delivery, but it did not help convey a sense of urgency.

24. See Clapham, *Transformation and Continuity*, pp. 213ff.; Markakis, *National and Class Conflict*, pp. 246ff.

Finally, a concept of compromise was absent from both the old and the new conflict. The EPLF and the government had not changed their positions in three decades. The TPLF and other groups had vague and changing goals, but these were becoming more ambitious, rather than more moderate. Under these conditions, a mediator would have had an impossible task. The parties did not just need technical advice on how to craft a mutually acceptable compromise. Rather, they still needed convincing that the purpose of negotiating was to reach a compromise, not to win the surrender of the other side. In fact, the very concept of compromise seems to be alien to the Ethiopian political culture. At best, compromise is seen as a temporary solution until victory becomes possible—Haile Selassie, for example, accepted the federal compromise in Eritrea until he found means to dismantle it.

CONCLUSION

In 1990, the chances for a negotiated solution to the spreading conflict in Ethiopia appeared very remote, more so, in fact, than they had even six months earlier. As the old conflict between the EPLF and Ethiopia turned into a new, broader conflict in which the TPLF figured prominently, conditions became more unfavorable to talks and compromise.

The major problem was the transitional nature of the conflict. A transitional conflict is by definition not stalemated. What makes it transitional is precisely the fact that new elements have been added and thus the balance of forces among the par-

ties has been altered. In the case under discussion here, the enhanced role of the TPLF and the collapse of the Ethiopian military broke the stalemate reached by the government and the EPLF.

The absence of valid spokesmen also appears inevitable in a transitional conflict, because the importance of the various parties changes, and so do relations among them. Taken individually, the EPLF and the TPLF had valid spokesmen. But the relations between the two changed as the TPLF became more successful militarily and spawned new groups such as the EPRDF, with the result that nobody could really speak for such a loose alliance of changing groups.

It thus appears that, in a transitional conflict, certain basic conditions are inherently unfavorable to negotiations. But conditions are equally unfavorable to a clear-cut victory, because the goals of the participants are in flux. In the case of Ethiopia, the defeat of the Ethiopian government was a definite possibility in 1990 and a certainty in 1991, but such defeat was unlikely to be a victory for both the EPLF and the TPLF. The EPLF wanted independence for Eritrea, but this would have thwarted the TPLF's greater-Tigrean nationalism or its ambition for a powerful role in the central Ethiopian government. The two groups have either to compromise or to come into conflict with each other and possibly other movements fighting the government.

The second possibility appeared the more likely. We have already pointed out some of the reasons. Both the EPLF and the TPLF have a history of suppressing rival organizations rather than finding an accommodation with them. The political culture shared by all groups in Ethiopia is inimical to compromise. The defeat of the central government undoubtedly increases the ambitions of all its opponents, increasing the chances of a clash among them.

Negotiations in Ethiopia are not likely to resume until the conflict emerges from the transitional phase and the new lines of cleavage are clarified. With the collapse of the Mengistu regime, the conflict eventually to be negotiated is between the two movements and the Amhara unionists who formerly supported the Mengistu regime. In such a scenario, negotiations may be unlikely to take place in the near future. The past history of the two movements suggests that they would attempt to maneuver politically or defeat each other militarily first and only consider negotiations at a later stage, if and when both sides perceived the situation finally as hopelessly stalemated.

No matter what, negotiations will have to take place in Ethiopia before the conflict, either in the old form of a bilateral Eritrean-Ethiopian conflict or in the new, broadened form involving the TPLF in a prominent position, can be brought to an end. The intervention of a mediator will be crucial in such negotiations, given the lack of experience of all parties and the difficulty inherent in negotiations in a culture where compromise is an alien concept. But the efforts of President Carter and Secretary Cohen show that, no matter how skillful the mediator may be, mediation efforts cannot succeed if the conditions are not favorable. As long as the conflict in Ethiopia remains in the present transitional phase, with poorly defined goals and ambiguous relations between the participants, conditions will remain unfavorable.

Regional Conflict and Regional Solutions: Lebanon

By MARY-JANE DEEB and MARIUS K. DEEB

ABSTRACT: The Lebanese conflict has gone through a number of phases, each with its own rationale, incorporating different issues and at times different players. Throughout there were attempts on both the domestic and the external level to find a solution to what was plaguing the country and eroding its political and social institutions. This article examines three major attempts at resolving the Lebanese conflict when the representatives of the domestic factions sat together and came up with formulae that appeared to address everyone's concerns. The process of multilateral negotiations, the asymmetrical structures of those negotiations, the ripe moment for negotiating, the role of external mediators, and the whole issue of the valid spokesman are analyzed within a theoretical framework based on I. William Zartman's model of government-insurgency negotiations.

Mary-Jane Deeb is assistant professor of government at the American University. Author of Libya's Foreign Policy in North Africa *and, with Marius K. Deeb,* Libya since the Revolution, *she received her Ph.D. from the Johns Hopkins School of Advanced International Studies.*

Marius K. Deeb, a senior fellow at the Center for International Development and Conflict Management, University of Maryland, has a doctorate in politics from Oxford University. His publications include Party Politics in Egypt: The Wafd and Its Rivals *and* The Lebanese Civil War.

THE Lebanese conflict has dragged on for 15 years and gone through a number of phases. Throughout there have been attempts at different levels, both domestic and external, to find a solution to what has been plaguing the country and eroding its political and social institutions. This article will examine three major attempts at resolving the Lebanese conflict when the representatives of the domestic factions sat together and came up with formulae that appeared to address everyone's concerns. The process of internal multilateral negotiations, the asymmetrical structures of those negotiations, the ripe moment for negotiating, the role of external mediators, and the whole issue of the valid spokesman will be analyzed within a theoretical framework based on I. William Zartman's model of government-insurgency negotiations.[1]

THE NATIONAL DIALOGUE COMMITTEE

Structurally, the Lebanese conflict is unique in that the government does not constitute an entity of its own or a distinct actor in the negotiation process. Whereas, the governments of South Africa, Sudan, or Sri Lanka can be considered primary actors in the negotiation process with a distinct insurgency movement, the Lebanese government represents the whole spectrum of political views and opinions, with most of the leaders of the so-called rebellion being part of the political system. Furthermore, the separation of powers between the executive and the legislative is blurred, with roles and jurisdictions overlapping. Consequently, the negotiation process takes place in most cases between the members of the executive and the legislative themselves rather than between the government and the insurrection.

The first attempt at resolving the conflict took place a few months after it erupted. It began with the formation of the National Dialogue Committee on 24 September 1975 and ended with the promulgation of the Constitutional Document of 14 February 1976. There were few actors then, and they were aligned primarily into two camps. On one side stood the predominantly Muslim Lebanese National Movement in alliance with the Palestine Liberation Organization (PLO); on the other, the Christian Lebanese Front.[2]

The National Dialogue Committee was composed of 20 members equally divided between Muslims and Christians.[3] Of the 10 Christian members, 5 were members of Parliament and 3 were cabinet ministers.[4] Only 3 were

1. See I. William Zartman, "International Perspectives on Regional Conflict Reduction" (Proposal, 1990). See also Saadia Touval and I. William Zartman, eds., *International Mediation in Theory and Practice* (Boulder, CO: Westview Press, 1985), pp. 7-16; I. William Zartman, *Ripe for Resolution: Conflict and Intervention in Africa* (New York: Oxford University Press, 1985), pp. 220-51.

2. See Marius Deeb, *The Lebanese Civil War* (New York: Praeger, 1989), chaps 2, 3, and 4, pp. 21-121, and, for the list of the various organizations, see pp. xiii-xiv.

3. Ibid., p. 3; *Al-Nahar*, 25 Sept. 1975, p. 1.

4. The most prominent Christian leaders in the National Dialogue Committee were three. First was Camille Chamoun, who was at the time a member of Parliament and a cabinet minister and who was also the president of the republic (1952-58). On the ground Chamoun

not prominent members of the political establishment per se, but two of them were protégés of leading politicians,[5] and one member belonged to both the cabinet and Parliament. On the Muslim side, 5 members were part of the political system, but 4 of them were cabinet ministers, and one was the prime minister himself. All were powerful traditional Muslim leaders.[6] Two groups were not repre-

sented in the National Dialogue Committee: the PLO and a new Shi'ite movement, the Movement of the Disinherited, headed by a charismatic cleric, which would eventually emerge as a major force in the Lebanese conflict.[7]

The issues that divided them were the Palestinian armed presence in Lebanon and the need for political reforms. The Christian Lebanese Front viewed the armed presence of the Palestinians in Lebanon as a threat to its sovereignty. It also perceived the PLO as having tilted the delicate balance of power between the religious communities in Lebanon in favor of the Muslims, and it

had, through his party, the National Liberal Party, controlled the second largest Christian militia. Second was Pierre Gemayel, a member of Parliament and a former cabinet minister. Through his Phalangist Party, he had controlled the most powerful Christian militia. Third was Raymond Eddé, who was then a member of Parliament and a former cabinet minister. He is the leader of the Christian National Bloc, succeeding his father, Emile Eddé, who was a president of the republic prior to 1943. Although Raymond Eddé refused to form a militia, he had tremendous political clout due to his independent character and charismatic personality. The two remaining members of Parliament, who were also former cabinet ministers, were René Muawwad, who was an ally of President Sulayman Franjiya and who hailed from the same Zgharta region, and Khatchik Babikian, a prominent politician representing the Armenian Tashnaq Party. Ghassan Tuwaini, a publisher and a journalist, and Philip Taqla, who had frequently served as minister for foreign affairs, were members of the cabinet but had no power on the ground. Ibid.

5. Only Raymond Rabbat, who was a prominent jurist, a former university professor, and an expert on constitutional law, did not belong to the political establishment. Ilyas Saba and Abbas Khalaf, who were former cabinet ministers, were, respectively, protégés of President Franjiya and the Druze chief and head of the National Movement, Kamal Junblat.

6. Three of the four Sunnis were prominent politicians. The prime minister at the time, Rashid Karami, was also a member of Parliament. The second of these politicians, Saib Salam was a member of Parliament and a former prime minister. The third, Abdallah

al-Yafi, was a former prime minister and a former member of Parliament. Only Najib Qaranuh, a physician by profession, was not a member of the political establishment, but he was a protégé of Saib Salam. The leading Shi'ite *muqatiji* ("feudal") politician, Kamil al-Asad, who was the Speaker of Parliament, was a member of the National Dialogue Committee. But the remaining Shi'ite members, Rida Wahid, Hasan Awadah, and Asim Qansu, were not members of the political establishment. The first two were prominent civil servants but with no political clout. Qansu, on the other hand, was a leader of the pro-Syrian Baath Party in Lebanon who was heading a militia and working for Syrian Intelligence Services; that is, he was Syria's protégé.

7. For more information on Amal—the successor organization to the Movement of the Disinherited—and its founder, Imam Musa al-Sadr, see Marius Deeb, *Militant Islamic Movements in Lebanon: Origins, Social Basis and Ideology* (Washington, DC: Georgetown University, Center for Contemporary Arab Studies, 1986); idem, "Shia Movements in Lebanon: Their Formation, Ideology, Social Basis, and Links with Iran and Syria," *Third World Quarterly*, 10(2) Apr. 1988; Augustus Richard Norton, *Amal and the Shi'a Struggle for the Soul of Lebanon* (Austin: University of Texas Press, 1987).

demanded that the PLO's power be curbed and its presence limited to certain regions of Lebanon.[8]

The Lebanese National Movement, on the other hand, considered irrelevant the armed presence of the Palestinians in Lebanon and claimed that the conflict was intra-Lebanese, stemming from an archaic political system based on a confessional division of power, which favored the Christian community. The National Movement demanded that major reforms be instituted that would curb the powers of the Christian president, increase the powers of the Sunni Muslim prime minister, and enlarge Parliament, which would be elected on a nonconfessional basis in order to secularize and modernize the system.[9]

Among the members of the National Dialogue Committee were three powerful politicians, a Maronite, who was Raymond Eddé; a Sunni, Saib Salam; and a Shi'ite, Kamil al-Asad.[10] These three attempted to find a compromise, namely limiting the Palestinian influence in Lebanon and introducing some reforms in the Lebanese political system. According to the theoretical model under consideration, those three leaders could have bridged the gap between the two sides and created a coalition "to settle the substantive issues and carry the

remaining members of the spectrum."[11] They were unsuccessful as they were unwilling to create their own militias, while both the Lebanese Front and the National Movement were using their forces on the ground to increase their bargaining power at the negotiating table.

The mediator in this attempt at resolving the conflict was Syria. Before the Lebanese conflict flared up, the Syrian government of President Asad had had good relations with most parties to the conflict: the PLO, the Christian president, and the leaders of the National Movement. It was, therefore, perceived as a valid mediator whose intentions were purely disinterested and based on a desire to see law and order restored in Lebanon.

The National Dialogue Committee met seven times. After each meeting, violence escalated as each party attempted to strengthen its position and undermine that of the opposition. The fighting continued until both sides reached a stalemate, with each scoring some victories and suffering a high number of casualties and losses of territorial control. Syria was then able to get the parties together to agree in February 1976 on a Constitutional Document, as it came to be known, which strengthened the power of the Sunni Muslim prime minister, weakened that of the Maronite Christian president, reallocated power in Parliament by equalizing the number of Christian and Muslim deputies, and called for Palestinians to abide by the agreements

8. For the views of the Lebanese Front, see Deeb, *Lebanese Civil War*, pp. 37, 41.

9. Ibid. pp. 75-77.

10. Al-Asad refused to attend the National Dialogue Committee meetings because, as the Speaker of the House, he believed that he, rather than Prime Minister Karami, should preside over the National Dialogue Committee. Ibid., p. 79.

11. See the preface in this volume.

between the Lebanese state and the PLO.[12]

The Constitutional Document was never implemented. An army insurrection led by a junior officer with strong leanings toward the National Movement and the PLO led to the disintegration of the army along sectarian lines. The National Movement and the PLO went on the offensive as they saw their chance to increase their power and control over the state. Syria, realizing that this was a golden opportunity to intervene, entered Lebanon militarily in April 1976, ostensibly on the side of the Christian Lebanese Front, to redress the balance and bring about a resolution to the conflict. It never bothered to implement the Constitutional Document it had sponsored.

THE GENEVA AND LAUSANNE CONFERENCES

By 1983 the structure of the conflict, the negotiating parties, a number of the divisive issues, and the ostensible mediator had changed. Whereas in 1975-76 there had been little or no asymmetry in the negotiations, by 1983 the situation had become completely asymmetrical. Syria had become the dominant power in Lebanon, with 30,000 troops in Lebanese territory. The old Lebanese army had disintegrated after the army rebellion of 1976, although a fledgling, American-trained, national army was being built. Armed militias proliferated, but none was as large, well-organized, or well-armed as the Syrian army.

12. Ibid., pp. 85-87.

The participants in the negotiations in Geneva and Lausanne were fewer in number and represented a much narrower segment of the political spectrum than those who met in 1975-76. They included nine members: four Christians and five Muslims. All the Christians were Maronites and included the Lebanese president and his father, the head of the Phalangist Party, as well as two other ex-presidents, who headed major parliamentary blocs.[13] The Muslim side included two former Sunni prime ministers, a Shi'ite former Speaker of the House, the traditional head of the Druze militia, and the head of the Shi'ite Amal militia.[14] Except for the latter all the participants were part of the political establishment.

The issues had also changed. Israel had destroyed the Palestinian military infrastructure in Lebanon in 1982, and Palestinian leaders and their forces had been forced out of the country. Consequently, the role of the Palestinians in Lebanon was no longer an issue in the negotiations. The Lebanese-Israeli Agreement of 17 May 1983 had become the principal issue of discussion, while political reform had been relegated to a secondary position in the negotiations.

Those who wanted to abrogate the treaty were Syria and its allies: the Druze leader, the leader of the Shi'ite faction Amal, the two Sunni leaders—one of whose constituency was

13. President Amin Gemayel, Pierre Gemayel, Camille Chamoun, and Sulayman Franjiya, respectively.

14. Saib Salam, Rashid Karami, Adil Usayran, Walid Junblat, and Nabih Berri, respectively.

in the Syrian-controlled part of northern Lebanon—and the ex-president of Lebanon, a Maronite who also represented a part of northern Lebanon under Syrian control. The Lebanese president and the two other Christian leaders were in favor of the agreement.

The mediator in those negotiations was Saudi Arabia. It called first for a cease-fire between the warring parties and Syria; Syria had been an active participant in the latest round of fighting. It then negotiated with Syria and the Lebanese factions to have a conference in Geneva, where they would come to some agreement over the main issues that divided them. Syria was represented in Geneva by its foreign minister and was technically an observer. In fact, however, it played an enormously important role in the negotiations by ensuring that the five Muslim leaders and the Maronite leader under its influence toed the line and did not break away from the position it wanted them to hold.[15]

The Geneva part of the negotiations was a result of an escalation of the fighting by the Syrian-supported factions of the Druze and non-PLO Palestinian forces who came from the Syrian-controlled areas of Lebanon in the Beqaa region. They attacked the Lebanese Forces, the principal Christian militia, in the area of Mount Lebanon under Christian control. The army intervened to stop their advance and impose a cease-fire. The fighting reached a stalemate

and all factions were ready for the Saudi-sponsored mediation that led to the negotiating table.[16]

The Geneva conference achieved very little except to recommend to the president the abrogation of the Lebanese-Israeli agreement and ending Israeli occupation of Lebanese territory. Each member presented a plan for political reform to the secretariat of the conference, but those plans were not discussed.[17]

The second round of talks was held in Lausanne four and a half months later, in March 1984. They were the result of further escalation of the fighting by Druze and Amal militias against the Lebanese army in West Beirut. The fighting was orchestrated by Syria, who financed the militias, gave them logistical support, and advised them on military strategy. The result of the fighting was the disintegration of the army for the second time, as the Shi'ite Sixth Brigade sided with the militias. It also led to the abrogation of the Lebanese-Israeli agreement, which had been the major demand of the Muslim participants at the conference in Geneva.[18]

The Lausanne conference of March 1984, therefore, was merely a way of formalizing the new redistribution of power on the ground. The Shi'ite and Druze militias were on the ascendancy. Syria, through them, had achieved its aim of abrogating the Lebanese-Israeli agreement, and the Christian forces were on the defensive. The Lausanne conference

15. George Bashir, Philip Abi Aql, and Fawzi Mubarak, Umara' al-Tawa'if min Geneva ila Lausanne (Beirut: Wikala al Anba al-Markaziya, n.d.), pp. 41-116.

16. Marius Deeb, "Lebanon's Continuing Conflict," Current History, Jan. 1985, p. 34.

17. Bashir, Abi Aql, and Mubarak, Umara' al-Tawa'if, pp. 114-16.

18. Ibid., pp. 139-41.

achieved a cease-fire and called for the formation of a National Unity Cabinet, which was created in April 1984. That cabinet included all the major participants of the Geneva and Lausanne conferences including militia leaders, such as the Shi'ite Amal leader, who now became part of the government.

THE TAIF CONFERENCE

In comparison to the other two attempts at resolving the Lebanese conflict, the Taif negotiations were, structurally, the least representative of the actual warring factions in Lebanon. Despite the fact that they included the largest number of Lebanese political figures, they did not include any of the major leaders of militias or parties actually involved in the fighting. Of the 71 surviving members of the 1972 Parliament, 62—31 Muslim and 31 Christian deputies—went to Taif in September 1989 to find a formula to end the conflict. However, the interim prime minister and commander of the army, General Michel Aoun, who had been battling Syrian and Syrian-backed forces for the previous six months, did not attend. Nor did the head of the Druze community and leader of the Druze militia, or the leaders of the two major Shi'ite militias, Amal and Hizbollah, all of whom had been involved in the latest round of fighting on Syria's side. Also absent from the negotiating table were the four external powers who were operating on Lebanese soil and whose ouster had been requested on a number of occasions: Syria, Israel, Iran, and the Palestinians, both PLO and non-PLO.

The Taif meeting took place as a result of intensive fighting, which started in March 1989, between, on one hand, units of the Lebanese army under the command of General Aoun, supported by the Lebanese Forces, and, on the other, the members of the Druze militia, Syrian army forces, and the Shi'ite Amal militia. The fighting continued almost uninterrupted for six months, during which General Aoun turned the confrontation into a war of liberation from Syria. By September 1989 a stalemate had been reached. The Syrians imposed a naval blockade on Christian ports, and the Arab world, France, and the United States had criticized Syria's actions and called for a settlement of the dispute.[19]

The role of mediator, in this case, was undertaken by a tripartite Arab committee composed of the three foreign ministers of Saudi Arabia, Algeria, and Morocco, assisted by a veteran negotiator: the Arab League's assistant secretary general, Al-Akhdar al-Ibrahimi. The committee was formed as a result of the decision made by Arab heads of state, at the Arab summit meeting at Casablanca in May 1989, to find a solution to the Lebanese crisis. The legitimacy of the mediator, therefore, rested on the fact that it had regional support and the backing of the League of Arab States. It had little power, however, to help implement such an agreement, and its only carrot appears to have been significant Saudi financial inducements to all of the parties concerned.

19. *FBIS Near East and South Asia,* 25 Sept. 1989, p. 38.

Three major issues were debated in Taif: political reforms, based primarily on the Constitutional Document of 1976; the withdrawal of all foreign forces from Lebanese territory; and the election of a new president.

The issue of political reforms presented few problems at those negotiations. The parties agreed to expand Parliament to 108 deputies from 99, with an equal representation of Christians and Muslims, instead of the existing 6:5 ratio between the two communities. The Maronite Christian president's powers were curtailed, and he could no longer appoint the Sunni prime minister, who was to be elected by Parliament instead. The Shi'ite Speaker of the House's term was extended from one to four years. Also agreed on was the disbandment of all Lebanese and non-Lebanese militias and the surrender of their weapons to the state.

The divisive issue at those negotiations was the role of the Syrian military forces. All but one of the Muslim deputies were hesitant about calling for the withdrawal of the Syrian forces, while the Christian deputies were divided. The majority wanted Syrian forces to leave Lebanon, but seven others, whose constituencies in northern and eastern Lebanon were under Syrian control, were on the side of the Muslim deputies.

After protracted mediation by the members of the tripartite Arab committee, and intensive Saudi-Syrian discussions, an agreement was finally reached on the wording of an accord, which was signed by 58 of the 62 deputies, with 3 Muslims and 1 Christian abstaining. The agreement stated that Syria would help the Lebanese state "impose its authority over all Lebanese territory" within a period of two years, after which it would redeploy its troops to specified areas of Lebanon.[20]

Two weeks after the accord was signed, the parliamentarians elected a new president, Rene Muawwad, as a first step to resolving the conflict. General Aoun refused to recognize him, claiming that he was Syria's candidate. Twenty days later the president was assassinated. The parliamentarians elected another president, Ilyas al-Hirawi, who was again rejected by the army commander. The standoff between the newly elected president and General Aoun eventually led to the breakdown of internal security. Fighting broke out between Christian forces: between those who supported the commander's view that Syria had to withdraw from Lebanon before free presidential elections could take place and those who were more willing to accept the Taif accord.

In August 1990 the Lebanese Parliament officially approved the Taif accord. Two months later Syria launched an all-out attack against Aoun, using its air force to dislodge him from the Presidential Palace, where his headquarters had been since September 1988, and forced him to seek refuge in the French embassy.

The Syrians then began implementing the first stages of the Taif agreement by supporting the forma-

20. Ibid., 23 Oct. 1989, p. 4.

tion of a new cabinet in December 1990. The majority of the cabinet members were hand-picked by the Syrian government. They convinced the militias to withdraw from greater Beirut and replaced them by a reorganized Lebanese army and Syrian troops.

THEORETICAL IMPLICATIONS OF THE LEBANESE NEGOTIATION PROCESS

The Lebanese case presents certain variations on the Zartman model of government-insurgency negotiations.

Triangulation and problems of asymmetry

Triangulation in the case of Lebanon is structurally different from the classic government, opposition, and host-neighbor model. Due to the de facto lack of separation of powers between the executive and the legislative, the government initially included all parties to the conflict represented either in the cabinet or in Parliament. There was no real opposition outside the political system as such. Consequently, negotiations on issues of political reforms, for instance, could very well take place between government leaders themselves.

The army—at the outstart, a national army—could not be used for or against any group because it was representative of all the religious communities in Lebanon. The conditions for asymmetry, therefore, did not exist at the start of the conflict but were created along the way.

Since the army could not be used initially, Lebanese politicians cre-

ated alternative paramilitary structures, that is, armed militias. The most powerful leaders in the cabinet and in Parliament thus became those with militias who fought their battles on the ground, taking over territory, expelling constituents from their homes, and expanding their power. Political leaders with no militias lost their bargaining power in negotiations. Consequently, in the case of the 1975-76 negotiations, the middle-of-the-road traditional leaders could not have their voice heard because they did not command any armed power on the ground.

A second way of creating asymmetry, where there had been none, was to form alliances with foreign paramilitary groups: in this case, the forces of the PLO. The Lebanese leaders who sought the military force of the PLO changed the balance of power between the various communities on the ground and increased their own bargaining power at the negotiating table.

With the Syrian intervention in Lebanon in 1976, the conflict became asymmetrical. Syria's armed forces increased in number and spread out over Lebanon, extending Syria's political and military control over two-thirds of the Lebanese territory by the time of the last set of negotiations. Meanwhile the PLO forces were destroyed by the Israelis and no longer play a significant role in the Lebanese conflict. Militias, on both the Christian and Muslim sides, proliferate, however, at times enhancing the power of their leaders in the political system and at times fighting among themselves and weakening their leaders while simultaneously increasing Syria's hold over the country.

It can therefore be concluded that the negotiations that had the best chance to succeed were the first ones, of 1975-76, when little asymmetry existed in the relations between all parties concerned. As asymmetry set in, and Syria became the major power in Lebanon, the issues at the negotiating table began to focus on Syria's interests rather than on those of the Lebanese parties concerned.

Thus the building up of asymmetrical relations, through the creation of militias, alliances with paramilitary organizations, and, later, accepting external military intervention, was counterproductive. It worsened the conflict, increased the number of players, undermined the power of moderate leaders, waylaid the original issues of the conflict, introduced new problems, and prolonged the conflict.

Structure of the negotiations

The groups that sought political reforms in Lebanon were not outside the pale of government. They were therefore not the typical opposition fighting for recognition and legitimacy. They had both. They were simply demanding a greater share of power. Furthermore, they were used to negotiating and compromising. The viability of the state for thirty years had been based on negotiation and power-sharing arrangements. The "most important deal," therefore, was not the "agreement to negotiate."[21] The conflict occurred when the traditional process of negotiation

broke down and the parties decided to resort to force to press for changes in the status quo.

Structurally speaking, therefore, the "most important deal" revolved around who was included in the negotiations and who was excluded or chose not to be involved in them. Again in the first set of negotiations, in 1975-76, the most important leaders of the warring factions, except for the PLO, were present at the negotiating table, unlike in the other two sets of negotiations, when many of the major parties were not represented. The Constitutional Document that was drawn up in the first negotiations remained through the years the most viable agreement on the basis of which all subsequent accords were made. The Taif accord was based on the Constitutional Document.

The role of the mediator

There were a number of attempts at resolving some aspects of the conflict in Lebanon that involved external mediators. Only the three attempts discussed in this article were undertaken to mediate the conflict internally between all major parties concerned. Syria was the primary mediator, although not always the official one. Its role was that of mediator as manipulator.[22] It had the "power, influence, and persuasion that can be brought to bear on the parties to move them to agreement."[23]

It is our contention here that some mediators initially, or eventually, be-

21. See Zartman, "Regional Conflict Reduction," p. 7.

22. Ibid., pp. 12-13.
23. Ibid., p. 12.

come active participants in a conflict. They become mediators not always to find a solution to those conflicts but to advance their own interests. This is the case especially when those mediators are neighboring states that are in a position to take advantage of a breakdown of law and order, for the purpose of extending their influence directly or indirectly over the various parties in the conflict.

It is therefore in the interest of such a mediator that the conflict be prolonged and that the parties concerned seek its help and become dependent on its political, economic, and/or military support. It is also to its advantage that negotiations take place, now and then, mediated by others, and that they fail so that the parties have no alternative but to seek its help once again to end the conflict.

It is also in the interest of such a would-be mediator that no party to the conflict wins politically or militarily over the other. That would make the role of mediator superfluous and undermine the mediator's influence in a country. Consequently, such mediators, usually the mediator-manipulator, will be seen as shifting its support to whichever party appears to be losing power during the conflict or during the negotiation process.

The ripe moment

One of the major reasons for the failure of the negotiations in the Lebanese case was the fact that the basic elements of the ripe moment were not present. Ripe moments, according to Zartman, occur when three elements are present: a mutually hurting stalemate, a formula for a way out, and valid spokesmen. Only in the first and third rounds of negotiation was there a mutually hurting stalemate. In the second case the Christian forces were hurting, while the Syrian-backed opposition was winning. Consequently the Geneva and Lausanne agreements formalized the gains made on the ground by the winning forces, rather than addressing the demands of all parties concerned.

The formula for a way out was found in only two of the three attempts at conflict resolution: the Constitutional Document of 1976 and the Taif accord of 1989. Both had well-formulated agreements that addressed the demands of all the factions. In Lausanne and Geneva, however, the issue of political reforms was never seriously addressed, although each member did submit a proposal for discussion.

It was only in the 1975-76 talks that all the valid spokesmen for the main parties to the conflict participated in the negotiations. Consequently, according to this formula, only the first set of negotiations, when the Lebanese conflict was only a few months old, occurred at the ripe moment and had any chance of succeeding.

One of the major obstacles to the resolution of the conflict, however, has been the assassination of the principal valid spokesman of each of the major communities in Lebanon. Those assassinations occurred when the leaders appeared ready for negotiation and for reconciliation. In almost every case they were replaced by weak leaders who were controlled or manipulated by Syria and who opposed reconciliation or negotiations.

The head of the Druze community and the founder of the National Movement, Kamal Junblat, was assassinated in March 1977. He was replaced by his only son, a weak leader, who has since opposed all major settlements of the conflict and has been one of Syria's principal allies in Lebanon.

In 1978, Imam Musa al-Sadr, the head of the Shi'ite Movement of the Disinherited, the movement that would later become the Amal movement, disappeared in Libya, where he was, presumably, assassinated. He was eventually replaced in 1980 by a Shi'ite lawyer, who became the major supporter of Syria's role in Lebanon.

In 1982, Bashir Gemayel, a young Maronite leader who had been elected president of Lebanon, was assassinated before taking office. He was replaced by his brother, who lacked his national appeal and did not force the issue of the withdrawal of foreign troops.

In 1987, the Sunni prime minister from northern Lebanon, Karami, was assassinated. He was replaced by a very weak Sunni leader, a university professor with no political base, who was completely dependent on Syria for his power. When the Taif agreement began to be implemented in December 1990, a new prime minister was appointed by the Lebanese president, who chose the members of his cabinet from among those Lebanese politicians who had Syrian backing.

In 1989, the Sunni Mufti Hasan Khalid, the highest religious author-ity of the Sunni community, was assassinated. He had called for reconciliation and for negotiation with the Christian leadership and had been publicly critical of the Syrian role in Lebanon.

Maronite President Muawwad, elected in 1989 after the Taif agreement, was assassinated. There had been hope that he would be able to implement the reforms and pull Lebanon out of its quagmire. Finally, in October 1990 one of the few remaining independent Maronite leaders, Dany Chamoun, was gunned down with his wife and children in their home in Beirut.

The assassination of those valid spokesmen who sought negotiations and reconciliation has prevented the nation from uniting. Its fragmentation has helped Syria consolidate its power and impose its own *pax Syriana* on the Lebanese. The fragility of this settlement, however, has already become apparent, as a number of leaders have refused to play the game and become part of a government completely controlled by a foreign power.

PROSPECTS FOR
FUTURE NEGOTIATIONS

The only mediator that has had the power to implement agreements has been Syria, which is the manipulator. But it has used that power, which is primarily military, to contravene negotiated agreements and promote its own interests instead. The interests of the Syrian regime in Lebanon are not served by a resolution of the Lebanese conflict. They are served by the perpetuation of the conflict, which allows the Syrian regime to control Lebanon politically and economically.

While blaming the various factions to the conflict in Lebanon, Syria has carried out acts of terrorism, such as the bombing of foreign embassies and the taking of Western hostages, to serve its foreign policy interests. Pretending to confront the Israeli threat in Lebanon by maintaining a low-intensity conflict on its borders, it has been able to justify domestically the continued state of emergency and regionally the presence of 40,000 Syrian troops in Lebanon. Economically, Lebanon has been a safety valve for the Syrians, who suffer severe shortages in their state-controlled socialist economy but can find what they need on the free-wheeling Lebanese market.

It is very unlikely, therefore, that this particular Syrian regime will opt to withdraw from Lebanon or that it will negotiate an end to its presence in the country. To withdraw from Lebanon, its forces would have to be defeated by a more powerful internal or external army; or maintaining the forces in Lebanon would have to become too costly politically and/or economically; or a domestic crisis would have to occur that would require their redeployment on their own territory. Unless any of these happens, the chance for a permanent resolu-

tion of the Lebanese conflict, as long as the Asad regime is in power in Syria, is dim.

On the other hand, if a new regime came to power in Syria, a number of steps for resolving the Lebanese conflict could then be considered. The withdrawal of Syrian troops would have to be negotiated first, and such negotiations could take place within a broader regional framework. Syria may require international assurances of a withdrawal of Israeli forces from southern Lebanon. Consequently, settling the Lebanese-Israeli border issue would be the next step in the negotiation process and would involve the United States in negotiations similar to those that took place in 1982-83.

It is only after the withdrawal of all forces from Lebanese territory that internal negotiations could proceed to resolve the third pending issue, namely, that of national leadership. Such negotiations would decide the structure of parliamentary elections. At the level of negotiations as well as at the level of implementation, there ought to be non-Lebanese mediators. The United Nations could be involved as a formulator during the phase of negotiation and, later, could supervise the elections to ensure that they are free and fair. The new parliament would then be required to elect a president.

ANNALS, *AAPSS*, 518, November 1991

Conflict Research and Resolution:
Cyprus

By JAY ROTHMAN

ABSTRACT: As the Cold War recedes and Europe moves into a new union, protracted ethnic conflicts raging around the world pose a major challenge to forging a more peaceful world order in the waning years of the twentieth century. The serious and fresh attention given to these conflicts may also provide valuable conceptual and practical tools for conflict management. This article describes a methodology used for conflict resolution training and intervention in the context of protracted ethnic conflicts, and its application to the Cyprus conflict as a vehicle for research. The methodology suggests that it may be fruitful if parties in conflict, or examinations of conflict, were able to systematically develop a variety of different ways of analyzing the conflict and posing solutions to it. Three different lenses for conflict analysis and management are suggested: adversarial, reflexive, and integrative.

Jay Rothman, Ph.D., is director of the Conflict Resolution Program at the Leonard Davis Institute for International Relations, Hebrew University of Jerusalem. He spends half the year as visiting assistant professor of political science, Haverford College. He is an educator, researcher, intervener, and trainer concerned primarily with conflict resolution in intercommunal conflict. Over the past six years, he has focused his efforts on the Israeli-Palestinian, Cyprus, and Sri Lankan disputes. He has just completed the book Thinking and Acting for Peace: International Conflict Resolution—The Israeli-Palestinian Case and Beyond *(forthcoming).*

NOTE: This article was prepared, in part, with support to the Leonard Davis Institute for International Relations, Hebrew University of Jerusalem, from the United States Institute of Peace and the John D. and Catherine T. MacArthur Foundation.

THERE is a new class of conflicts in the world. Actually, it is not new; rather, it is newly noticed. These conflicts are the ethnically rooted ones that rage primarily within states but also transcend their borders. Among the most prominent, protracted, and apparently intractable are the Eritrean-Ethiopian, the Northern Irish, the Israeli-Palestinian, the Lebanese, the Sri Lankan, and the Cyprus conflicts. They stretch conventional ways of analyzing and addressing international conflict; in fact, they pose important challenges to concepts about what constitutes "international." In the sense that they are contained within single states, or at least occur in situations in which two separate sovereign states are not yet clearly defined, they may be called domestic disputes—and many are thus beyond the mandate of the United Nations. Yet, they are clearly about discord between contending nations, even if not embodied in sovereign states, seeking to perpetuate or change the status quo of the single state in which their conflict occurs.

CONFLICT RESOLUTION: ANALYSIS AND INTERVENTION

Over the last few decades, many academics rooted in the Lewinian tradition of action research have been coupling their role as analysts of international conflict with new roles as third-party interveners. This has led to a fruitful interaction in which theory and practice have informed each other.[1] Donald Schon

lauds this link and calls those who make it "reflective practitioners."[2] Chris Argyris and colleagues developed a methodology whereby, through promoting a critical discourse between parties in conflict as they search for peaceful means of problem solving, the academic engages in what they term "action science."[3]

Combining conflict resolution theory and practice requires a delicate balance. On one hand, such a combination contributes to the broadening of analytical insights into conflicts and possible solutions. Social scientists may constructively apply their theoretical insights, comparative analyses, and methods of critical thinking to the management of deep conflict. On the other hand, theorists without necessary practical training, caution, or humility may be manipulated by parties to the detriment of peaceful solutions, they may create false expectations, and, for the sake of their own research and writing, they may offend sensibilities or betray the trust and confidentiality of their sources.

1. Edward E. Azar, *The Management of Protracted Social Conflict: Theory and Cases* (Hampshire, England: Dartmouth, 1990); John W. Burton, *Resolving Deep-Rooted Conflict: A Handbook* (Lanham, MD: University Press of America, 1987); Michael Banks, ed., *Conflict in World Society* (Sussex, England: Wheatsheaf Books, 1984); Diane B. Bendahmane and John W. McDonald, Jr., eds., *Conflict Resolution: Track Two Diplomacy* (Washington DC: Department of State, Foreign Service Institute, 1984).

2. Donald A. Schon, *The Reflective Practitioner: How Professionals Think in Action* (New York: Basic Books, 1983).

3. Chris Argyris, R. Putnam, and D. M. Smith, *Action Science: Concepts, Methods, and Skills for Research and Intervention* (San Francisco: Jossey-Bass, 1985).

This article is written to contribute to the positive potential of the theory-practice balance by presenting my experience with, and research into, the Cyprus conflict such that it is in some small way constructive to a peaceful solution, contributes to the connection of conflict theory and conflict management practice, and enhances the trust that the Cypriot parties may have or gain for the role of academic-interveners in general. Balancing these various objectives may lead to some compromises in which, for example, in order to protect sources, full identification or direct quotation will not be possible. On the other hand, seeking this balance may create a fruitful intersection between the various considerations brought to bear in preparing this article. For instance, a number of members of this article's constituency— including theorists, Greek Cypriots, Turkish Cypriots, and some who were both theorists and members of one of the conflict communities— were asked to review and comment on this piece before it was submitted for publication.[4]

CONFLICT RESOLUTION METHODOLOGY AS RESEARCH

While different parties will trace the origins of the Cyprus conflict differently, its modern expression may be most clearly marked by the uneasy

founding of the Republic of Cyprus in 1960.[5] Three years after its establishment, a political power-sharing relationship between the Greek Cypriots and the Turkish Cypriots broke down. As one analyst writes:

From its creation the new regime showed all the signs of succumbing to immobility. In the cabinet, Greek Cypriot ministers accused their Turkish Cypriot colleagues of obstructionism, and the latter retorted that the government circumvented them. The failure to establish constitutionally mandated separate municipalities in the five largest towns brought about the final deadlock, which [President] Makarios sought to resolve in November 1963 through the introduction of constitutional amendments that proved unacceptable to both the Turkish Cypriots and to Turkey . . . civil war erupted.[6]

4. While I, ultimately, retain all responsibility for the limitations of this article, I am grateful to several politically and/or academically influential Turkish Cypriots and Greek Cypriots who provided valuable criticism and suggestions. The Cypriots will remain unnamed to maintain the confidentiality of my sources.

5. For various historical accounts of the Cyprus conflict, see Michael A. Attalides, *Cyprus: Nationalism and International Politics* (New York: St. Martin's Press, 1979); Rauf R. Denktash, *The Cyprus Triangle* (London: Allen & Unwin, 1982); Ahmet C. Gazioglu, *The Turks in Cyprus* (London: K. Rustem & Brother, 1990); Peter Loizos, *The Heart Grown Bitter: A Chronicle of Cypriot War Refugees* (New York: Cambridge University Press, 1981); idem, *The Greek Gift: Politics and Solidarity in a Cypriot Village* (New York: St. Martin's Press, 1975); Kyriakos Markides, *The Rise and Fall of the Cyprus Republic* (New Haven, CT: Yale University Press, 1977); Pierre Oberling, *The Road to Bellapais: The Turkish Cypriot Exodus to Northern Cyprus* (New York: Brooklyn College Studies on Society in Change, 1982); Naim M. Necatigil, *The Cyprus Question and the Turkish Position in International Law* (New York: Oxford University Press, 1989); Polyvios G. Polyviou, *Cyprus: Conflict and Negotiation 1960-1980* (New York: Holmes & Meier, 1981); Vamik Volkan, *Cyprus—War and Adaptation: A Psychoanalytic History of Two Ethnic Groups in Conflict* (Charlottesville: University of Virginia Press, 1979).

6. James H. Wolfe, "A Historical Review of the Dispute," in *Perspectives on Negotiation:*

Tension and hostilities between the communities continued on the island until a coup staged by a military leader from Greece in 1974 brought about intervention by Turkey, leading to the subsequent division of the island. As in this instance, foreign involvement, be it by Greece, Turkey, the North Atlantic Treaty Organization, the European Economic Community, Britain, the United States, or others, has played a significant role in the evolution and course of the conflict. In 1983 the Turkish Cypriot legislative assembly established the Turkish Republic of Northern Cyprus, a status immediately and fully rejected as illegal by Greek Cypriots and, to this day, by all others in the world community, except Turkey. With the election of the new leader, George Vassiliou, on the Greek side in 1988, prenegotiations between him and the Turkish Cypriot leader Rauf Denktash have been held through the good offices of the United Nations. Time and again, however, they have been getting stuck on the mutually exclusive positions of the sought-for return to a unified state, desired by the Greek Cypriot side, and the acceptance and creation of two separate federated states, sought by the Turkish Cypriot side.

Concerning the brief and inadequate factual summary of the conflict just provided, it should be noted that describing the history of protracted ethnic conflicts, like that in Cyprus, to the mutual satisfaction of all parties is about as difficult as externally

arbitrating a solution that the parties in such conflicts would accept—which is to say, nearly impossible. Parties' own historical descriptions of such conflicts are loaded with diametrically different interpretations of past and future. If there is any historical fact about such conflicts, it is perhaps best found in the intersubjective meanings that may be discovered in exploring the separate interpretations that each party has about the conflict, its definition, its causes, and its possible solutions.

A major purpose of this article is to give voice to various interpretations of the Cyprus conflict—to attempt to enable parties to give their own explanations, as interpreted by me—and to explore possible intersections between them. Primary data for this article were gathered by me during a week-long visit to Cyprus in the fall of 1989, when I met with a number of high-level actors and third parties involved in the conflict. Since then, ongoing correspondence has been maintained with some of these actors, and many secondary sources have been surveyed. Research and interviews were conducted to conform with a specific conflict resolution workshop methodology designed to enable parties in deep conflict to articulate interactively their separate and intersecting interpretations of the conflict, its causes, and possible solutions.[7] These workshops, primarily conducted in the context of the Israeli-Palestinian conflict, move parties through three different

---

Four Case Studies and Interpretations, ed. Diane B. Bendahmane and John W. McDonald (Washington, DC: Department of State, Foreign Service Institute, 1986), p. 110.

7. Jay M. Rothman, "Supplementing Tradition: A Theoretical and Practical Typology for International Conflict Management," Negotiation Journal (July 1989).

FIGURE 1
COMPARATIVE CONFLICT MANAGEMENT FRAMEWORK

Framing:	Conflict Analysis		
	Adversarial	Reflexive	Integrative
Definition	Blaming (them) / Factual	Introspection (us) / Contextual	Relational (we) / Interactive
Causes	Competition / Disposition	Experiences / Trauma	Needs / Situation

Solving:	Conflict Management Strategy		
	Distributive Bargaining	Reflexivity	Integrative Bargaining
Alternatives	Zero-Sum / Exclusive	Aspirations / Internal	Positive-Sum / Inclusive
Implementation	Coercive	Buy-In	Mutual-Aid

modes of analyzing their definitions of the conflict and its causes and posing alternative solutions to the conflict and strategies for implementing them. As the methodology is based largely on the Socratic method of asking questions of parties in conflict such that they may gain new insights about their conflict situation and options for creatively managing it, it is quite adaptable as an instrument for conflict research.

Intervention methodology

The methodology includes the application of three approaches. (See Figure 1.) First, an adversarial approach is utilized. In it, the parties are asked to frame the conflict in terms of how they define it and analyze its causes. Such frames regularly blame the other side and attribute aggressive disposition to the adversary. This commonly leads to distributive and often win-lose, or zero-sum, approaches to settling the dispute. Such settlements are regularly sought in ways that are at least partially at the expense of opponents' concerns and therefore are achievable only through some type of external coercion.

Next, a reflexive approach is employed. Suggesting to parties engaged in exploratory dialogue that adversarial definitions and solution strategies are the norm and may well be in part why so little progress toward a lasting solution has been made, the parties are asked to articulate those underlying motivations, hopes, and fears in the conflict that must be addressed in any lasting solution. Having articulated these concerns and hearing similar concerns expressed by the other side, parties often begin to acknowledge the serious limitations of adversarial and coercive approaches for adequately addressing such deeply rooted disputes.

Finally, an integrative approach is used. After parties have described their reflexive analyses of the situation and what must be addressed for a lasting peace to be built, they are asked to find intersections and try to merge their underlying hopes, fears, and motivations. This leads to an attempt at integrative bargaining in which they are invited to invent creative and largely win-win, or positive-sum, solutions to their destructive and common problems. Such an approach may foster a lot of mutual aid between the parties in solution implementation.

From intervention to research

Based upon the intervention methodology just summarized, data about the Cyprus conflict have been gathered and analyzed. Just as in workshops where participants are asked to first articulate their adversarial frames and suggest resulting distributive solutions, so in this research and presentation of data, the adversarial mode is first presented. This is followed by presentation of the reflexive and, finally, the integrative modes of conflict framing and solving as articulated by various actors in the conflict. It should be noted that while the presentations of the parties' adversarial, reflexive, and integrative modes of conflict framing and solving are designed to reflect their perspectives, the role of the researcher in gathering this information and presenting it mitigates its objectivity. Conflict management, in both the analytical and solving phases, is a largely interpretive process. This article parallels this circumstance.

Adversarial frame

Ethnic conflict often leads to a vicious cycle in the way that each side regularly interprets the other side's expressions and actions about the situation and its solution in the most aggressive light possible. Either side's national symbols, expressions of national solidarity and historical grievance, articulation of aspiration, and so forth are commonly viewed by their opponents as inherently hostile. As Kelman writes about the Israeli-

Palestinian conflict, so too in the Cyprus conflict and in other deep communal conflicts "there is strong tendency to see the other's movement and its ideology as exhausted by—exclusively dedicated to—the desire and purpose of destroying one's own national existence."[8] Thus, for example, many Greek Cypriots see evidence of such hostile intent in the close relations between Turkish Cypriot leaders and Turkey. From the other side, many Turkish Cypriots believe that the long-term objective of the Greek Cypriots continues to be the full incorporation of Cyprus into Greece. While they share a common island, emotionally, for the most part, the Greek Cypriots identify themselves as Greeks more than as Cypriots, and the Turkish Cypriots identify themselves as Turks more than as Cypriots.

In this context, the very articulation of self, experience, and aspiration often leads the other side to feel threatened. Each attributes to the other's self-assertions memories of past traumas whose repetition is feared. To the Turkish Cypriots, an important and painful part of their past, as they recall it, was characterized by insecurity and disenfranchisement at the hands of the Greek Cypriots. These memories shape their vision of the future. To the Greek Cypriots, a foreign state, Turkey, has, in their view, usurped at least a third of their island and pushed many of them out of their homes. This injury, as they feel it, shapes their vision of the future. Expressions by either side of identity, aspiration, and hurt are interpreted by the other side as evidence of perfidy and hostile intent.

For example, in the five-finger mountain range that runs across the northern part of Cyprus, I saw, during my visit to the North in 1989, two gigantic flags that had been painted on the side of a mountain. One was the Turkish Cypriot flag, the other was the Turkish flag. Below the latter was written in Turkish, "I AM PROUD TO BE A TURK." The Greeks point to this and say, *"You see, they are merely a colony of Turkey, which has designs not only on the northern part of island, which they have de facto nearly absorbed already, but on the whole island."*[9]

On the other side, at the U.N. neutral zone dividing the part of Cyprus controlled by the Greek Cypriots from that controlled by the Turkish Cypriots, a sign has been placed stating:

Beyond this checkpoint is an area of Cyprus still occupied by Turkish troops since their invasion in 1974—the invaders expelled 180,000 Cypriots of Greek origin from their ancestral houses and brought over colonists from mainland Turkey to replace them. ENJOY YOURSELF IN THIS LAND OF RACIAL PURITY AND TRUE APARTHEID. Enjoy the sight of our desecrated churches.

---

8. Herbert C. Kelman, "The Political Psychology of the Israeli-Palestinian Conflict: How Can We Overcome the Barriers to a Negotiated Solution?" *Journal of Political Psychology*, 1987, p. 361.

9. The use of italics indicates that the italicized passage is not a direct quotation but a composite of representations, orally or in writing, made by various individuals to the author and drawn from various essays. This method was employed in part to protect sources and in part to provide flexibility in portraying various interpretations of the situation.

Enjoy what remains of our looted heritage and houses.

From the inhabitants of the area that were forbidden to return.

The Turkish Cypriots point to this sign and say, "*You see, they do not recognize our distinct identity as Turkish Cypriots, nor do they understand our legitimate security needs, which are protected by Turkey against an aggrandizing and aggressive Greek majority.*"

These cryptic messages and the wholly negative interpretations that the parties give to them illustrate the type of attributional communication patterns that have been established between the two sides. Such an analysis leads to an atmosphere of suspicion, mistrust, and disbelief in the possibility of cooperative problem solving.

Adversarial solution

Having framed the problem in adversarial and attributional ways, both parties view the other's intransigence as the main obstacle to a just and lasting solution. Since they have come to feel that the other side cannot or will not listen to reason, each side spends a great deal of energy trying to gain external sympathy and support for its cause against the other side and trying to gain external sanction for its particular cultural and political identities.

The Greek Cypriot side suggests that an important reason there is no solution is that the Turkish Cypriot leadership are merely puppets and pawns of the Turkish government in Ankara and its perceived strategic interests in the region. These include economic, military, and historical interests, which they attribute to the ongoing rivalry between Greece and Turkey played out in proxy on the island of Cyprus. A favored solution derived from such an analysis is to get the international community to put pressure on Turkey to give up what the Greek Cypriots commonly perceive as unjust and illegal claims over the northern part of Cyprus. Thus a lot of effort is placed on gaining access to the European Common Market and the legitimacy it would afford the Greek Cypriot government, on ensuring that the regime in the North is not recognized as legitimate, and on getting friends and allies to stand by and promote the Greek Cypriot cause.

The Turkish Cypriot side suggests that an important reason there is no solution is due to the lack of genuine desire on the Greek Cypriot side to resolve the situation fairly such that the Turkish Cypriots will gain equal status with the Greek Cypriots in some future two-state arrangement with possible federation and not just to return to what they recall as a dangerous past in which the Turkish Cypriots were merely afforded an inferior minority status within a single Greek-dominated entity. This lack of desire, they will suggest, is derived from the fact that the Greek Cypriots feel they have already won the support of the international community, which has been treating the Greek Cypriot administration as if it were the sole legitimate government of Cyprus. They enjoy this status, the Turkish Cypriots will say, and feel no reason to accommodate the Turkish

Cypriots. Therefore the Turkish Cypriot leadership expends a great deal of energy attempting to persuade the international community to support the Turkish Cypriot cause.

Conclusion: Adversarial mode

This mode is the norm of conflict framing and solving in intense conflicts. This pattern can be found wherever ethnic groups are in deep conflict usually expressed in terms of rivalry for control of tangible territorial, economic, or military resources and for a monopoly over international support. It is a vicious cycle in which the conflicting parties frame the situation by looking outward toward their adversaries and placing the lion's share of blame on them; furthermore, the parties look outward toward international actors who might coerce their opponents into accepting an imposed solution. This outward-looking approach, while certainly based in deeply rooted perceptions on each side, is nevertheless reductionist. At best, it perpetuates fruitless negotiation; at worst, it leads to regular outbursts of violence.

Reflexive frame

To break the vicious and fruitless cycle of adversarial conflict framing and solution seeking, a reflexive telling of self can serve as a powerful transition. In other words, changing the frame of the parties from a complete outward view of the conflict to incorporate a greater inward-looking perspective can significantly broaden the parties' analysis of their conflict and lead to a wider range of possible solutions. This telling of self in the presence of adversaries when possible, or filtered through the mind of a third-party intervenor or researcher, can create a new range of possibilities for creative problem framing and solution generation than does the stale, outward-focused adversarial mode.

Kurt Lewin spoke of the need for parties in intense intergroup conflict to "unfreeze" their analyses and attitudes about the situation and each other.[10] One method for doing this is to convince the parties to reflexively tell about their hopes, fears, and needs in the conflict such that the other side can truly understand—if not necessarily believe or sanction—that these concerns are genuinely and in significant ways what motivates the other side.

When pushed for this analysis about the numerous failures to launch successful negotiation, a high-ranking U.S. embassy official in Cyprus, who had been involved for years in both tracking and brokering high-level talks between Greek Cypriots and Turkish Cypriots, suggested that there is a culturally determined inability—"mentality"—to be introspective about acts or deeds that he viewed as necessary for building confidence and promoting peace. *People don't hear the other side's needs, fears, or aspirations, nor do they comprehend their own role in making the situation difficult for the other side.* This interpretation about the lack of introspection as a major obstacle to effective negotiation is

10. Kurt Lewin, *Resolving Social Conflicts* (New York: Harper & Row, 1948).

apt; however, there is a good deal of evidence emerging that the "mentality" this official spoke about in frustration is not unique to the Cyprus conflict but is found in one protracted conflict after another.[11]

While it may be very difficult for parties in deep conflict to be reflexive about their conflict, it is less difficult for third parties to glean a great deal of introspective analysis by listening to the parties' passionate stories, hopes, and fears beneath their blaming of each other. The following two statements summarize what this third party, as analyst, heard when listening for the reflexive narrative of the two sides.

Turkish Cypriot: *The main features of our situation are fear of the other side based on our experience at their hands, and our need, therefore, for externally ensured security and, perhaps most important of all, recognition of our distinctive identity and our equal rights to express our national and cultural selves. The first two features of this situation, fear and security needs, have grown up over the many years of intercommunal strife, in particular through the denial of our distinctive identities—not merely as Turks, not merely as Cypriots, but as a mixture of the two: Turkish Cypriots.*

Greek Cypriot: *My home across the border calls to me. I and so many of my friends and family have not been able even to visit our places of birth since the country was divided nearly two decades ago. Moreover, I feel as if a piece of myself has been irreparably maimed, as the church in which I grew up is now a mosque. And it is not*

just mourning for a past lost: we all feel insecure with a military giant poised to grab more from us. Cyprus is a great country, but she weeps now, and we feel like a minority in our own land.

Reflexive solution

The reflexive approach to conflict framing provides a vehicle for conflict resolution evaluation and prescription. For a solution to be mutually acceptable, one that the parties want to implement and protect in the long run, it must address the parties' various deep-felt motivations, hopes, and fears. Thus, for instance, each side may articulate solutions in terms that will further its own separate, though not necessarily exclusive, needs for identity, safety, recognition, justice, participation, and so forth. The extent to which proposals for peace on the island address these sorts of existential concerns may play an important role in determining if they will be accepted and implemented. If solutions further threaten or frustrate these concerns, it is likely that they will be rejected as unrealistic and potentially damaging.

Conclusion: Reflexive mode

The reflexive mode of conflict management serves to unfreeze parties from total reliance on the adversarial mode and provide room for a more integrative mode. In the Cypriot situation, the adversarial and outward focus that both sides display in their most common analyses of the conflict and methods for solving it leads to a stale and stagnant conflict

---

11. Azar, *Management of Protracted Social Conflict*; Ronald C. Fisher, *The Social Psychology of Intergroup and International Conflict Management* (New York: Springer-Verlag, 1990).

status quo. Focusing primarily on in-compatible positions—for a unified state or two states—and on gaining the support of external actors who can perhaps influence the eventual solution, discussions break down time after time.

If parties would instead articulate their underlying concerns that are at stake in the conflict—the real and very pressing human concerns for dignity, justice, safety, identity, and so forth—they could perhaps make more progress in articulating what must be addressed for a mutually acceptable solution to be forged. As Zartman and Berman write, "Issues of recognition, of dignity, of accep-tance, of rights and justice may be more important than the actual dis-position of a material good, and tak-ing them into account may facilitate a solution." They go on to cite master negotiator Averell Harriman: "In-stead of people going to extremes of trying to explain what 'nefarious plans' the other side has, we ought to spend our time trying to understand what motivates these other people."[12]

By shifting the emphasis to the common human needs for identity, safety, recognition, and fairness that lie beneath the established adversar-ial positions of the conflict status quo, the possibility of a new agenda for joint problem solving may be launched. It is at the integrative mode of problem framing and solu-tion generation that this new agenda is built.

12. I. William Zartman and Maureen Ber-man, *The Practical Negotiator* (New Haven, CT: Yale University Press, 1982), p. 84.

Integrative frame

When the integrative mode is reached, participants in an actual conflict resolution workshop between the parties would be asked to get into the skin of members of the opposing side and articulate, in the voice of that side, what most deeply moti-vates them. This exercise serves as a test of the extent to which parties have understood the other side's ex-pression of itself. It also serves as a broadening mechanism whereby par-ties in deep conflict hear, often for the first time, that the other side can understand, if still not necessarily agree with, one's own perception of the conflict. Most substantively, this perspective-taking exercise is used to articulate the intersections in the parties' underlying concerns.

Instead of primarily blaming the other and jockeying for the preemi-nence of their mutually exclusive po-sitions, the parties would articulate common hopes and fears for full ex-pression of identity, for dignity, for safety, and for recognition. They may even be able to move from an articu-lation of the conflict in terms of "us versus them" to an expression that "we are in this together and perhaps can best, or maybe only, get out of it together."

Integrative solutions

This article is based on interviews and research and not on third-party conflict resolution intervention. Par-ties were not brought together to ar-ticulate a merging of stories. Instead, a merging of stories was constructed during research into each side's introspection about the situation. Also, parties were asked to describe ways in which they might articulate shared concerns and ideas for addressing them.

Both sides spoke of the need for and possibility of cooperative efforts in areas of agriculture, the environment, and rural development. Greek Cypriot and Turkish Cypriot planners told us about immediate and concrete benefits to be derived from joint planning. *"Tourism could flourish, our markets could be expanded, our limited water resources could be fruitfully coordinated, our industrial base developed, and so forth, if only we could divert our resources and energy from conflict to cooperation."*

On the Turkish Cypriot side, one leader spoke about the need for curriculum reform whereby students in both communities would learn more positive images of the other side—their cultural heritage, their historical legacy, their values, and basic decency. *"Each side skews the picture of the other and not only perpetuates but also promotes enemy or devil images between the two sides."*

A third-party actor interviewed about creative efforts told of his government's activities to continue educating all children on the island in the link language of English to ensure that when the communities do again meet they will have a common tongue in which to communicate. *"This will help to ensure that the future generations, now born without friends or contacts from the other side but rather raised in the milk of enmity, will at least have a common language with which to address each other."*

Perhaps the most complete and evocative story of self-interested and integrative problem solving was the program described separately by the two "representatives of the Greek Cypriot and Turkish Cypriot communities of Nicosia."[13] After the city of Nicosia was formally divided following the war in 1974—it had been functionally divided in many respects long before then—the populations in the two halves of the city were left without adequate sewage facilities. The water was on one half of the divided city, the physical plant on the other. The parties had two choices: to muster the resources to replace the missing half, or to cooperate with the other side. Each side, however, was resource poor. Quietly, over a number of years, these two leaders drew up and implemented plans for cooperation.[14] This effort,

13. This is the mutually agreed-upon phrase that Mr. Mustafa Akinci and Mr. Lelos Demetriades used to describe their roles. Within their respective communities each was called "Mayor," but as use of this title is viewed, particularly on the Greek Cypriot side, which does not recognize the legitimacy of a government structure separate from its own, as capitulation to the other side, they agreed that when they met in public they would use this broader appellation. Unlike other sources consulted directly for this article, their names are provided in this footnote as they publicly, and sometimes on shared podiums, have spoken about their cooperation, which is described herein. Thus the concern for confidentiality in their case is absent.

14. One of the Turkish Cypriots from whom I requested prepublication critique of this article, a private adviser to Rauf Denktash, commented as follows on my description of this cooperation: "The story of this particular cooperation is, obviously, more complicated than your presentation space allows. It had an intense relationship to internal politics and the

beginning with sewage resources—about as prosaic an effort as one can imagine—has built confidence between some leaders and within their communities that negotiations, at least around issues of urban development, are useful. Indeed, built on this foundation there has emerged a regular meeting of a joint planning commission constituted of Greek Cypriot and Turkish Cypriot city planners, architects, economists, sociologists, engineers, geographers, and outside experts who come together to discuss and design, through functional cooperation, broader plans for city development.

In attempting to work on these broader plans, the Nicosia masterplan team was faced with a serious dilemma. As a nonpolitical body, how could it design cooperation when the political future of the city they were discussing was completely unknown and in the hands of negotiators and politicians? They agreed on a creative solution. They accepted that there were two main sets of political scenarios to work with. One assumed an eventual solution in which two separate sovereign states would exist; the other envisioned a binational, bicultural unified island state. The team then was able to proceed by developing two sets of cooperative plans for rebuilding Nicosia, given either eventuality.

economy of both sides. It was done, at least on the Turkish side, under a perceived separateness from the Greeks." While this criticism surely has some merit and thus is useful to note, examples of integrative problem solving and functional cooperation in situations of intense ethnic conflict are rare and thus this one, while imperfect, is still relatively unique and evocative and therefore illustratively powerful.

Conclusion:
Integrative mode

One of the serious obstacles to successful negotiation and conflict management in protracted social conflicts is that compromise regularly appears unacceptable to the parties involved. Though often expressed in terms of instruments of state like territory and political control, these conflicts are most essentially about deep existential human concerns. Thus compromise of any kind appears highly threatening. To build a willingness to make concessions—indeed, at some point parties do have to give a little in terms of the institutional dimensions of their conflicts—parties must first have a sense of the benefits that may be derived from cooperation and joint problem solving. Integrative and positive-sum solutions over joint problems that can build confidence, enhance mutual safety while strengthening separate identities, and so forth are very likely to be necessary preconditions for successful distributive bargaining and compromise in intense ethnic conflicts.

In the interactive mode the problems are framed in common. For instance, insecurity of either side is viewed as a concrete problem for both. In feeling insecure, each side will often act in ways that will lead the other side to feel insecure as well. Through articulating common threats and frustrations to deep needs and values on both sides, an agenda for joint problem solving is set. This agenda is one that can be both incremental and wholistic at the same time. It can be designed to work on pieces of peace, as in the Nicosia example, in ways that both symbolically and practically are part of a total fabric of peace.

CONCLUSION

One of the most useful aspects of the conflict resolution methodology described in this article is that it is cybernetic and self-correcting. In this approach there are built-in criteria for success in the extent to which solutions will enhance the fulfillment of human needs and values for both sides as the sides have introspectively expressed them. This article began with setting criteria for success that will now be reviewed in conclusion.

Three key objectives were stated for writing this. The first was that it be, in some small way, at least minimally constructive for peacemaking. It is hoped that an implicit suggestion emerging from this article is that, instead of continuing with heretofore relatively fruitless negotiations over territorial compromises for one or both sides, negotiations beginning with exploration of ways to enhance each community's sense of safety, dignity, and identity given all possible territorial arrangements are useful. The Nicosia example of looking at various ways to solve specific problems given various political scenarios provides a useful model.

A second criterion was that this article would contribute to a merging of theory and practice. Deriving a new agenda for conflict management as just suggested from explorations of various conceptual frameworks—adversarial, reflexive, and integrative—for conflict analysis and management is perhaps some evidence that analysis can provide new foundations for practice. With respect to the contribution of practical experience to theoretical development, perhaps showing how an intervention methodology that was developed in the course of running conflict resolution workshops can be usefully adapted as an analytic tool demonstrates that not only is good theory eminently practical but that good practice can be theoretically useful as well.

Finally, the third criterion for success was that this article enhance the trust that the parties to the conflict have or gain for academic intervenors in general. With this goal in particular, only time will tell whether success has been achieved, although stating it self-consciously as an objective and asking a few parties who are closely involved in the conflict to comment on it prior to publication may in itself be helpful.

ANNALS, *AAPSS*, 518, November 1991

Steps versus Solutions in the Arab-Israeli Conflict

By IRINA D. ZVIAGELSKAIA

ABSTRACT: Partial solutions can present way stations en route to complete resolution of regional conflicts, or they can actually hinder those resolutions by providing comfortable resting places with no incentives to move on. The step-by-step peace process in the Middle East took account of local and global realities, but it left the conflict stuck in its progress after the Camp David Accords and the Egyptian-Israeli Peace Treaty. Saddam Hussein erred in seeing in the end of the Cold War an opportunity to carry out aggression with impunity, but there will be other Saddam Husseins as long as a general settlement is not produced in the region. What is needed is joint U.S.-Soviet action and a balanced formula that provides for the return of a few Palestinians to Israel in exchange for the maintenance of some Israeli settlements on the West Bank, sealed by an international conference.

Irina D. Zviagelskaia graduated from Leningrad University and joined the Institute of World Economy and International Relations, where she earned her Ph.D. in history. Since 1982, she has been a senior researcher at the Institute of Oriental Studies. She specializes in the field of international relations in the Middle East, particularly in conflict situations there. Her main publications include two books, The Role of the Israeli Military in State Policy Formation *(1982) and* American Policy toward Conflicts in the Middle East, Mid 1970s to 1980s *(1990).*

THE bulk of regional conflicts have a complex nature. They are conditioned by territorial, national, ethnoconfessional, and ideological contradictions between their participants and by expansionist policies of regimes and leaders who try to realize their ambitions in the course of a conflict with their neighbors. In addition to sharp local differences that act as causes of conflict and at times are deeply rooted in history, an important role in maintaining conflict situations has been, until recently, played by global international relations.

THE SHADOW
OF THE COLD WAR

In the Cold War period, international relations were to no small extent shaped under the impact of dogmatic notions of autonomous and parallel development of two social systems. Unwillingness to look at problems in terms of their interconnection and interdependence resulted in rigid ideologization of interstate relations and unfriendly and even hostile moves by states belonging to different social systems.

In such a confrontational context, the relations between the United States and the Soviet Union acquired the nature of an acute rivalry, which, naturally, was not restricted to the bilateral relations but also involved the periphery. The thesis that the destinies of the East and the West would be determined in the Third World, which gained currency in the period of national liberation wars and revolutions, made the developing regions a sphere of struggle for influence. While the "Comintern approach" frequently dominated the Soviet leadership's attitude toward regional problems, the United States no less stubbornly sought to contain the Communist threat even where there was not a trace of it.

In regional conflicts, the confrontation of the two powers had a negative effect. It became an important additional factor hampering the search for compromise settlements. Moreover, it was frequently the case that a conflict—the Arab-Israeli in the first place—in the course of its development and the greater involvement of the United States and the USSR, started indirectly to reproduce their confrontation, though the initial causes of the conflict were in no way connected with the interaction of the two powers in the world arena.

A black-and-white interpretation of the complex socioeconomic and political processes, manifested as a zero-sum game, inevitably led the two powers to blur the dynamics of the behavior of the local forces whose interests did not necessarily coincide with those of the power toward which they gravitated.

Taken together, the previously mentioned factors complicated both the possibilities of unblocking conflicts and Soviet-American relations. On one hand, confidence in the support of one of the powers weakened the factors deterring the parties to the conflict, which led to manifestations of political extremism. On the other hand, the aggravation of the situation in the region favored the efforts of the local forces to involve their global ally more deeply in the regional confrontation and undermined the chances of stabilization of Soviet-American relations.

The end of the Cold War has proved to be a mixed blessing for the Third World in general and for the Middle East in particular. With normalization of Soviet-American relations, the view has arisen that the period of global confrontation, dangerous as it was, gave the two superpowers a great measure of control over developments in conflict zones. With the Cold War over, certain regimes in the Third World that possess relatively strong military capabilities have obviously come to the conclusion that they might now have a free hand in using military force against their neighbors. The other point of view that has gained currency during détente is that the end of the East-West confrontation will contribute to fast democratization in the Third World countries, which in turn will make peaceful interaction between various states possible.

There is perhaps some truth in both statements. But neither of them can be fully applied to what is going on in the potential conflict zones. First, the control exercised by the USSR and the United States over their regional partners during the Cold War can be seriously doubted. No regional ally has ever been a puppet. All of them have had interests of their own that have not necessarily coincided with those of their patrons. Second, the containment exercised by both superpowers left enough room for local actors to use force, as long as it did not threaten direct nuclear confrontation between the United States and the USSR. Third, a détente that obviously creates favorable conditions

for joint or parallel actions of the two superpowers in the context of regional conflicts does not liquidate deep contradictions between various countries or between ethnic and ethno-confessional groups inside them. It can neither block development of nationalist, Islamist, and other destabilizing currents nor neutralize ambitions of totalitarian regimes.

The Iraqi invasion of Kuwait is an example of a crisis that unfolded in the new international framework. It is not so much a product of the Cold War as of internal causes, the ambitions of the Iraqi regime, its own motives and goals. There is, unfortunately, a high probability of new crises and even new Saddam Husseins. But though the Persian Gulf crisis demonstrated the importance of internal causes of conflicts, it showed that détente had made it possible for the superpowers to work out a common approach and joint measures to counter the aggression.

The reaction of the USSR and the United States to the Iraqi invasion gives hope that, despite the asymmetry of their interests, there exists a basis for a joint search for common ground, for optimal models of conflict settlement, and, first and foremost, for the settlement of the Arab-Israeli dispute. The problem of this dispute's settlement or at least reduction has become even more acute in the context of the gulf crisis, which demonstrated an interconnection between the two conflicts. The *intifada* clearly reflects this interconnection or linkage—of course, not in the sense in which the term was used by Saddam Hussein. If the Arab-Israeli confrontation is not seriously dealt with, the situation in the region might easily reach a point of no return.

THE WEAKNESS OF INTERIM SETTLEMENTS

The complex tangle of mutual claims and contradictory interests, the high level of distrust and suspicion, and the long-time enmity hinder the creation of conditions for the settlement of such conflicts as the Arab-Israeli conflict at one go. Consequently, it becomes necessary to find some interim solutions, which many experts regard as a logical and realistic way of settling conflicts. The American expert Linda Miller emphasized the notions of accommodation and resolution of conflicts when she wrote:

Through accommodation actors may come to accept the legitimacy of divergent interests or goals; through conflict resolution, specific disputes or controversial issues may be settled by interested parties. But often distinctions between the two are blurred by both participants and observers. Moreover, usage of terms varies greatly. . . . Such [an] impression reflects the fluidity of the contemporary system in which instances of "pacific nonsettlement" and "non-pacific settlement" are numerous.[1]

Whatever terms are used to denote an interim or overall settlement, an interim solution should be viewed not as a lesser evil as compared with the continuation of confrontation but as a stage opening up a possibility of further steps in the direction of the elimination of the causes of the con-

1. L. Miller, ed., *Dynamics of World Politics: Studies on the Resolution of Conflict* (Englewood Cliffs, NJ: Prentice Hall, 1968), p. 5.

flict. Its principal difference from separate arrangements lies in the existence of a close linkage with the measures aimed at the establishment of a final peace. Consequently, an interim solution should be placed in the framework of general principles determining the main settlement's parameters. In the first place, this will provide an additional incentive to start talks for the party that considers itself weaker and is not sure that it will be able to gain its goals through negotiation. Second, such linkage will prevent the opposite party, which believes that it will make sufficient gains at the initial stages of the talks, from becoming complacent and discontinuing the negotiation process, leaving its opponent in an unfavorable position.

One can ask whether an interim settlement that does not liquidate all the causes of a confrontation but merely reduces the confrontation to a less dangerous level can be interpreted as a form of conflict management. Methods used in both cases will probably be similar. But results or, rather, perceptions of these results by the participants to the conflict should be different. For them the result must mean a real breakthrough, a qualitative change in the situation—if not a full peace, then some peace. Conflict management can hardly create such a perspective because the term itself is interpreted as a complex of measures directed at conflict stabilization or reduction, and for the participants it will be even psychologically difficult to accept something less than peace.

To achieve a breakthrough in a settlement in the context of a protracted confrontation, certain conditions should be created both at the regional and the global levels. Clearly, the parties directly involved in the conflict should be convinced that military methods are unable to resolve the accumulated problems and will only aggravate the situation. The hopelessness of military solutions was convincingly demonstrated by the situation in the Iran-Iraq, Afghan, and Arab-Israeli conflicts. Besides, in light of the mutual influence of the regional and global levels of international relations, normalization between the external forces directly or indirectly involved in the conflict situation under the impact of historical circumstances becomes a sine qua non of the progress of the settlement. The continuation of rivalry instead of a search for a balance of interests and the use of the settlement process for that purpose may lead to extremely undesirable results. Suffice it to recall in this connection the rather cool response of the USSR to the Fahd Plan or the United States' skeptical stance vis-à-vis the Soviets' 1984 peace proposal.

American leaders who were engaged in the Middle East settlement brought about the separate Egyptian-Israeli accord, which did not create conditions for tackling other problems, but they took into account both the regional realities and the character of their relations with the USSR. The structure of the conflict itself created difficulties for American policy. The line of confrontation stretched not only between Israel and the radical Arab regimes but also between Israel and Arab countries oriented toward the West. In the 1970s, stabilization of the situation in a way that would suit the principal U.S. ally, Israel, and be acceptable to the conservative Arab wing became the order of the day for the United States. Its recognition of the fact that the continuation of the conflict was fraught with serious consequences that would hinder the pursuit of its policy in the Arab world prompted it to try to work out and implement a scheme that would ensure American dominance in the region on a broad and stable basis not affected by crisis fever. Successful progress toward this goal could seriously change the balance of forces in a vast area adjoining the Soviet borders.

Thus the context of Soviet-American relations strongly influenced the American approaches to the settlement. This was confirmed by Alfred Atherton, former assistant secretary of state for the Middle East and South Asia, while describing the approaches of the "globalists" and "regionalists" to the problem of the Middle East settlement. According to the "globalists," Atherton wrote, "considerations of global strategy and efforts to enlist the support of the Middle East nations against the Soviet threat take priority over initiatives designed to resolve the underlying causes of regional conflicts, and, specifically, the Arab-Israeli conflict." As for the "regionalists," he wrote,

While we cannot ignore external threats to our interests in the region, efforts to deal with root causes of the Arab-Israeli conflict, including above all the conflicting Israeli and Palestinian claims in the west of the Jordan River, must be dealt with before we can realistically hope to enlist the support of the Middle Eastern states on our side of the global conflict with the Soviet Union.[2]

In such a confrontational context, particularly precluding any joint or parallel actions of the two powers designed to stabilize the situation, American settlement efforts could hardly result in anything but a separate agreement.

The simplification of complex problems alone does not ensure successful progress of settlement. "Issues that are defined too broadly may never be solved. . . . Issues that are defined too narrowly may leave no room for compromise."[3] From a technical point of view, one may agree with that statement. But the use of fragmentation should not entail refusal to formulate the main principles of the settlements. Entering negotiations, each party runs a risk. Such a decision in the context of a protracted enmity requires giving up certain stereotypes and a readiness to take extraordinary steps. And it is especially important to be clear about the purposes for which these steps are taken. For example, without offering statehood to the Palestinian people in accordance with the "one people, one state" formula as well as talks with the Palestine Liberation Organization (PLO), the Israeli government not only blocked the possibility of starting Israeli-Palestinian talks but, in fact, provided additional arguments to the forces in the Pales-

tinian movement who continue to reject a political solution to the problem.

It is, no doubt, always possible to find in the set of the root causes of a regional conflict some issues that are easier to solve than others. But uncoupling them from the totality of contradictions without providing a close linkage to subsequent steps for a settlement may provoke a new spirit of tension. Exactly such a role was played by the Camp David Accords, despite the fact that they ensured calm on the Egyptian-Israeli flank and led to the signing of the first peace treaty in history between Israel and an Arab country. Israeli author Naomi Chazan wrote that

the Camp David Accords indirectly curtailed for a time the prospects of territorial compromise in the West Bank and Gaza. By decoupling peace from territories, they actually encouraged Israeli settlement. By leaving the notion of Palestinian autonomy purposefully vague, they permitted the gradual elaboration by various Israeli leaders of functional autonomy as a palliative to the demand for self-determination. By giving successive governments a false sense of security, they blinded Israeli leaders to Palestinian responses to the consequences of Israeli rule. And by minimizing the sense of urgency previously associated with the occupation, they deferred negotiations on alternative solutions.[4]

Thus there may be a reason behind an interim agreement, and such an agreement might help the general reduction of tension in a conflict, but

    2. Foreign Affairs, 62(5):1195 (Summer 1984).
    3. T. R. Gurr, ed., Handbook of Political Conflict: Theory and Research (New York: Free Press, 1980), p. 453.

    4. N. Chazan, "Domestic Developments in Israel," in The Middle East: Ten Years after Camp David, ed. W. B. Quandt (Washington, DC: Brookings Institution, 1988), pp. 155-56.

only if it provides a possibility for tackling other issues of the conflict, or for parallel searches for approaches to those groups of contradictions that have not as yet been directly included in the package of issues under discussion. For example, the Israeli-Palestininan negotiations on an interim solution for the West Bank and Gaza, placed in the framework of general principles, should be accompanied by parallel contacts with Syria and other Arab countries, talks on lowering the risk of war, and so forth. Were parallel contacts to take place, the continuation of the peace process would be assured, and parties to the conflict who did not participate in the talks on the Palestinian problem at the first stage would not feel a natural apprehension about being disregarded, about the adoption of decisions behind their backs, and about the weakening of their security and political positions.

SECURITY AND SETTLEMENT

When an interim settlement is necessary and is the only possible step on the way to conflict resolution, it should fulfill a number of important functions. Through it, confidence-building measures should be worked out and implemented, including the establishment, *inter alia*, of demilitarized zones. In the Middle East, deeply affected by the gulf crisis, the problem of security has become of greatest importance. Taking into consideration very serious concerns about security that the Arabs and the Israelis share, one should include the possibility of a dialogue on security along with eventual talks

on territorial and national issues. In other words, it is necessary to create a new and more favorable climate for the continuation of negotiations. Both sides should see that political solutions are profitable to them, that their efforts to find a compromise are successful, and that none of them has been driven into a corner and forced to retreat, thereby losing face.

Interim settlements, which may start with the solution of relatively less painful issues that have more room for compromise, cannot ignore principal issues, however difficult they might be. The Israeli settlements and the return of Palestinians seem to be very complex problems in the Arab-Israeli conflict. As the Israeli and Palestinian people historically have lived in one and the same territory and are to continue to live together, the future should provide a possibility for them to move freely and have the right to acquire property in the entire territory of Palestine. William Quandt observes that the gap between the Israeli and the Palestinian stances cannot be narrowed on the basis of "classical concepts of sovereignty," and therefore it is necessary to find a possibility of "overlapping sovereignty," mixed regimes, and "shared authority."[5] This idea can prove to be especially useful during a transitional period in the framework of an interim settlement. It might at last extend to the Palestinians the right to self-rule and also minimize the Israeli sense of insecurity.

5. William B. Quandt, *Camp David: Peacemaking and Politics* (Washington, DC: Brookings Institution, 1986), p. 333.

The issue that arouses the strongest passions is the Palestinians' right of return. From the point of view of the vast majority of Israelis, the great influx of Palestinians to the West Bank and Gaza would create conditions for their expansion into Israel, something of a "Green March." Israelis are especially adverse to even the symbolic return of the Palestinians to Israeli territory proper.

In fact, however, these fears are greatly exaggerated. Some Palestinians would like to return to the West Bank and Gaza, but, according to existing estimates, their number will hardly exceed a million. The returning Palestinians could be absorbed by the Palestinian state with international assistance. Most of the rest will probably prefer to receive compensation.

Evidently, a symbolic return of Palestinians to Israel is also necessary, at least for reunification of families. Ignoring the Palestinians' demand to be able to return in the course of the conflict settlement may have extremely negative implications, putting a time bomb under any agreement.

It is impossible for the Palestinians living in the refugee camps to give up their dream of returning to Palestine. If they are not granted that right of return, they not only will reject the idea of the Palestinian state in the West Bank and Gaza but will become, in their desperation, a nutrient medium for various extremist elements who will prefer armed struggle to political solutions. Taking this prospect into account, as well as the Israelis' apprehensions, Abu Iyad, a prominent PLO leader assassinated in 1991, said in an interview, "Thus, in order to minimize disaffection and discontent, we believe that Israel should remain open to discuss the right of return while we shall for our part remain flexible regarding its implementation."[6]

This flexible stand of the PLO makes it possible to achieve a compromise on that sensitive issue. Moreover, if a small number of Palestinians returned to Israel and acquired property there, it would, in a measure, balance the maintenance of some Israeli settlements on Palestinian lands.

Thus, from a functional point of view, an interim settlement might play an important role in the establishment of genuine peace in the region. But it is essential that both sides regard it as an interim step, which may be facilitated by the elaboration beforehand of a schedule of further steps to be taken.

The gulf crisis has put a serious brake on the eventual start of the Israeli-Palestinian peace process and has made the Middle East situation more complicated. At the same time, factors that, according to Harold Saunders, "enable the parties to see the present situation as unacceptable in the light of their interests and hopes," continue to operate.[7]

The positive processes taking place at the global level, the *intifada* and growing Palestinian self-consciousness, and new Arab coalitions have brought about shifts in the

6. *Foreign Policy*, Spring 1990, no. 78, p. 103.

7. H. Saunders, "Reconstituting the Arab-Israeli Peace Process," in *Middle East*, ed. Quandt, p. 415.

postures of the parties directly involved in the conflict, though, due to the acuteness of local contradictions, the trend toward political settlement is developing very slowly. Particular mention should be made of new elements in Syria's approach to the problems of settlement and its readiness to hold talks. At the same time, no consolidation of positive shifts in the position of the Arab world is feasible without a reciprocal response from the Israeli government. Unfortunately, despite the existence in Israel of forces realizing the necessity of a political breakthrough, the policy of Israel's ruling circles leaves little room for optimism.

Yet there are grounds for considering the situation in the Middle East as other than hopeless. Both the USSR and the United States must contribute to the launching of the peace process, as both of them recognize the necessity of finding a solution. There seems to be a rapprochement of the stands of the USSR and the United States, though differences still exist. They concern the mechanism of settlement, which, according to the vast majority of the international community, should take the form of an international conference on the Middle East. The United States is not enthusiastic about this idea. If an international conference is to be effective, it is obvious that it should be well prepared for. Here a positive role is played by the Soviets' very flexible approach: recognizing the existence of a variety of ways to prepare the conference, including the usefulness of bilateral and multilateral talks and contacts.

The indispensability of joint action arises from the fact that in recent years processes dangerous to both superpowers have been developing in the Middle East. Among them are fundamentalism and terrorism, victimizing citizens of third countries. The scale of the arms race grows and includes weapons of mass destruction.

At the same time, the previous experience of joint efforts and the practice of Soviet-American interaction in the conflict zones in the Middle East requires a thorough study in order to avoid repetition of old mistakes. Besides the use of the settlement process for the continuation of rivalry, the mistakes include the search for universal models of settlement, the absence of regular consultations, and insufficient information about the steps already taken. Joint efforts of the USSR and the United States aimed at the resolution of the conflict would mean not the establishment of a condominium of which the participants in the conflicts are apprehensive but a search for a balance of interests, which is so much needed in the contemporary world. Whatever the differences are between the Soviet and the American approaches to the Middle East conflict, one thing is quite clear: peace in that long-suffering region is a sine qua non of further normalization of international relations as a whole, of the removal of the threat of war.

ANNALS, *AAPSS*, **518**, November 1991

U.S.-Soviet Cooperation: The Role of Third States

By EDWARD A. KOLODZIEJ

ABSTRACT: U.S.-Soviet cooperation in the developing world must be pursued within a multilateral setting since neither, alone or together, is capable of defining regional security systems. In eliciting the cooperation of regional states in defining peaceful security regimes around the globe, the United States and the Soviet Union should base their cooperation on the following assumptions or principles. First, current understandings should be codified to establish a solid foundation for future cooperation. Second, impediments to further cooperation should be clearly delineated to limit misunderstandings. Third, both should be sensitive to the limits of their power as a function of the demands of other states to have a say in regional security. Fourth, these limits should not hinder cautious but optimistic expectations of advancing cooperation because both Washington and Moscow, whether under centralized or federated authority, have powerful incentives to continue to expand the scope and depth of their cooperation at the regional level.

Edward A. Kolodziej is research professor of political science at the University of Illinois, Urbana-Champaign, and director of the Project on European Arms Control and Security. He has written or edited over 100 journal articles and 10 books on security and foreign policy, including The Uncommon Defense and Congress: 1945-63 *(1966);* French International Policy under De Gaulle and Pompidou *(1974); and* Making and Marketing Arms: The French Experience and Its Implications for the International System *(1987). His most recent work, edited with Roger Kanet, is* Cold War as Cooperation: A Regional Understanding of Superpower Conflicts *(1991).*

DEFINING the prospects for U.S.-Soviet regional cooperation requires some notion of what has succeeded in the past and why. Such knowledge is the basis for identifying the realistic limits and opportunities that the post-Cold War international system and the specific circumstances of these two great powers afford for enlarging and deepening the cooperation that has been achieved. The discussion in this article is a modest start on these difficult tasks.

The discussion is divided into three parts. The first makes the often neglected point that a necessary, if not sufficient, condition of U.S.-Soviet regional cooperation is the cooperation of third parties—states, regional and international organizations, and nongovernmental actors. Of particular importance are the power, roles, and resources of regional states in resolving or managing their own problems. As a cursory review of the Cold War struggle suggests, the successful resistance of third states to the pretensions of Moscow and Washington as well as their ability to use both, or either, for local purposes led both powers to the gradual realization that they had more reason to cooperate in order to cut losses, reduce risks, and protect perceived gains than to engage in unrestricted conflict and competition. The shared frustrations experienced by Moscow and Washington in working their regional wills oriented both progressively toward cooperation rather than collision. That process of reorientation needs now to be extended to third states.

Building on the assumption that third parties—most critically, regional states—must be incorporated into any regional cooperative design, the second part of this discussion attempts to define several conditions that have to be met if U.S.-Soviet cooperation is to be fostered. The third section, drawing on the preceding, more general, discussion, briefly sketches how U.S.-Soviet cooperation might be advanced in league with third parties to promote regional accord in North and West Africa and southern Africa.

THE ROLE OF THIRD STATES
IN CONTAINING THE COLD WAR

As the Cold War expanded to regions around the globe, it absorbed the national, ethnic, racial, and communal conflicts that divide the world's populations against themselves. The efforts of the two big powers to impose their preferred regional solutions on other peoples and states were resisted at every turn. Interventions that once appeared to American and Soviet leaders as vital national interests were gradually reevaluated as the costs and risks of projecting U.S. or Soviet power mounted, as domestic opposition to intervention grew, and as international censure spread. The harshest tests in the developing world for Washington and Moscow were, of course, Vietnam and Afghanistan. Resistance elsewhere to U.S. and Soviet expansion in the developing world was also strong. Rising global powers, like China, and regional powers, like Pakistan and India, also sought a say over local affairs and had the will and resources to get their way, or at least to frustrate great-power designs.

Third states in the developing world have also been remarkably resourceful in using U.S. and Soviet power for their own purposes. Despite Israel's critical economic and military dependency on the United States, it has repeatedly acted on its own, often with U.S. military equipment, to pursue its strategic interests even when they were opposed to American policies. Its contraventions of U.S. preferences ranged from the invasion of Lebanon to aerial attacks on Palestine Liberation Organization headquarters in Tunisia and on Iraq's nuclear facilities. Pakistan has served its own and U.S. interests in Afghanistan, but it has also relied on its crucial role in checking Soviet military power to diffuse U.S. pressure, aimed at blocking the development of a nuclear arms capability.

Large-scale Soviet arms shipments to Egypt similarly failed to make Cairo a Soviet satellite, as evidenced by President Anwar Sadat's expulsion of thousands of Soviet advisers and, later, his launching of the Yom Kippur War without Moscow's approval. Cuba's aims in Central America and in black Africa have also been often at odds with Moscow's priorities, and not seldom at its expense and embarrassment. So, too, despite massive aid, the Kremlin had little influence on Ethiopia's Mengistu regime to end the war in Eritrea or even over North Korea's campaign of terrorism against South Korea.

Over time, recognition of the countervailing power that each big power disposed in a region to check its rival, the constraints imposed by regional states either in checking or in channeling U.S. and Soviet power for their own purposes, and an increasingly heightened understanding of the costs and risks, not to say dubious gains, of intervention abroad induced the leadership cohorts of the big two to find ways to accommodate their nations' conflicting regional interests and aims.[1] As early as the Berlin crisis of the late 1940s and the Korean War of the 1950s, leaders on both sides of the ideological divide clearly understood that regional conflict might escalate to global conflagration. Fear of the consequences of unregulated escalation became more acute as the balance of terror crystallized in the middle 1950s. The mutual perception of these risks led both countries to qualify their strategic commitments to clients and allies. The Soviets, for example, reneged on nuclear assistance accords to China and qualified their aid to Beijing in the latter's conflict with Washington over Taiwan; the United States, in turn, insisted on a strategy of flexible response in Europe, making the continent vulnerable to conventional war, to inhibit rapid escalation to the use of nuclear weapons in any armed conflict with the Soviet Union.

Both powers also attempted to control the supply and use of their military arms and equipment by clients and to constrain their suppliants from using force to press their particular regional claims when these clashed with the guarantor power's interests. Gradually there

1. These are delineated at length in Roger E. Kanet and Edward A. Kolodziej, eds., *The Cold War as Cooperation: Superpower Cooperation in Regional Conflict Management* (London: Macmillan; Baltimore, MD: Johns Hopkins University Press, 1991).

arose, in the action-reaction cycles of successive tests of will and of compromise in their regional competition, an ever-expanding encrustation of understandings—most tacit, some explicit—about what forms of power might or might not be acceptably deployed in a region—no Soviet supersonic aircraft for Nicaragua, for example—and what spheres of influence were permissible—Soviet presence in Cuba, but no deployment of strategic nuclear missiles; conversely, no U.S. invasion to topple the Castro regime.

Big-power cooperation during the Cold War was most evident in Europe before the revolutions of 1989 in Eastern Europe ended the postwar bipolar bloc system. It assumed the form of tacit agreement on the division of Germany,[2] explicit accord on Big Four occupation rights in Berlin, and the Helsinki understanding that created the Conference on Security and Cooperation in Europe. Cooperative arrangements also emerged in Central America, in the Cuban missile outcome; black Africa, as seen in resolution of the Angolan civil war; and South Asia, as in U.S. deference to Soviet mediation of the 1965 Indo-Pakistan war and Soviet toleration of U.S. assistance to the Afghan rebels.

Galia Golan notes similar instances of cooperation in the Middle East. She lists at least 25 such tacit or explicit understandings between 1948 and 1984.[3] Some of the most notable include the creation in 1948 of the state of Israel; U.S.-USSR condemnation of the Suez war in 1956; negotiations during the years 1967-70 for Middle East peace in pursuit of U.N. Resolution 242; efforts between 1973 and 1977 to moderate Palestine Liberation Organization behavior and policy; and tacit acknowledgment of the legitimacy of each other's presence in Lebanon, with Syria as Moscow's client and the United States as Israel's guarantor.

As long as the Cold War persisted, neither party was able to get its way at acceptable cost and risk. Each had incentives to optimize mutual gains and to limit losses and risks by cooperating with its rival-partner. Cooperation did not imply an accord on values or a congruence of interests between Moscow and Washington. Tacit cooperation—however reluctant, reserved, or publicly repudiated—still offered more than unilateral attempts to dictate regional strategic and political outcomes. It is in this sense that the Cold War can be viewed, paradoxically, as cooperation. More as the consequence of pragmatic responses and mutual power adjustments with respect to a series of often unforeseen crises than as the outcome of a shared design, Washington and Moscow gradually constructed a functioning, if fragile and jerry-built, structure of regional arrangements that restrained their conflict and those of local powers.

2. Anton DePorte, *Europe and the Superpowers*, 2d ed. (New Haven, CT: Yale University Press, 1986).

3. Galia Golan, "Superpower Cooperation in the Middle East," in *The Cold War as Cooperation*, ed. Kanet and Kolodziej, pp. 125-26.

See other chapters in this volume for a discussion of U.S.-Soviet regional cooperation in other regions. The appendix provides a complete list of instances of U.S.-Soviet cooperation identified by the authors.

ASSUMPTIONS AND PRINCIPLES FOR U.S.-SOVIET REGIONAL COOPERATION AFTER THE COLD WAR

As the foregoing line of analysis suggests, this process of cooperation has been evolving for some time. If further progress is to be made in the developing world through U.S.-Soviet cooperation, policy coordination should be built on tested lessons of past successes, however limited, and on a realistic assessment of the degree of mutual interest, resources, and will at the disposal of the United States and the Soviet Union—or its major republics—to coordinate their policies, to dampen regional conflict, and to promote peaceful relations.

First, U.S.-Soviet regional understandings need to be codified. The record of cooperative accord by the two countries on each other's legitimate presence in a region and on the range of policy instruments that may be employed to advance national or joint interests should be systematized, say, through joint memoranda of understanding at working levels to provide a framework within which to base future expectations about mutual cooperation.[4] Unless the "shadow of the past" is understood by both sides in the same way, leadership cohorts in the United States and the Soviet Union may send the wrong signals to each other about their aims and motives and might act in a manner that may well be misperceived in untoward ways.[5] Or, in challenging

an understanding in one region, Washington or Moscow may be unaware that it may provoke a counterproductive defection in another region and, conceivably, damage the global cooperative structure that had been built. Future progress hinges, then, on a shared understanding by political decision makers in the United States and the Soviet Union—and by the publics to which they are responsible—about the levels, scope, and depth of their cooperation, about the mutual gains of cooperation, and about the factors that have encouraged convergence and that now advise its extension and deepening.

Second, the obstacles impeding Moscow and Washington from moving from a conflict mode to one of conflict resolution should be clearly and candidly understood. The Cold War remains institutionalized in the foreign and security bureaucratic organizations and military forces of each state and embedded psychologically in the conditioned behavior and political memory of its leadership cohorts who have done battle for decades. One should not expect Moscow, for example, to be indifferent to a hostile reversal of alliances in Eastern Europe any more than Washington would be expected to be indifferent to civil strife in the Caribbean or in Central America. Washington and

---

4. This was one of the principal objectives of Kanet and Kolodziej, eds., *Cold War as Cooperation.*

5. As the extensive discussion in ibid. argues, the "shadow of the past"—the experience

of rival-partners in compromising their differences—is as important as the "shadow of the future"—the prospects of future interaction—in eliciting cooperation between opponents. For a contrasting view, consult Robert Axelrod, *The Evolution of Cooperation* (New York: Basic Books, 1984); *World Politics,* 37(1) (Oct. 1985), a symposium on the prospects of cooperation under so-called conditions of anarchy.

Moscow will not see eye to eye on such matters for a long time to come. Moreover, Moscow's efforts to maintain its rule over the Soviet republics and nationality groups pressing for independence, as the failed August coup suggests, could be major obstacles to East-West understanding and mutual confidence.

Third, even with the best of will in Washington and Moscow, formidable, if dissimilar, socioeconomic constraints preclude Soviet and American leaders from contemplating ambitious designs for expanded cooperation. The United States has irretrievably lost its postwar hegemonic economic position, and its current status is heavily assailed by strong competitors in Europe and Asia. Greater European Community market integration promises to enhance the global market shares of European firms, while Community rules threaten to shut out or hamper U.S. access to European markets.

These European competitive pressures are reinforced by those arising from Japan and from the smaller but highly competitive Asian states of Taiwan, Singapore, and South Korea. Chronic U.S. trade imbalances with these nations, as well as with China, are annually reckoned in the tens of billions of dollars with little sign that these shortfalls will be redressed in the near future. These structural weaknesses in the U.S. competitive position are complicated further by persistent and mounting budget deficits that saddle the United States with heavy debt payments, a weakening dollar, and high interest rates, which are a drag on investment and competitiveness.

The Soviet Union is even less favorably positioned than the United States to increase its economic assistance and security commitments abroad.[6] It competes with its former East European allies and with developing states for credits, loans, assistance, and trade concessions from Western states and Japan. It must also focus its scarce resources on its socioeconomic and political reforms. So far progress has been slow. Backsliding threatens what advances have been recorded, and the possibility of a complete reversion to former authoritarian rule cannot be dismissed if the reforms fail. The possible breakup of the Soviet Union or its fundamental political reconstruction along more decentralized or federated lines of government also cautions against optimistic assessments of the willingness and ability of Moscow, preoccupied with domestic upheaval, to cooperate with the United States. The prospects for Soviet cooperation may, then, be essentially reduced to acquiescence to U.S. or Western initiatives. Instructive is the limited and reactive role played by the Soviet Union in fashioning the events leading to U.N. sanctions against Iraq and to the military attack by the coalition arrayed against Baghdad in January 1991.

Fourth, while it is prudent to harbor sober expectations about the possibility of surmounting the limitations of U.S.-Soviet cooperation, it is

6. Edward A. Kolodziej and Roger E. Kanet, ed., *The Limits of Soviet Power in the Developing World: Thermidor in the Revolutionary Struggle* (Baltimore, MD: Johns Hopkins University Press, 1989).

just as important not to set one's sights too low. The big two will remain the strongest military powers on the globe for some time. Both are still the major producers of arms and the world's leading suppliers. Each also spends more for defense than any other country. The gross national product of the United States approaches $5 trillion, the largest of any nation on earth; the country possesses a large, energetic, and talented people and is endowed with great natural resources and favorable geopolitical assets.[7]

These U.S. assets can be mobilized for joint ventures with the Soviet Union in the service of regional cooperation. The current political upheaval and lagging economic and social development in the Soviet Union do not necessarily spell that country's definitive demise as a major force in international relations. It enjoys close working relations with peoples and nations around the globe. These are important assets that can be traded to aid regional peace in the Middle East and South Asia. The task is to define, first, how the assets of Washington and Moscow can be effectively employed to advance regional peace and, second, what their division of labor should be to best exploit the strengths that each dis-

7. Joseph Nye, Jr., *Bound to Lead: The Changing Nature of American Power* (New York: Basic Books, 1990), states the case for continued U.S. power. The secular decline of the United States is delineated in Paul Kennedy, *The Rise and Fall of the Great Powers* (New York: Random House, 1988). For a parallel, though more contemporaneous, analysis of declining Soviet influence, see Paul Dibb, *The Soviet Union: The Incomplete Superpower*, 2d ed. (Urbana: University of Illinois Press, 1988).

poses in a particular region without damaging the interests of the other or those of its local clients.

There is ample reason for close U.S.-Soviet cooperation. Acute regional conflicts, like those in the Middle East and the Persian Gulf, will not recede simply by ignoring them. Those that may have temporarily abated in Afghanistan, southern and central Africa, and South, Southeast, and Northeast Asia may well erupt again if they are left unattended and allowed to fester. They constitute continuing challenges for big-power diplomacy. How Moscow and Washington respond to them, unilaterally or jointly, are touchstones for long-term détente and cooperation.

Since crises do not arise in sequential order, permitting time to deal with each on its own terms, there is a need for new mechanisms and understandings to be in place between Moscow and Washington to reduce regional conflicts and to eliminate or ameliorate their sources as opportunities for initiative arise. The appropriate bargaining model for big-two cooperation might be somewhat akin to the one employed by the European Community to enlarge and deepen economic and political cooperation. Package deals between members are constructed across policy areas. Success in these efforts has tended to have, over time, a spillover effect that encourages further progress.

In the same vein, as the size of the bargaining framework and the number of differing issues and stakes increase, opportunities for cooperative trade-offs between the United States and the Soviet Union are more likely to arise if they do not treat each region separate from others or react to crises with ad hoc measures only after their outbreak. Good-faith actions by Moscow and Washington in one region of the globe may offset the almost inevitable misunderstandings that will emerge between them in other regions, not to mention the misperceptions that each has of the other's motives and aims as a consequence of their profound national and ideological differences. The negative and threatening taint of linkage politics, associated with balance-of-power and spheres-of-influence maneuvering, might be utilized under a new and positive guise to facilitate great-power cooperation in a post-Cold War world.

Finally, and this is the trickiest part of the problem, greater U.S.-Soviet coordination in the developing world will have to be premised on active third-state participation. Here, the past is prologue. If regional rivals can block efforts to impose a peace thrust upon them by others or if other states, in and outside the region, can undermine a political accord or an arms control and disarmament measure, it makes little sense to cut these actors out of negotiations and to isolate them from participating in arrangements that affect them. The successful negotiation of the Soviet withdrawal from Afghanistan and the resolution of the Namibian question, leading to South African and Cuban military disengagement, illustrate the point.

There are, of course, limits to the unreserved application of this principle. Too many participants, especially those with little power to influ-ence results or with little stake in making a peace accord work, unduly complicate negotiations and hamper the realization of accommodations designed to arrest or dampen strife. It is hardly constructive just to enlarge the number of participants involved in resolving a conflict when some parties will have no direct standing nor the will or relevant resources to contribute to workable solutions. Moreover, some third states or parties may well be a major source of regional upheaval; an example is Libya in its support of terrorist organizations. Their disruptive behavior may have to be contained rather than simply co-opted.

Which states should participate and on what terms will have to be determined according to the problem at hand. Relevant criteria include historical presence and established interest in a region, such as the case of Britain in South Africa; availability of resources to encourage economic cooperation between former rivals, as with the European Community and Japan vis-à-vis economic aid; a high level of regional penetration through such avenues as trade, arms and technology transfers, investments, and labor flows, such as the case of France with respect to North Africa; cultural, communal, racial, ethnic, or ideological affinities with rivals in a region, as Brazil has with Angola and Mozambique; and rising future claims to a regional presence, as Italy has within the Mediterranean. These criteria, among others that might be identified, qualify a state to be considered as a participant and to be assured that it will be consulted by other engaged states, including the big two, in the management and resolution of regional conflicts that affect its interests.

As Paul Schroeder persuasively argues, one of the reasons why the nineteenth-century Eurocentric system preserved relative peace for a century can be traced to a complex and finely tuned system of understandings, based on mutually accorded and respected rights and roles of big and small powers, that gradually developed in the wake of the chaos of the Napoleonic Wars. For some time, statesmen were sensitized to respond to the concerns of other states that perceived their interests or status at risk in a regional conflict or in the negotiations leading to a conflict's containment or resolution.[8] Part of the explanation for the breakdown of the nineteenth-century system, leading to World War I, can be attributed to the atrophy and ossification of this consultative process and to the destruction of those delicately constructed sets of national equilibria of interest—not just crude power balances—that undergirded peace in Europe.

We now turn to a discussion of how the United States and the Soviet Union might compose their joint interests in regions around the globe in cooperation with relevant third states. The aim would not be the redrawing of the world's map into big-power spheres of influence—a futile enterprise—but the creation of zones of relative peace and prosperity based on security, welfare, and regime assurances more than on threats directed at interested parties. These zones would depend for their functioning on U.S.-Soviet cooperation, the support, or at least the tacit tolerance, of regional rivals, and especially the contributions of third parties.

These clusterings might well be sanctioned by the United Nations and subsequently incorporated in some formal way into an expanding system of U.N. peacekeeping responsibilities under the aegis of the Security Council. Whether such formalization is seen to be useful or feasible will depend on the contribution that institutionalizing regional conflict management and resolution arrangements will have on the participants most relevant to a regional accord. If the participation of the United Nations or of a regional association would impede conflict reduction, then there appears little reason to press collective solutions that may affirm some abstract legal norm or moral principle or that are simply appealing on grounds of comprehensiveness or symmetry. How this clustering of third states and international actors might be composed and the leadership of the big two in constructing them occupy the remainder of this discussion.[9]

8. Paul W. Schroeder, "The Nineteenth Century System: Balance of Power or Political Equilibrium," Review of International Studies, 15:135-253 (1989).

9. Axelrod and the World Politics group also contend that cooperation increases in inverse proportion to the number of participants. Whatever the logical attractiveness of this proposition may be, research on U.S.-Soviet relations with developing states suggests that enlarging the scope of peace negotiations and increasing the number of interested parties can have positive results.

GLOBAL COOPERATION
THROUGH REGIONAL CLUSTERS

Since neither the United States nor the Soviet Union, alone or together, is fully capable of containing or concluding regional conflicts, it would appear more fruitful—and consistent with the historical record since World War II—to group or cluster states and third parties, including the big two, and to focus their collective resources on a region in order to promote peace. Clustering promises to restrain and resolve regional conflict better than a more narrowly based approach restricted solely to Moscow and Washington or one that automatically invokes regional organizations or the United Nations as much to preclude serious negotiations between principals to a conflict as to facilitate accord. It goes beyond the scope of this analysis to survey all of the regions of the globe where this cluster principle might be applied. For illustrative purposes, the discussion will be limited to North and West Africa and to southern Africa, where clusterings have already worked to an appreciable degree. The success achieved in these regions by counting relevant parties in, not out, and by creating denser and more intricate networks among clustered parties in support of regional peace might well be relevant and even directly applicable to other regions.

North and West Africa

The North African states have been remarkably successful in resisting U.S. and Soviet penetration and in establishing mutually satisfactory relations with both power centers.[10] Morocco has enjoyed a beneficial contractual arrangement with the Soviet Union, bartering phosphates for capital equipment, infrastructure improvements, and road creation. Algeria trades gas and oil to the West while purchasing most of its weapons from the Soviet Union. Algiers has also represented U.S. interests at times in dealing with such ticklish questions as the release of American hostages held by Iran. Tunisia is also on friendly terms with both the East and the West. The revolt in the western Sahara still lingers, but it is no longer a threat to Rabat, partly because Morocco has succeeded in minimizing great-power and intraregional intervention.

Libya has been a source of irritation to the United States, embarrassment to the Soviet Union, and a threat to French interests in the region. France's diplomatic and strategic containment of Libya under Qaddafi's rule since 1969, while negotiating the treacherous waters of ceaseless Chadian strife, contrasts favorably with U.S. efforts to restrain Libyan meddling abroad. The clumsy attempt of the United States to eliminate Qaddafi by bombing his headquarters and sleeping sites failed. While, arguably, this assault by technological overkill may have temporarily discouraged Qaddafi from launching additional provocations

10. For an excellent overview of why North Africa has been largely insulated from the Cold War struggle, see I. William Zartman, "Superpower Cooperation in North Africa and the Horn of Africa," in *Cold War as Cooperation*, ed. Kanet and Kolodziej, pp. 147-70.

against American interests, the fact remains that he is still in power. Meanwhile, with less fanfare and with far more discipline and consistency—though lapses can be readily cited—French military assistance to the Chadian government then under Hassène Habré defeated a superior force of Libyan troops and largely contained Libya's threat to Chad. French success in this venture was all the more a bitter pill for Washington to swallow since the Mitterrand government refused overflight rights for U.S. aircraft stationed in England on their bombing mission over Libya.

France has also demonstrated more restraint than the United States and the Soviet Union in transferring arms to its clients. However much France may have commercialized its arms sales, it has essentially pursued a policy of restraint in supplying arms to Francophone West Africa.[11] The United States and the Soviet Union have not always exhibited the same restraint. At some expense to its trading position and economic advantage, France has also continued to assign priority to its relations with the Francophone West African states, principally for strategic and political considerations, rather than pursue, as some French ministers have argued for,[12] a more global approach toward developing states that promised more economic benefits for

11. See Edward A. Kolodziej, *Making and Marketing Arms: The French Experience and Its Implications for the International System* (Princeton, NJ: Princeton University Press, 1987), pp. 367-83.

12. E.g., Jean-Pierre Cot, as minister of cooperation in the first Mitterrand government, whose insistence on a global strategy contributed eventually to his ouster.

France and a lowered postcolonial burden than one that concentrated on its former dependencies. It has also skillfully executed timely interventions in Francophone countries to rid populations of unpopular and inhumane leaders, like Jean-Bedel Bokassa in the Central African Republic. Again, these calibrated initiatives can be contrasted with the sledgehammer blows associated with the U.S. military interventions in Grenada and Panama or the bombing of Libya.

The European Community also has a critical economic role to play throughout Africa. The Mediterranean and black African states, thanks partly to French leadership, already enjoy special access to European markets for their products, particularly fruits and vegetables. The extensive immigration of the peoples of this vast region into Europe binds the nations of these two continents together. The socioeconomic development, stability, and peace of Africa will depend on European economic assistance, increasingly regularized in successive Lomé accords, as an essential ingredient in building regional clusters of peace.

In sum, if the United States and the Soviet Union contemplate any joint policy toward North Africa or the Francophone states of West Africa, their initiatives will have to be coordinated with those of France and the European Community for unnecessary friction to be avoided and for the chances of success of any joint venture to be enhanced. These two regions provide good opportunities for Moscow and Washington to assume a low profile. The states in these regions have contained the spread of violence better than other areas have while maintaining relatively stable, if authoritarian, regimes. Even long-standing disputes like those between Morocco and Algeria have not been allowed to get out of hand by the parties most directly affected. Regional stability depends not only on knowing when Moscow and Washington should cooperatively intervene but also when they should not.

Southern Africa

Significant and continuing U.S.-Soviet cooperation was indispensable in reaching accords on Angola and Namibia. Neither the truce reached in the Angolan civil war, with the departure of Cuban troops and a slowdown in Soviet military assistance to the Luanda regime, nor the independence of Namibia, with the end of South African rule and the withdrawal of Pretoria's armed forces, would have been possible without U.S.-Soviet cooperation and the determination of Moscow and Washington to prevail over the objections of their regional clients to these settlements.

The role of the Front Line States should also not be minimized as a stabilizing force in bringing the warring parties to the bargaining table. They still have a vital role to play in assisting Namibia through its transition to full independence and nation building, where their experience is valuable. Finally, the process of ending apartheid in South Africa and preparing the way to black rule has

only now begun in earnest. These problems, however much they are interlocked, will require different mixes of states, including but not restricted to the United States, the Soviet Union, and the Front Line States, to effectively address the diverse issues raised by each.

Except for Margaret Thatcher's Britain, most of the other states of the European Community cooperated with the United States and the Soviet Union in pressuring Pretoria, through an economic embargo on trade and investment, to embark on negotiations aimed at the sweeping reform of racial relations. Other states also have a role in aiding this process to a successful conclusion. Countries like Sweden, which ordinarily strive to stay out of the limelight of international conflict, have been particularly generous in supporting the African National Congress and in providing economic assistance to embattled African states. The participation of the member states of the European Community and neutrals is critical if a combination stick-and-carrot diplomacy is to be successful in inducing the minority white government to dismantle all vestiges of racial discrimination and to prepare the way for black majority rule. In any event, however, unless the white minority can be integrated into a South Africa under black rule, post-apartheid South Africa will hardly inherit a viable political order, already threatened by civil war among blacks, nor will a productive economic system be created that is attractive to outside investment from the West and Japan.

CONCLUSION

U.S.-Soviet regional cooperation should be based on certain assumptions and principles. First, the United States and the Soviet Union should begin the arduous process of codifying their understanding of the cooperation that they have already achieved in regional affairs and of laying the political groundwork for its extension. This codification process is all the more important now that the state structure and Communist party of what was the Soviet Union is in the process of fundamental transformation. If past is prologue, there will eventually emerge a new political force—conceivably several—among the peoples that previously formed the Soviet Union. These centers of decision are likely to be defined by national and ethnic identity, with the Russian people who compose the largest of the Soviet republics assuming their historic leadership role in the region. Those republics which will form what is likely to be a weak union and central government will essentially inherit the legacy of international commitments made with other states. They will also be expected to abide by the understandings that comprised U.S.-Soviet cooperation before the demise of the Soviet state and the Communist party.

Second, and for reasons outlined earlier, both the United States and the emerging republics and the new union in the Soviet Union should adopt an across-the-board multiregional approach toward resolving local strife. All parties should cast their conflict-reducing and resolution initiatives in post-Cold War terms. Emphasis should be placed on establishing scenario-specific equilibria of interests between relevant states rather than on just creating spheres of interests or narrowly conceived balances of power. Regional stability and peace depend as much on assuring states and peoples that their interests will be protected and promoted as on creating military alliances to deter war and would-be aggressors. While it would be naive to believe that military power, threats, or incipient coercion, illustrated by the economic embargo raised against Pretoria and by U.N. sanctions against Iraq, will have no role in negotiations leading to regional peace, it is no less true that post-Cold War regimes at the regional level cannot long survive unless they also incorporate measures for economic development and for the expression of what local populations conceive to be legitimate principles of rule.

A post-Cold War politics affords the world community a rare opportunity for the incorporation of assurances as well as for addressing threats in building regional systems that ameliorate, if not eliminate, regional conflicts. As regional strife in North and West Africa and in southern Africa suggests, neither the United States nor the Soviet Union, alone or jointly, can ensure regional peace. Other actors, including third states, regional groupings such as the Front Line States, and the United Nations will also have to be enlisted into service under joint Soviet and American leadership. Regional states have earned a place at the bargaining table not only by checking the hegemonic pursuits of Moscow and Washington but also by their ability today to significantly preclude or promote regional cooperation. The Cold War struggle was never as bipolar as many believed; much of its stability can be attributed to the efforts of third parties, particularly regional states, as well as to the United States and the Soviet Union.[13] The aim of U.S. cooperation with the peoples of the Soviet Union is, then, to enlarge the scope of international efforts to include the resources, talents, and commitment of as many other states as possible in building the post-Cold War order. A multipolar world will certainly be complex and, arguably, more difficult to manage, but it need not be more conflictual and globally threatening than the politics and political struggles of the Cold War era.

13. For a nostalgic interpretation of the Cold War as stable and under the control of the United States and the Soviet Union, see John Mearsheimer, "Back to the Future: Instability in Europe after the Cold War," *International Security*, 15(1):5-56 (Summer 1990).

Regional Organizations
in Conflict Management

By THOMAS PERRY THORNTON

ABSTRACT: The end of colonialism and the decline of Cold War bipolarity mean that the United States and the Soviet Union must find new ways of relating to a Third World that is growing increasingly influential and is seeking ways to be master of its own destinies. Over the past decade and more, there has been a marked growth in regional organizations within the Third World designed to deal with the related problems of solving internal disputes and reducing the role of outside powers in regional affairs. These organizations have mixed records, and some could pose threats to broader global interests, including those of the United States and the USSR. Nonetheless, the trend toward regionalization is pervasive, and in many cases regional groupings can deal with problems that the superpowers no longer can or want to handle. Moscow and Washington must judge each case on its own merits, but their general approach should be to let regional groupings carry as much of the burden as possible.

Thomas Thornton is adjunct professor of Asian studies at the Paul H. Nitze School of Advanced International Studies of the Johns Hopkins University. He previously served as senior member of the Policy Planning Staff of the Department of State and, during the Carter administration, as director of North-South affairs on the staff of the National Security Council. He has written extensively on Third World matters, especially concerning South Asia.

THE bipolar system under which the United States and the Soviet Union contested for primacy on a global basis—in Europe, first of all, but also throughout the Third World—is weakening. The contest was not always equal nor was it always pursued with the same intensity; nevertheless, there were few substantial political events in which one or the other superpower did not take an interest. In many cases, one or both of them came to dominate the state of play in regions that were often distant from their homelands and not evidently very relevant to their vital interests. In several of these, events slipped so far that the United States and the Soviet Union came near war because of their involvement on opposite sides of a dispute. More recently, however, the Soviet Union and the United States have been reassessing their involvement in distant, Third World affairs in order to save scarce resources and reduce risk.

The likely future involvement of the superpowers in Third World affairs will vary according to place. For the United States, Central America is of special significance, as is South Asia for the Soviet Union. The Middle East is important for both. One cannot assume that declining trends of activism will be necessarily reflected in these areas, where perceived vital interests, not just matters of prestige, are at stake. Reactions to the Iraqi takeover of Kuwait are a case in point.

It will be important to see whether and how the policies of the superpowers can be brought better into phase, whether they will be able to cooperate broadly, or whether they will trend toward a more clearly defined spheres-of-influence approach, whereby each one asserts its preeminent and uncontested concern in areas of vital interest to it. While important, however, these are specific exceptions to an overall process of devolution of responsibility away from the United States and the Soviet Union—in effect, the end to the era of bipolarity as the organizing factor of the global system.

AUTONOMY

A second process is closely related to the end of bipolarity: the end of colonialism and the assertion of autonomy by the nations of the Third World themselves. This is a still less tidy evolution than is the pulling back of the superpowers. The nations of the Third World are immensely varied in capability and interest, and there are murderous disputes among them. Nonetheless, here, too, one can see the broad outlines of an epochal development in international relations.

The assertion of autonomy by the Third World nations occurs in two broad forms. The first is military: nations such as India or Vietnam have set about building a military capability that will enable them, perhaps, to expand their own influence and will at a minimum keep outsiders at bay. For the most part, however, the search for autonomy has taken place in political forms. The Afro-Asian and Nonaligned movements of the 1950s and 1960s represented initial attempts at the assertion of autonomy and met with some success. They have not, however, proved fully effective and cannot do so since the membership is so diverse geographically and so badly riven by disputes. Continentwide organizations—the Organization of American States and the Organization of African Unity—have also not proven very helpful to Third World security concerns. The demand for autonomy is, of course, even stronger at the national level, and individual states pursue autonomy as best they can. In most instances, however, they lack the power to achieve it.

There is, however, a middle ground, and in fact there has been a significant tendency in the past decade and more toward the evolution of regionally specific subsystems that can be more effective in meeting the needs of their participants. The geographic definition of some of these systems is imprecise, even variable, and they are often characterized more by conflict than by cooperation. We should not expect Third World equivalents of the European Community. It is convenient to discuss these groupings in their organizational forms such as the Association of Southeast Asian Nations (ASEAN) or the Gulf Cooperation Council (GCC), and I will do that later. The key to the broad development lies not, however, primarily in the organizational forms, which may be ephemeral, but in the dynamic that underlies them, a dynamic that must be conceptually understood as prior to the organizational form. That dynamic, in its broadest form, is the search for autonomy, that is, the exclusion of powers external to the region—generally

the superpowers—from a management role in regional security and political matters. Such exclusion takes on particular meaning when one realizes that loss of autonomy has in the past resulted—and could again result—in the merging of regional problems into the rivalries of the global system. When that happens, the Third World states are rarely long-term winners.

The greatest danger to regional autonomy arises from conflicts between Third World states—generally within the same region. These are the Achilles' heel for any attempt to assert autonomy, providing the point of entry for outside interventions. The classic case is the Indo-Pakistan dispute: Pakistan, fearing India, calls on the United States, and the Indians then call on the Soviet Union. The case of the Middle East is almost as striking. In addition, rifts in the Southeast Asian and Caribbean systems provided entrée for outside powers, and other examples can be adduced in Africa, such as the Horn. A key, then, to regional autonomy is the composition of disputes internal to a system, and this fact is clearly appreciated by all of the emergent systems—at least in theory!

An additional problem is the relationship between regional groupings and states in or near the region that are especially strong. Such states have sometimes been called "regional influentials" and can play both a positive and a negative role in the formation of regional systems. On one hand, it is extremely useful for a region to have a strong member around which it can coalesce. On the other hand, it is often very difficult for a regional influential to establish a balanced relationship—that is, one in which the larger nation's superior position is acknowledged and in which the smaller neighbors feel that their concerns get fair consideration. The integration of a regional influential into a regional system has often been the major task confronting emergent systems.

A similar challenge arises when a strong regional actor external to the system poses a security threat to it. Such a challenge can be helpful in bringing the members of the system closer together—for example, it puts their own internal disputes in a different perspective—but the rivalries between a regional subsystem and powerful neighbor can themselves become dangerous and can best be solved by achieving a *modus vivendi* in which the neighbor actually joins the system as a leading member. More likely, however, it will remain external to the system and be a course of continuing tension.

REGIONAL SYSTEMS

The most penetrated regional systems have taken the initiative in soliciting the involvement of the United States and the USSR—and China—in their affairs. This pull factor was, of course, complemented by a push factor—the superpowers' attempts to extend their global role—but it does not automatically follow that the reduction in the push factor, described in the previous section, will automatically eliminate pressures for U.S. and Soviet involvement in the security and political affairs of Third World states and regions. The pull factor must also be brought under control lest pressures—and temptations—lure one or both of the superpowers back into regions from which they have withdrawn—or, especially as in the Middle East, prevent the superpowers from disengaging at all. Limiting the U.S. and Soviet roles means, therefore, not simply declarations of abstinence on the part of Moscow and Washington; it also entails the settlement of regional disputes or, where that is impossible, their containment, so that they do not pull outsiders into a competition for regional security management.

A detailed examination of the dispute-settlement capabilities of the various regional groupings goes beyond this article. It is useful, however, to review briefly the more important of the regional attempts at assertion of autonomy through dispute settlement or containment.

For analytical purposes, we can consider each of the regional groupings in such terms as its membership; its origin; the factors that hold it together; its weaknesses; the origin, source, and degree of penetration from outside; whether it has a deviant member; what its principal tasks are; and how successful it has been in solving regional disputes and promoting autonomy for the system. The consideration at this stage will be very schematic and not all-inclusive; the point of the exercise is to get a general picture of the phenomena we are dealing with.[1]

1. For a more detailed discussion, see Thomas Perry Thornton, *The Challenge to U.S. Policy in the Third World: Global Responsibil-*

ASEAN, embracing Thailand, Malaysia, Singapore, Indonesia, Brunei, and the Philippines, is something of a model. It was organized mainly as a way for these countries to look to their own security concerns as it became clear during the later phases of the Vietnam war that the U.S. protective presence would be scaled back. ASEAN styled itself an economic organization, moved very slowly in elaborating a political agenda, and even waited some years before its chiefs of state met officially under the ASEAN aegis. ASEAN has not been very successful in promoting economic integration—its members' economies are too similar—and it has had only limited success in representing its economic interests in international fora. On the political front it has been successful in asserting its right to be the *interlocuteur valable* for Southeast Asian interests in the Kampuchean matter, albeit not able to exclude all external influence on that question. For the states of a region that had been considered a set of dominoes, the playthings of the United States, the USSR, and China, that is no mean achievement.

A major contribution to ASEAN's success has been Indonesia's willingness to play a role that is still very prominent but rather less than it might feel entitled to on the basis of size and power. ASEAN faces a number of other internal difficulties, however, and is weakened by the fact that it does not fully cover its logical region, Southeast Asia. Until Indochina is brought into the system or is

otherwise neutralized, ASEAN will remain vulnerable.

The South Asian Association for Regional Cooperation (SAARC) was consciously modeled on ASEAN but has not progressed nearly as far. SAARC, which embraces India, Pakistan, Bangladesh, Nepal, Sri Lanka, the Maldives, and Bhutan, was formed at the urging of Bangladesh and encountered great initial—and understandable—resistance. Pakistan was skeptical about any regional organization that might be dominated by India; New Delhi, on the other hand, feared that SAARC would provide a forum for the smaller regional nations to gang up on India. For this reason, it was agreed that the new organization would not be concerned with security and political matters. SAARC has provided some useful channels for promoting regional economic, cultural, and law enforcement cooperation and, like all such established organizations, provides a forum within which leaders can unobtrusively meet with each other to discuss difficult political and security subjects, such as Indo-Sri Lankan relations.

SAARC's most difficult obstacle lies in the structural problem of the system, which is the overwhelming predominance of India constrained by the presence of a Pakistan that is too strong to be dominated by India. South Asia must develop a framework in which India can find a style of regional leadership that the smaller states find acceptable. Clearly, SAARC as such will not be able to solve that problem; at most, it can provide a stabilizing framework within which India and its more important neigh-

---

ity and Regional Devolution (Boulder, CO: Westview Press, 1986), chap. 6.

bors become more comfortable with each other. That, however, could be a critical contribution.

The Gulf Cooperation Council is a collection of the small sheikhdoms of the Persian Gulf plus Saudi Arabia. It was formed in order to give these militarily weak states a political base from which to counter possible threats from neighboring Iran and Iraq, as well as to limit the role of outside powers in gulf affairs. In addition, it has served to facilitate internal security cooperation between states whose small size and vast wealth make them attractive targets for takeover in the highly charged atmosphere of Arab politics. The members of the GCC had been successful in maintaining their independence and a freedom of action well beyond expectations. Disputes between the member states have been settled without untoward incident; the leading role of Saudi Arabia is recognized and accepted and the Saudis have played it with considerable grace. Through the heat of the Iran-Iraq war, the GCC nations were able to maintain a substantial degree of autonomy and flexibility in their policies. Even in the tanker war they gained a strong voice in shaping the terms of inevitable external involvement. In a sense, the Iraqi attack on Kuwait was testimony to their success. An inroad was possible only through direct aggression.

The GCC's failure was its inability to develop structures that would enmesh its powerful northern neighbors in a security system that would protect the interests of all. The nations of the GCC simply lack the military strength to protect themselves and have had to rely on outside powers for protection in the face of the Iraqi attack. That is clearly not a comfortable situation, as evidenced by the many calls for an Arab—that is, regional—solution to the Iraq-Kuwait crisis. The security of the gulf states can probably be assured only in a much larger framework, but the fissures within the Arab world make that extremely difficult. In the meantime, they are fortunate in that their oil wealth has brought the outside world to their rescue. That, however, cannot be a permanent solution.

The Front Line States (FLS) of southern Africa—in their economic incarnation, the Southern African Development Coordination Conference—are an extremely informal group of black African nations in the southern third of Africa brought together by the need to counter white colonialism and the apartheid regime of the Republic of South Africa. The membership of the group varies. The FLS eschewed formal organization and have never acted as a dispute-settling organization between group members as such. The FLS did, however, play an impressive role in coordinating the policies of a membership that was far from unanimous in how to deal with the problems that they faced. They enjoyed striking success in shaping the role and extent of outside powers' involvement and largely excluding Cold War considerations in the lengthy process of bringing independence to Zimbabwe.

With all colonial vestiges gone from the subcontinent and Pretoria dismantling apartheid, the political task of the FLS appears much less difficult; it is to hold the line until

South Africa sorts out its domestic problems. When majority rule comes to the republic, however, the FLS will have to rethink their goals. They may find that their main concerns are encapsulating the new black regime into their system, for the South African dream of a constellation of states is not dependent on the skin color of the rulers in Pretoria.

In the Western Hemisphere, the Contadora Group as such has been superseded by a somewhat different collection of Central American states. It was, however, the first and has provided the foundation for later groupings that grew out of concern for the deteriorating political situation in Central America—focused on Nicaragua and El Salvador—and the danger that this could become swept up into the Cold War competition between the United States and the Soviet Union, the latter through its Cuban ally. Even absent superpower competition, Central Americans need some sort of cooperative structure to partially offset the overwhelming power of the United States. Although severe problems persist in Central America, ad hoc groupings of Central American states have played a significant role in bringing a settlement to Nicaragua—thereby reducing its role as a potentially deviant member of the system—and limiting the ability of the United States to dominate the proceedings.

The Central Americans will continue to face major challenges to solve problems within their own countries and between the individual states—in addition, of course, to staking out an increasing role for themselves in determining how outside powers, especially the United States and Cuba, relate to Central America. Ultimately, they may also find the need to encapsulate Mexico, which, thus far, has chosen to maintain considerable distance.

There are other more or less formal, more or less effective groupings of regional states, and throughout the world there are systems that are defined by geographical proximity and some mixture of conflict and cooperation. The Middle East is the most visible example. Others are West Africa, where the regional states showed some skill in dealing with the collapse of Liberia; the Horn of Africa; the Southern Cone of Latin America; and, potentially, the states of Eastern Europe. The latter will have an interesting time composing the many differences between themselves while coping with their Soviet and German neighbors.

No one subsystem has a guaranteed bright future. External pressures, internal dissension, or even the social and economic problems that face individual members could bring any of them to ruin. Their very existence, however, is more remarkable than their weaknesses. A decade or so ago, few of them existed, and, although the logic of the situation was in their favor, few observers predicted such a widespread phenomenon. What we are seeing here is not single, isolated cases but a trend that is literally worldwide and seems to be growing. Nothing in international politics is inevitable or irreversible, but the movement of weaker states toward regional system formation is one of the most interesting and most promising trends of recent decades.

THE VIEW FROM THE
UNITED STATES AND THE USSR

The approaches of the Soviet Union and the United States to regional organization with political and security overtones have been mixed. In the years of their exuberant interventionism, neither of the superpowers could look with unmixed pleasure at the existence of regional groupings seeking autonomy. For the United States in the 1950s, for instance, the only proper regional groupings were those that were tied into the Western alliance system and thereby contributed to the containment policy.

Moscow also showed little enthusiasm for regional groupings while it was moving toward greater global involvement. It took a decidedly negative view of ASEAN in the early years of that organization and was even dilatory in expressing its approval of SAARC a decade later. In the early years, the Soviets may have been reluctant to see the emergence of dispute-containing organizations, for it was through disputes that the Soviet Union could gain access to systems that were otherwise closed to them, such as Southeast Asia. That could hardly have been the case with SAARC, however, and concern that Western, capitalist-inclined governments would come to dominate such groupings and tie them into the Western system economically as well as politically was increasingly the cause of Soviet caution.

Soviet attempts to promote regional security systems were rare. The ill-fated Brezhnev proposal, in 1969, for an Asian security system was rejected by the Asian states. Proposals for a regional security arrangement in the Persian Gulf in 1980 received little more support. These were perceived as programs with their own agenda—maximizing the political position of the Soviet Union with little regard for regional organization as such.

More recently, both of the superpowers have come to speak approvingly of SAARC, the Front Line States, and ASEAN, in no small part, apparently, because neither the United States nor the USSR sees them as threats to their own shifting interests. When Washington saw the efforts of Contadora running counter to its own interests, however, it showed little tolerance. It is not clear how seriously Washington and Moscow take these organizations as actual or potential security managers for their respective regions. Nor is it clear whether either has really thought through the implications should the regional groupings succeed.

The implications are, in fact, mixed. On the negative side, there is no guarantee that regional groupings, having achieved autonomy, will act in ways that are compatible with the interests of either or both superpowers or, indeed, with the interests of global order. This could involve disregard for human rights, proliferation of weapons of mass destruction, attacks upon neighboring states, or even direct attacks on the interests of one of the superpowers.

Second, the way in which the regional grouping organizes itself to achieve autonomy may be repugnant—specifically, the brutal imposition of regional hegemony by one nation upon its neighbors. In this process, a nation that had long and friendly ties with one of the superpowers might find itself oppressed. If, hypothetically, India imposed its will on Pakistan, or Egypt on Syria, there would be great pressure on the United States or the USSR to come to the aid of its client. It is encouraging, however, that the superpowers maintained considerable solidarity in their approach to the recent Iraq-Kuwait situation and in the Indo-Pakistan tensions over Kashmir in 1990.

On the positive side, there is an impressive array of factors. First, of course, any regional mechanism that can contain conflict and disputes, reduce the likelihood of war, and reduce wasteful defense expenditures and the like must be welcomed. The United States and the USSR have, one hopes, passed beyond the stage where they saw regional conflicts as an opportunity to insert themselves into regional affairs. The costs are simply too high for all sides—and not least of all for those in the Third World whose blood and treasure are being wasted.

More important from my point of view is the contribution that regional dispute management can make to improved relations between the superpowers. That is to say, the pull factor of regional disputes, mentioned earlier, will have been greatly reduced and thereby facilitate the disengagement that the reduction of the push factor has made desirable.

Finally, if regional groupings can work out their own internal problems, the solutions that they find are likely to be more lasting, if not necessarily more just, than solutions imposed from the outside by Moscow or Washington or—as is more often the case—the simple postponement of a solution as a result of outside pressures.

PRESCRIPTION FOR SUPERPOWER INVOLVEMENT

The behavior of the Soviet Union and, especially at this point, the United States remains a crucial factor affecting the ability of regional groupings to achieve autonomy, at least in the short to mid-range. It goes beyond the scope of this article to discuss in any detail the various arrangements that the United States and the USSR might seek to implement severally or jointly. Among the possibilities are a U.S. attempt to seize leadership of a new world order, the division of the world into spheres of influence, a U.S.-Soviet condominium, or limited and ad hoc cooperation in maintaining some semblance of international order.

The two great powers, joined increasingly by the Europeans and Japan, are not going to abandon the field completely; each will seek to maintain a strong voice in immediately neighboring areas—Eastern Europe, Central America—and regions of great economic importance such as the Persian Gulf. They will also want to maintain a strong voice in certain functional areas, especially nonproliferation of nuclear weapons but also environmental concerns with global implications.

It would fly in the face of reality, however, if either or both were to attempt to maintain the kind of global reach and influence that they have had in the past. The pursuit of policies that run counter to growing political and security capabilities in the Third World would be anachronistic and could be maintained only for short periods and in limited areas. The decline in the relative, if not absolute, capabilities of Moscow and Washington should dictate a policy of very selective, cooperative involvement—wherever possible under a broader international aegis.

The series of routine discussions that are held between U.S. and Soviet officials concerning Third World issues is a constructive move—as long as they accept the fact that these regional forces are no longer simply the objects of First and Second World policy but increasingly the subjects of international affairs in their own right. This acceptance will be difficult for two nations with the histories and national proclivities of the United States and the Soviet Union.

With that understanding in mind, they can move on to a more positive appreciation of the usefulness of regional groupings in managing their own security and dealing with their mutual conflicts. In addition, they can better calculate the levels and forms of cooperation that they should strive for in their dealings with the Third World. It is essential in this regard that both sides critically assess their ongoing policies toward the Third World and consider the implications of the gaps discussed earlier in this article. The United States needs to consciously build down its involvement; the Soviet Union should consider whether masochism

is a suitable substitute for policy. Americans found, after Vietnam, that it was not.

The next step is to appraise carefully just what the situation and trends are in the more important regions of the Third World: What are the dynamics of conflict and cooperation among the nations of the region and in relationship to neighboring regions and neighboring states that might be drawn into the scope of the region? Are there useful formal organizations in existence? What are their capabilities in dispute settlement? Beyond that, is the region as a whole, or one individual state within it, likely to pursue policies that are unacceptable as international behavior, such as aggression, mishandling of neighbors, human rights violations, or acquiring of weapons of mass destruction? Finally, how deeply engaged are the interests of one or both of the superpowers in the region, how important is it to their interests, and are elements within the region hostile to one or the other of the superpowers and likely to make that hostility effective?

In most cases, as was suggested earlier, the United States and the Soviet Union will find that they can live with, indeed welcome, the more probable forms of assertion of autonomy and methods of conflict resolution that are applied in the individual regions. Where that is not true, it is extremely important that this be made clear, both between the superpowers themselves and to the world at large. They apparently failed to convey their message with adequate clarity to Saddam Hussein.

Where, however, the situation is acceptable, Moscow and Washington should consider how they should relate to it. On one hand, they could remove themselves as much as possible from the security affairs of the region in question on the grounds that they need not and/or cannot influence the probable outcomes.

Alternatively, they could take steps, individually or jointly, to strengthen regional forces by their own actions. This, at an essential minimum, means not doing anything that might harm the emergence of an effective regional security management system. Positive steps are much more problematic but might include public statements supportive of regional groupings, taking actions—such as in the structure of international negotiations—to put responsibilities on the regional grouping, or meeting officially with representatives of the regional organization. There may be interesting precedents for these steps in the way the United States dealt with the emerging European Community. When specific crises arise, the United States and the USSR should consider meeting with the regional group, making clear to it their own concerns but, even more, underlining the fact that both Moscow and Washington look to the group to take effective action and that as long as the regional group does so, the superpowers will stay out of the situation. Particular thought might be given to holding such consultations within the framework of the appropriate articles of the Charter of the United Nations.

Finally, of course, the superpowers should strive for some understanding of how they will respond should the political and security situations get out of hand in ways that seriously threaten international norms and order. Unilateral action—most likely by the United States—is in almost all instances undesirable and joint U.S.-Soviet action only somewhat less so since neither of the two nations should try to play the role of global policeman any longer. Wherever possible, the two should work cooperatively within the framework of the United Nations or other suitable international organization to deal with the situation. The strengthening of global institutions is also an important part of the devolution of responsibility that should be the goal of both the United States and the Soviet Union in this new phase of history.

ANNALS, *AAPSS*, 518, November 1991

Rules of Conduct in the Settlement of Regional Conflicts

By VICTOR A. KREMENYUK

ABSTRACT: The settlement of regional conflicts has definitely joined the U.S.-Soviet agenda. Both superpowers have become engaged in talks on the approaches to such settlement in their bilateral relations and in their relations with third parties-participants to conflicts. This development has emerged only recently and demands more attention on the part of researchers. What makes this task even more attractive is the necessity of finding an approach shared by the United States and the USSR in dealing with regional conflicts. For this purpose, it is necessary to analyze the past experience of the superpowers when they adhered to a collision course in their attitudes toward regional conflicts and, first of all, to find what types of actions and decisions they should avoid in order to establish the necessary level of trust and, second, what type of actions they could envisage in order to establish a pattern of cooperation. Without such a study, it would be difficult to expect a positive result from the superpowers' efforts to settle conflicts in different areas of the world.

Victor A. Kremenyuk is deputy director of the Institute of the USA and Canada of the Soviet Academy of Sciences. He received his Ph.D. in international economics at the Moscow Institute for International Relations (1968) and a doctorate in sciences in history of international relations at the Institute of the USA and Canada (1980). He publishes his works mainly in Russian, among them eight monographs on U.S. foreign policy, and also contributes to publications in the United States, Great Britain, the Federal Republic of Germany, and other countries.

THE resolution of regional conflicts is a matter of practical implementation in U.S.-Soviet relations. Agreements on Afghanistan and South-West Africa have been reached recently. There has been tangible progress in the settlement of the thorny issue of Cambodia. Intensive steps are being undertaken regarding a Middle East peace settlement, especially in the wake of the Persian Gulf crisis. Definite changes have occurred even in such long-standing conflicts as that between North and South Korea. In quite a number of regional conflicts, then, there is movement, albeit at different rates of speed, by the conflicting parties toward finding peaceful settlements to their disputes. At the same time, the impact of the Persian Gulf crisis on Soviet-American relations has highlighted the need for a much more advanced type of relationship between the superpowers since, without their cooperation, it would be irrelevant to hope to manage the existing conflicts or prevent new ones.

All of these developments can be described as a consequence of the changes in Soviet-American relations generally. The changes that have taken place in Soviet foreign policy; the development of a new approach to the peaceful settlement of conflicts, which puts a greater emphasis on the policy of national reconciliation; the promotion of greater U.N. involvement; consultations with other great powers; mediation efforts; and so forth—all have radically changed the status of regional conflicts and have paved the way to a more favorable international climate.

It is hoped that the future course of events in this area will continue in their current direction and, as time goes on, will become more stable. In this context, the gulf crisis has raised a set of issues including not only how to resist local aggression but also how to speed up settlement of the existing conflicts in order to avoid reversing the present trend and fueling the existing hotbeds of tension. It is obvious that what is involved is an issue of extreme delicacy, complexity, and diversity, an issue that does not lend itself to easy solutions. It is not enough to proclaim a policy of peaceful settlement and national reconciliation. What is needed is to find ways to do away with multiple layers of mistrust and suspicion, to understand the underpinnings and the real nature of various positions taken by the conflicting sides. What is also needed is to define a model of the settlement of conflicts and to work out reliable mechanisms for practical implementation of decisions that are taken. This problem presents the task of reconsidering U.S.-Soviet attitudes toward regional conflicts and the realistic possibilities of their cooperation in this area.

U.S.-SOVIET CONSULTATIONS

In their capacity both as permanent members of the U.N. Security Council and as countries that have developed an extensive network of allied and friendly ties, the great powers certainly have their share of responsibility for the settlement of regional conflicts. While emphasizing in every way the significance of local, or regional, factors in the development of conflicts, one must not picture the great powers as mere observers of the regional situation. They supply weapons and munitions to their friends and allies, provide them with economic and technical assistance, train their troops, and render diplomatic support. In many cases, though by far not all, the great powers encourage decisions by local governments, which lead to an aggravation or, on the contrary, to a relaxation of tensions in a conflict. Respecting the inalienable sovereignty of the sides involved in a given conflict, the great powers are nonetheless real, though indirect, participants in it.

An insurmountable wall of rivalry and mutual suspicion on these issues separated the USSR and the United States for many years. The established practice in U.S.-Soviet relations during those years made any fruitful dialogue between the two powers impossible, not withstanding earlier cases when they had undertaken joint steps to find solutions of some conflicts, such as the Geneva Conferences of 1953 and 1954, which put an end to the bloodshed in Korea and Indochina, and the conference on Laos of 1962. Even at the Soviet-American Summit in May 1972, following the U.S. decision to withdraw its troops from Vietnam, there was no consistent or meaningful discussion of the settlement of the conflict, according to former Secretary of State Henry Kissinger.[1]

The bizarre nature of this situation was striking to any observer dur-

1. H. A. Kissinger, *White House Years* (Boston: Little, Brown, 1979), p. 1249.

ing the 1970s. All attempts by the Carter administration, which used its own method of linkage at the Soviet-American Strategic Arms Limitation Talks, to deal with this unnatural situation failed. The method of linkage was far-fetched in itself, but, primarily, it was conceived and used as a means of putting pressure on the Soviet Union, which could not but stem the development of a normal dialogue on regional problems and, instead of promoting the negotiations, actually slowed them down. The brief period of 1977-78, when the USSR and the United States attempted to negotiate on the issue of the demilitarization of the Indian Ocean, on the Middle East—concerning which they even signed a joint statement—and on conventional arms trade, left no appreciable imprint upon bilateral interaction. Because of the disillusionment it produced, the period of 1977-78 created obstacles, which emerged later, to promoting productive dialogue and building trust.

In spite of all this, both sides—in dire need of interaction during the early 1980s, when Soviet-American relations had already entered a period of crisis—began to exchange views on regional problems. The first round of such exchanges, which took place in 1981 and 1982 between Soviet Foreign Minister Andrei Gromyko and U.S. Secretary of State Alexander Haig, was not particularly successful. The significance of this series of exchanges for regional problems, however, should not be underestimated. It was a breakthrough in this particular area of confrontation between the two powers, and it enabled each side to present to the other a general outline of its interests in regional conflicts. Bilateral discussions of these interests had a far-reaching impact, because prior to them, each side, turning a deaf ear to the other and insisting on the legitimacy of its own regional interests, simply did not recognize any interests of the other side in any region of the world. The explicit presentation of each superpower's interests during the bilateral exchanges of 1981-82 made it possible subsequently to work out and put forward the fruitful idea of the balance of interests, though it happened much later, after 1985.

Generally, before 1985 it was both premature and unrealistic to speak about any substantial Soviet-American consultations on regional issues. At that stage, interaction between the Soviet Union and the United States in this area, using the terminology employed by A. Rapoport, remained at the level of "debates,"[2] and the emphasis was clearly on confrontation, even though a number of both written and unwritten rules were followed by both sides, including the "Hot Line" Agreement of 1963, the 1971 agreement on incidents on and over the sea, the "Hot Line" Modernization Agreement, and the Basic Principles Agreement of 1972. Under these conditions, sporadic meetings and discussions could only tone down somewhat the disagreements between the two coun-

tries and prevent the disagreements from worsening; by no means could they disentangle them.

This situation could not last. The fact that it was unbearable became particularly obvious in the fall of 1985, on the eve of the first Reagan-Gorbachev summit, in Geneva in November 1985. The U.S. president's speech on 24 October 1985 at the United Nations General Assembly dealt extensively with the issue of regional conflicts and, in fact, became a prelude to the Reagan Doctrine, which was proclaimed later. In his speech, the president again referred to foreign interference as the main cause of all conflicts, claiming that conflicts can be done away with only through struggle against "alien ideology" imposed upon the Third World by force.[3] There were some constructive ideas in the speech, particularly concerning stage-by-stage settlement of conflicts—dialogue between the opposing sides in a conflict, Soviet-American negotiations, and participation of the world community in the settlement of conflicts. The overall tone of the president's speech, however, was so ideologized that it could not evoke anything but a negative response.

At the same time, this period marked the beginning of regular discussions of regional conflicts, among other issues, at Soviet-American meetings. Both formal and informal meetings of experts from the two countries took place. Serious and painstaking efforts were applied for the first time to reach a settlement in

2. A. Rapoport, *Fights, Games, and Debates* (Ann Arbor: University of Michigan Press, 1963).

3. *The Department of State Bulletin*, 85(2105):1-7 (Dec. 1985).

Afghanistan, and they were consummated by the agreement signed in April 1988. Official Soviet and U.S. representatives began a series of contacts with the goal of finding a solution to the conflict in southwestern Africa. Overall, a fairly consistent and streamlined system of consultations on issues involved in regional conflicts had begun to take shape.

SOME BASIC DIFFERENCES
IN APPROACHES

Even with the advent of a new climate in Soviet-American relations, some basic differences continue to exist in the approaches of both nations toward conflicts. The basic Soviet approach was forged by the Marxist-Leninist doctrine that was for many years implanted into the thinking of the policymakers and into the existing practices. This approach, based on the theory of the class struggle, was oriented toward a permanent conflict of interests between the ruling elite and the rest of society and, in the international dimension, toward a permanent conflict between two "world systems," as well as between the "oppressed"—the Third World—and the "oppressors," or the developed nations of the West. In the American approach, based mainly on the general theory of conflict, the thrust was toward a kind of conflict-cooperation type of relationship that envisaged the possibilities of war as well as of durable peace.

The Soviet approach, combined with the ideology of the class struggle, in the area of international relations, produced a strong inclination toward forceful, violent methods of conflict resolution. The American approach, which had the same inclination toward violence, at the same time did not exclude the possibility of a peaceful settlement; a large part of the American political community was inclined to support a nonviolent approach in the resolution of conflicts. This was illustrated by the development of the conflict resolution approach by American academicians.

There is mutual benefit in the interplay between practical policymaking and scholarship: the former is enriched by the results of academic deliberations, the latter by concrete, practical results. This interaction is no closed cycle of continuing reproduction of the same ideas but a process of mutual enrichment, in which new concepts and recommendations are continually produced. Practical policymakers are also winners in the interchange because they obtain a variety of informal recommendations and points of view, which are helpful to them either in extending the sphere of possible solutions or, through the evaluation of the criticisms of their methods from the vantage point of scholarly theory, in analyzing their current positions.

In any case, an environment of a plurality of views is created. Such an environment makes it possible, each time a new difficulty arises, to ascend to a new level in the quest for compromises, instead of deep-freezing a given official position in the sterile permafrost of rigidity and intransigence. The role of theory in this case is to keep the options that present themselves in this quest within the reasonable framework of a common objective, which is dictated by the national interest.

Viewed according to the theory of conflict resolution, regional conflicts present themselves as fairly complicated phenomena. It is only from the standpoint of Soviet-American relations that they can be considered as a specific type of conflict having both the limiting factors to take into consideration—in the American literature these factors came to be known as rules of prudence[4]—and, simultaneously, a certain freedom of action. From the viewpoint of the main antagonists, however, each conflict can comprise a number of components— ideological, including confessional; racial; ethnic; and many others— which more often than not result in its becoming a zero-sum game, where a gain of any of the sides is tantamount to a loss to the others. It was this particular aspect that somehow escaped the attention of theoreticians for quite a long time—probably because everybody was strongly convinced that any regional conflict must be a direct result of foreign interference—and that prevented them from coming any closer to a more or less realistic model of conflict resolution.

Regardless of the real sources of multilayered regional conflicts, they were always crammed into the procrustean bed of global confrontation as new bridgeheads of antagonisms and were thus assigned their roles in the global relationship of forces. The inevitable corollary of this analysis

4. G. T. Allison, W. L. Ury, and B. J. Allyn, eds., *Windows of Opportunity: From Cold War to Peaceful Competition in U.S.-Soviet Relations* (Cambridge, MA: Ballinger, 1989), p. 9.

was the conviction that finding solutions to conflicts was not so much a matter of the domestic or foreign policies of the countries that were directly involved as it was an issue on which understanding between the great powers should be reached. For example, it was on the basis of this conviction that the agreement to convene the International Conference on the Middle East in Geneva, in December, 1973, had been reached. The complete fiasco of the agreement at the time did not even make anyone wish to review the reasons underlying the conviction.

The impossibility of finding viable solutions to regional conflicts during the 1970s was explained not only by the current, incorrect understanding of the nature of such conflicts but also by the acute and irreconcilable contradictions between measures to find positive solutions on the global level —strategic arms limitation—and the ineffectiveness of those measures on the level of regional conflicts. Assisted by the theoretical postulate that the ideological struggle was becoming more intense as the process of the relaxation of international tensions continued—mainly because of the aggravated human rights problem—Soviet policymakers concerned with foreign policy in the Third World concluded treaties of friendship and mutual cooperation with India, Iraq, the People's Democratic Republic of Yemen, the Socialist Republic of Vietnam, Mozambique, Egypt, and many other countries.

By the mid-1980s, however, a new knowledge had been accumulated in the area of regional conflicts by both superpowers. Official consultations between the USSR and the United States on regional issues developed on the basis of a long-standing exchange of opinions between unofficial experts from academic institutions of the two countries, which began in late 1970s and early 1980s. Meetings of experts on regional problems within the framework of the Dartmouth Conferences are held regularly. Research institutions of the USSR Academy of Sciences, which study regional issues—the Institute of World Economy and International Relations, the Institute of Oriental Studies, the Institute of Africa, the Institute of Latin America—are also engaged in active exchanges of opinion with American colleagues on questions related to the Middle East, Africa, Latin America, and the Asian-Pacific region. All of these issues are also among the questions that are discussed at an academic level between American specialists and specialists of the Institute of the USA and Canada of the USSR Academy of Sciences, in various projects organized by Brown, California, Southern California, Harvard, Indiana, and the Johns Hopkins universities.

The importance of these contacts for practical policymaking is difficult to overestimate. They made it possible for each side to discuss, in a substantive way and in a frank atmosphere, the other's policies in various regions of the world, to work out their estimates of the other's actions, to express their views concerning the reasons underlying the conflicts and possible ways of managing them, and to discuss the nature of possible solutions of these conflicts.

In these exchanges, there was not even a trace of great-power hubris in approaching the problems of third countries; on the contrary, it was repeatedly stated that the problems of regional conflicts posed a serious challenge to the foreign policies of both countries and to international stability in general and that in tackling them particular care was required, as well as thorough discussion and, if solutions were to be found, the active involvement not only of the direct participants in the conflicts but of the United Nations as well. This perspective of the problem area was particularly characteristic of discussions of regional conflicts that took place under the aegis of the International Peace Academy in New York.

POSSIBLE APPROACHES TO SETTLING REGIONAL CONFLICTS

Soviet-American consultations, along with some other concomitant factors, can play a significant role in the settlement of regional conflicts. It is clear, however, that a minimum of mutual understanding and a willingness to move toward each other are needed. It is important in this context to define exactly the scope of the opportunities that are at the disposal of the great powers—in contrast to the steps that must be undertaken by the parties directly involved in the conflict—and to concentrate attention on this particular aspect of conflict resolution.

It is in this area that the role of the ideological factor needs serious and substantive elaboration on a priority basis. Certainly, it would be unrealistic to speak about the complete elimination of ideology. The sympathies and antipathies of the great powers to a large extent are determined by the dominant ideology, and it is impossible to completely exclude ideology from the policy-formulation process.

In addition to the ideological factor, it is necessary to take into account the legal aspects of any conflict and of any decisions that may be taken by the parties in the conflict. In this respect, international law can and must function as a foundation on which to build mutual understanding and rapprochement between the sides, be they the parties that are directly involved in the conflict or the countries supporting them. Without international law as a foundation, it is impossible even to hope to find a solution to regional conflict.

A serious and substantive review of the role of violence in regional conflicts could become another important aspect of an approach of the USSR and the United States to resolving such conflicts. The military and political situation in the world completely rules out any possibility of a military victory or of a one-sided settlement of a conflict as a result of such a victory. The two great powers—the United States and USSR—have come to know this by their own bitter experience: in Vietnam for the United States, in Afghanistan for the USSR.

A serious question arises in this connection with respect to the attitude of the two great powers to the use of military force, either their own military force or that of friendly and allied countries. Both great powers supply these countries with weapons and munitions, explaining that they —the great powers—need to assure them of the right of legitimate self-defense, which is fully in accordance with international law and does not in principle leave room for any doubt or criticism. But then the question arises, What are the limits of this self-defense and how is it defined by the governmental and military circles of the countries involved? As a rule, this sphere is clothed in mystery and, as a result, either weapons that are supplied for the purposes of self-defense are used by the recipient for aggression—as in the case of Iraq— or the other side responds by acquiring weapons of its own. This sequence of events leads to an arms race in some parts of the world.

In this connection, development of some rules of conduct, which should apply to both the USSR and the United States with respect to regional conflicts as well as to situations between them, could become another component of the new approach to conflict resolution. The 1985 agreement between the two countries on the establishment of nuclear risk-reduction centers seems to be the only positive result of the development of the ideas contained in the agreement on the basic principles of relations between the USSR and the United States. The absence of a clear-cut and unambiguous understanding between the USSR and the United States concerning rules of conduct is a factor that has negatively affected the possibilities of both countries to exercise mutual control of each other's activities in different regions of the world and has also served as a source of numerous mutual claims, counterclaims, and accusations.

Finally, a much greater and substantially more intensive utilization of the mechanism and the opportunities of the United Nations for resolving regional conflicts could become a most important aspect of a possible new approach of the USSR and the United States to regional conflict resolution. Otherwise, any actions that might be undertaken by the two powers, even those motivated by the best of intentions, could be considered by third countries as something like the dictate of superpowers or a policy of condominium. Considering the important role that both countries could play in finding solutions to regional conflicts, such an attitude on the part of the world community, including the attitude of the direct participants in these conflicts, could become an obstacle to genuine settlement.

What could be achieved on the basis of such a balanced and mutually acceptable approach to the settlement of regional conflicts? First of all, it could certainly help the two great powers to distance themselves with respect to these conflicts and to each other. The distance is needed, on one hand, to drive away the feeling of direct involvement in particular conflicts—in other words, to make each of them cease to perceive these conflicts as ones in which they are involved and to bring back the realization that these conflicts impinge primarily upon the interests of other countries, groupings, and political organizations. On the other hand, it is needed to create a situation in which these conflicts are no longer perceived as a continuation or special case of conflicts between East and West or between the USSR and the United States.

It is of utmost importance to bring back the realization and to understand the fact that regional conflicts are concrete and self-contained situations that are certainly connected with the basic contradictions existing in the world arena but that at the same time do have their own root causes and sources. This would be useful both to the great powers—because there would be no danger anymore of the escalation of a conflict or of its aggravation to a point of confrontation between the great powers—and to the direct participants of the conflict because they would be more independent and responsible for their decisions.

Second, such an approach would be minimally tied to military solutions; on the contrary, it would promote peaceful resolution of conflicts. Reduction of violence, or of the threat of the use of force, besides being of great value objectively—because the number of victims, particularly among the civil population, would be greatly reduced—would simultaneously create incentives for those who adhere to the national reconciliation policy and would make them more disposed to seek compromise solutions.

Third, such an approach would not just be based on international law but would put it into the forefront of practical policymaking and would make it really take a place of pride in international relations, a place that the international law needed to take a long time ago in the system of relations between civilized nations. International law, reinforced by the prestige both of the great powers and of the United Nations, solemnly proclaiming the respect of the right of each country and of each nation to sovereignty in its domestic affairs, can successfully govern their international relations, particularly in such areas where controversial problems arise. International law, which is currently undergoing a period of intensive development, can also exert a beneficial influence on the domestic situation in many countries, especially in such spheres as respect for and strict observance of the rights of individuals, of separate communities, and of ethnic minorities.

Fourth, and finally, such an approach could help to focus attention on the problems of regional conflicts as an area of concern not only for the direct participants of these conflicts or for the great powers supporting the direct participants but for the entire world community of nations, the U.N. Security Council, its mechanism, and the U.N. Secretariat.

Conflict and Cooperation:
Between the Cold War and the Gulf

By CHARLES F. DORAN

ABSTRACT: Several myths about Soviet-American relations vis-à-vis third actors—unlimited military competition during the Cold War; perfect future political harmony; international political status quo and lack of significant change—may get in the way of possible cooperation in conflict avoidance, management, and resolution. This article examines the historical and structural setting that has created a proper climate for parallel U.S. and Soviet initiative and joint diplomatic efforts regarding Third World disputes. Conflicts that may lend themselves most to joint U.S.-Soviet involvement on behalf of conflict regulation or resolution are (1) conflicts outside local spheres of influence, (2) conflicts where the leverage available to Washington and Moscow with respect to one or both disputants is greatest, (3) disputes that can be paired and are subject to workable quid pro quos, and (4) conflict situations that can be submitted to international organizations within which the superpowers hold significant membership. Pragmatism and flexibility will serve the superpowers well in their quest to generate a more stable and secure Third World political environment.

Charles F. Doran, professor of international relations at the Johns Hopkins School of Advanced International Studies, Washington, D.C., is the author of many scholarly works in international politics and international political economy and has pioneered work in political risk analysis. He is a member of the Council on Foreign Relations. A regular adviser to business and government officials, he has provided congressional briefings and testimony on trade, security, and energy policy, most recently regarding Persian Gulf security.

IN the warm light of the Cold War's aftermath, several myths about Soviet-American relations, both past and present, vis-à-vis third actors must be laid to rest lest they get in the way of possible cooperation in conflict avoidance, management, and resolution. First is the myth of unlimited military competition during the Cold War. Even at the height of the Cold War period, the two superpowers understood each other well and shared a deep respect for each other's position and capability. While, to outsiders, only the tensions and suspicions were apparent, to the participants, a set of restraints on behavior and norms for competition were quite clear.[1] For example, even under Stalin, who was scarcely reluctant to use severe coercion for domestic political purpose, there was a reluctance to take steps that would lead to a high-risk diplomacy and the possibility of direct confrontation with the United States. Soviet support under Stalin for the Greek Communists following World War II was never conducted in a fashion that would have invited a direct military confrontation with the United States. Likewise, even with American presidents who felt very strongly about individual human rights considerations and the virtues of a market economy, there was no disposition to intervene militarily in Eastern Europe, for instance, during the 1956 Hungarian revolution. The Soviet Union was fully aware of this disposition.

Second is the myth of perfect future political harmony. Even though détente has mellowed the statecraft of the two superpowers, and in all likelihood will continue to do so, and even though ideological shifts have occurred and a new domestic preoccupation with policy problems in both polities is evident, the two principal military powers have awesome capability, necessitating management of that military capability with careful stewardship. Each continues to be able to destroy the other—and itself; each exercises far more power over the actions of other states than they in turn can exercise over either superpower. Thus very little room for balance exists in the present international system with respect to third states, and therefore the logic of power relationships still facilitates a division of international political focus when the interests of the great states do not entirely coincide.

Third is the myth of the international political status quo and lack of significant change. From the perspective of world politics, the year 1990 could scarcely look more different from the year 1980, yet only a decade elapsed, so rapid was the ideological and structural change.[2] While many would point to the decision of many East European countries to opt for a market economy, following the lead of *perestroika* but in fact pushing beyond in terms of pace, if not intent, others would emphasize the capacity of the superpowers to work out mutual force reductions and operational withdrawals of standing armies as

1. John Lewis Gaddis, *The Long Peace: Inquiries into the History of the Cold War* (New York: Oxford University Press, 1987), pp. 237-45.

2. William G. Hyland, "America's New Course," *Foreign Affairs*, 69(2):12 (1990).

the most important single change. From another perspective, the unplanned yet seemingly inevitable reunification of the Germanys creates the most visible and influential change on the map of Europe and thus on the future interaction of the great states themselves. But in the aftermath of both Vietnam and Afghanistan, both superpowers have learned how costly is the effort to employ force in the Third World to defend regimes that are otherwise incapable of sustaining themselves without very sizable external support. Hence the 1980s was a decade of astonishing structural and strategic change.

Debunking the first two myths might appear to reinforce the third, that of continuity with the past. This is not true. Some continuity exists, but the remarkable set of events since 1986 suggests that those who make policy solely on a rejection of the first two myths will end up stumbling upon the third. Its rejection makes the remainder of this article feasible analytically.

DÉTENTE AND THE HISTORICAL-STRUCTURAL CLIMATE FOR COOPERATION

Albeit at somewhat different levels of overall power, the United States and the Soviet Union are at points in their power cycles,[3] defined as capability relative to the other

leading states in the system, where their dynamism is, for the present, turned inward toward the resolution of domestic political problems and toward meeting thorny challenges to internal economic development. External involvements have not been particularly kind to them, such as Vietnam and Afghanistan, respectively, on one hand, and the international debt crisis and the evident attitude of Eastern Europe regarding the Soviet legacy, on the other. Each country is at or near the apex of its relative power curve. There can be no doubt about their military preeminence within the international system. In nuclear capability and missile sophistication, no other government is even close. But this great preeminence has for each state been purchased at a correspondingly great cost in goods and services forgone, a much greater comparative cost for the Soviet Union but, as U.S. deficits reveal, a substantial cost for the United States as well.[4] Their security assured, with only each other as a military threat of any consequence, it is not a surprise that they have come to realize that they have some common interests within the international system.

Given the realization that at this point in their respective power cycles they have other preoccupations than creating difficulty for each other, and given their comparative complacence with their positions in the interna-

3. Charles F. Doran, *The Politics of Assimilation: Hegemony and Its Aftermath* (Baltimore, MD: Johns Hopkins University Press, 1971); idem, "Systemic Disequilibrium, Foreign Policy Role, and the Power Cycle," *Journal of Conflict Resolution*, 33(3):371-401 (1989); idem, *Systems in Crisis: New Imperatives of High Politics at Century's End* (Cambridge: Cambridge University Press, 1991).

4. Christine A. Bogdanowicz-Bindert, *Solving the Global Debt Crisis: Strategies and Controversies* (New York: Harper & Row, 1989).

tional hierarchy, and with respect to their overall security situations, but accompanied with not a little anxiety over the possible future relationship with third powers—China for the Soviet Union, Japan for the United States—each government would like to see the present structure of the international system preserved as much as possible.[5]

A downturn in ideological rhetoric on each side is a response to these changes in the structural position in which each state finds itself, not a cause of the relaxation of tensions in East-West relations.

Cooperation between two such large centers of power in world politics is always difficult. A political realist assumption is that cooperation emerges only in the face of a common external threat, and there is no such identifiable, cohesive, and common threat. Yet the aroma of latent potential for considerable parallel behavior, whatever its origin and justification, is in the international political air.

Moreover, cooperation is feared by third parties almost as much as it is welcomed.[6] It is feared because they feel that the superpowers may gang up on them. The only prospect worse than open conflict between the superpowers is a too-close coordination of superpower interests at their own expense. Heard in Africa, for example, regarding Eritrea, this same anxiety

about U.S.-Soviet cooperation is echoed in many quarters where the actors have no right to register such mistrust. Indeed, a far greater concern for Third World countries does stem from a reduction in the Soviet-American competition. This concern is that much of the assistance, both economic and military, that each recipient has been getting, usually justified in terms of the East-West confrontation, may now simply disappear. Thus potential recipient governments in the Third World who for decades have been able to play the Soviet Union and the United States against one another may discover that East-West détente is really for them just a recipe for hard times.

On the other hand, cooperation between the superpowers is what many governments at the regional and systemic levels have long been seeking. Moreover, the conditions for the distribution of economic assistance to other governments on grounds of equity and the prospect for economic development can begin to shape the policies of the United States and the Soviet Union such that economic need becomes more clearly the grounds for aid. Such criteria are likely to lead to better results for aid distribution than the often more political justifications.

Most important, however, the new international context may prepare the way for cooperation in the avoidance, management, and even resolution of some Third World disputes through parallel U.S. and Soviet initiative and action.[7] This cooperation permits

5. Charles H. Fairbanks, Jr., "Bureaucratic Politics in the Soviet Union and in the Ottoman Empire," *Comparative Strategy*, 6(3): 333-62 (1987).

6. Philip E. Mosely, "Soviet Search for Security," in *Soviet-American Rivalry in the Middle East*, ed. J. C. Hurewitz (New York: Academy of Political Science, 1989).

7. I. William Zartman and Maureen Berman, *The Practical Negotiator* (New Haven, CT: Yale University Press, 1982), pp. 42-86;

the superpowers to carry on with their internal programs, to lower the prospect of crisis and international political distraction, and to back the efforts of some Third World governments to reorient their own policies toward more productive goals.

POTENTIAL SETTINGS
FOR U.S.-SOVIET
CONFLICT RESOLUTION

Natural areas of communality in conflict reduction and resolution may develop in disputes in which the interests of the superpowers tend, for various reasons, to converge. A logical area of convergence emerges out of a conflict situation in which each government perceives a serious and comparable danger from a protracted dispute. The Iraqi invasion of Kuwait is one such example.

One reason for such a sense of comparable danger is that the dispute is not perceived to be controllable. If the dispute is violent, or potentially violent, and is subject to escalation, it may receive far more attention than if it is marginal to the security of each state. A dispute that knows no easy territorial boundaries, or is likely to spill over into surrounding areas for reasons of communal, religious, or ideological affinity, may be regarded as dangerous and therefore as a subject for containment.

Likewise, interests may converge where a dispute is getting in the way

Gilbert R. Winham, *Negotiation as a Management Process* (Halifax, Nova Scotia: Dalhousie University, Center for Foreign Policy Studies, 1976); Daniel Druckman, *Human Factors in International Negotiations* (Beverly Hills, CA: Sage, 1973).

of an improvement of overall relations. This presupposes that the dispute is in fact finite and subject to the influence of outside parties. The impulse here is to regard the dispute itself and the stakes in the dispute for each party as far less important than the overall relationship between the superpowers. Thus the timing of a resolution with respect to the changing global pace of events may be crucial to its success.

Finally, the interests of the superpowers may converge where both see financial and political costs rapidly increasing without a prospect of winning on a unilateral basis.[8] This combination of rising costs and mutual pessimism about the course of an altercation may be as great an incentive to resolution as the prospect of an immediate or easy end to such a dispute. For the superpowers to engage themselves actively in attempting to end a dispute, through a coordination of effort, the evolution of the dispute and its prospects for resolution are no more important than how an outcome will affect the interests of each actor.

In some ways, the dispute between the Germanys corresponds to the criteria for an end to a dispute along lines that are mutually acceptable to the superpowers. Put differently, in the absence of acquiescence by Washington and Moscow, this dispute between the two halves of a single nation probably would not have ended. That local antagonism existed despite an underlying propensity of the

8. Seweryn Bailer, *The Soviet Paradox: External Expansion, Internal Decline* (New York: Vintage Books, 1986), p. 330.

German people to become whole again is scarcely open to question. Moreover, the superpowers held the cards that would determine the pace and direction of unification, if not the matter of whether unification eventually would occur. A sense that the resolution of this dispute had to be handled very carefully prevailed. Its potential for spillover was large. Similarly, the costs of continued acrimony were great for each principal actor. The mutuality of interest in seeing this visible symbol of the Cold War finally overcome exemplifies how larger interests can subordinate smaller differences.

Another potential area of converging superpower interest lies with disputes in the Third World in which a new type of weapons technology threatens an existing equilibrium, an equilibrium from which both states in the past have benefited. The new weapons technology presumably must have the capacity to shift military balances or to target populations or military installations in a way that is provocative and not easily countered unilaterally.[9] Resulting shifts of role and power, or suspected potential shifts, must be less attractive than the existing order. Suddenness of perception and massiveness of potential impact are prerequisites to new foreign policy initiatives that normally would not stem from incremental arms changes.

Since the armistice in the Iraq-Iran war, and the advent of the Iraqi invasion of Kuwait, a whole new arms situation has developed in the Middle East and the Persian Gulf area. Both long-range missiles and chemical weapons have proliferated in an area where nuclear weapons currently exist and may spread among dyadic opponents. Iraq and Pakistan are recurrent candidates for nuclear weapons acquisition. In a region where there is a history of surprise attack; where populations are small, urban, and concentrated; and where no possibility of the stability of second-strike capability exists, the prospects for conflict avoidance are bleak without outside sympathy and restraint.[10]

But just as the presence of nuclear missiles combined with chemical and, possibly, biological warheads has transformed the nature of warfare inside the region, these new weapons now put Soviet populations at risk in a way not heretofore experienced. Likewise, the oil fields in the Persian Gulf area have become hostage to a regionwide conflict potential.

Under these circumstances, perhaps the impact of new weaponry in the midst of old regional antagonisms will be sufficient to elicit joint Soviet-American interest in assisting governments within the region to formulate nascent arms control proposals. While without doubt the pressures on the side of supply are as great as on the side of demand to accelerate local

9. Paul Doty, "Strategic Arms Limitation after SALT I," in *Arms, Defense Policy, and Arms Control*, ed. Franklin A. Long and George W. Rathjens (New York: W. W. Norton, 1976), p. 72.

10. That is why both a two-track arms control policy and a larger U.S. military presence in the gulf were advocated in April of 1990, although in the complacence of the interval they were largely ignored. Charles F. Doran, "Gulf Security in Perspective," in *The Gulf, Energy, and Global Security: Political and Economic Issues*, ed. Charles F. Doran and Steven W. Buck (Boulder, CO: Lynne Rienner, 1991).

arms races, and while political reconciliation must often precede meaningful arms control measures, a communications vacuum is a very bad context in which to base regional security. Right now a dearth of communications exists between the various dyadic contenders. A positive attitude on the part of the two superpowers toward regional negotiations would surely further both the peace process and related arms control initiatives.

A further set of circumstances that might allow the superpowers to get more serious about conflict resolution in the developing world is the situation in which third parties begin to impinge heavily on superpower interests. At the height of bipolarity, very little third-party activity occurred because balancing was a quite futile exercise given the relative preeminence and isolation of the superpowers. Diminution of the Non-Aligned Movement occurred for reasons not only internal to the movement but for external reasons of ineffectiveness regarding influence over the actions of either superpower. While in many respects bipolarity continues to characterize international relations, at the margin, within specific regions, third parties have begun to have a much larger impact.

Provided that such a third-party impact is large, and provided that it affects each of the superpowers in a fashion that is mutual—if not congruent—a raison d'être emerges for the Soviet Union and the United States to respond.[11] Where the problem at issue is a festering local or regional dispute, joint attention may be far more helpful than unilateral and separate attention. Even benign indifference on the part of Washington or Moscow may be less propitious for conflict avoidance or management than mutual support for tension reduction.

An example of the type of third-party involvement that this theoretical circumstance envisions could focus upon either China or India. In the case of China, two disputes with direct relevance are (1) the matter of Korean relations and the possible eventual desire for reunification and (2) the struggle between Kampuchea and Vietnam as well as the civil war within Kampuchea itself. Concerning the involvement of India, a number of disputes come to mind, ranging from the ongoing quarrel over Kashmir to the civil war in Afghanistan. Pakistan's role may or may not be affected by a growing Indian presence in some of these disputes as well.

A key point here is that as the influence of these regional powers grows, the influence of the superpowers may change or diminish in disputes over which timely action might lead to advantageous international political stability. Recognition by Washington and Moscow that a dynamic of power is at work within each region may enable them to see clearly the wisdom of acting together now rather than separately or not at all, because of the negation of influence in a later historical interval.

11. George Liska, *Russia and the Road to Appeasement: Cycles of East-West Conflict in* *War and Peace* (Baltimore, MD: Johns Hopkins University Press, 1982), pp. 176-201.

REGIONAL CONFLICTS AND CONFLICT ISSUES SUSCEPTIBLE TO JOINT AMENABILITY

The natural targets for amenable management include, first, conflicts outside the putative spheres of influence of either superpower. Inside spheres of influence, unilateral measures are not only likely to be more productive but are perhaps the only instruments that can generate benefits without causing negative side effects for the relations between the superpowers themselves. The principal rationale of the sphere of influence is that it is a way of limiting direct conflict between the major powers themselves.[12] What happens within the sphere in terms of stability is derivative of and secondary to this desire to regularize relations at the larger global level. Aggravated domestic and international conflict within such spheres, of course, can occur. Dependence upon individual core states by other states within a sphere limits the potential for global cooperation as well as competition and often has a very negative, even internally oppressive effect upon politics and policies within the individual states inside the sphere.[13] Such a lack of democracy is lamentable and, although not solely the result of a sphere-of-influence framework, is perhaps strengthened by such a framework. Yet the primary logic of the sphere of influence from the

12. Charles F. Doran, *Domestic Conflict in State Relations: The American Sphere of Influence* (Beverly Hills, CA: Sage, 1976).
13. Marshall I. Goldman, *USSR in Crisis: The Failure of an Economic System* (New York: W. W. Norton, 1983).

global perspective is that it limits interference and even the prospect of intervention by outside principal powers, thus reducing the probability of major war over a local or regional issue. Internal costs to polities involved in the sphere approach are reasonable to assess, but they must always be measured against the stability that the major powers think they are obtaining from acknowledgment of the sphere arrangement.

From the perspective of joint conflict amelioration by the superpowers, however, the most likely possibilities quite clearly would fall in areas outside any implicit or explicit spheres of influence. These areas may also be among the most politically volatile. They also may be geographically distant from the territories of the superpowers, involving logistical and other costs of involvement. Finally, these nonsphere areas may be the least interesting in strategic or other terms to either or both of the superpowers, thus creating less enthusiasm for any kind of sustained or earnest attention.

Yet it is in the areas that lie outside the spheres of the respective superpowers where, in some ways, the largest probability of mutually constructive cooperation on conflict reduction can occur. For the very reason that the superpowers are less directly involved in such areas, with less perhaps immediately at stake, they have the luxury of experimenting and of trying out solutions that may not be as financially expensive or as strategically risky as for disputes closer to home. Disputes in these nonsphere areas are not marginal, but they are more approachable. They provide a good place to begin.

Second, conflicts that are likely candidates for some positive Soviet-American attempts at management or reduction virtually necessitate the potential for leverage by Washington or Moscow—preferably both—with either or both disputants. That such is not always the case despite the global reach of the superpowers, and that it may increasingly not be the case as the structure of the system changes, requires emphasis.[14]

Part of the reason that the war between Iraq and Iran dragged on for as long as it did—some eight years—is that neither Moscow nor Washington had particularly certain rapport with either Tehran or Baghdad. This does not mean that no leverage existed, as the naval presence in the Persian Gulf attests. Nor does the statement that little rapport existed indicate that communications were impossible between these governments during the hostilities. But for really concrete results, the superpowers must enjoy a type and level of interaction with the belligerents to get beyond merely good offices.

The essence of leverage is that if something is added or something is removed from the participants in a regional quarrel, their level of costs, risks, or stakes is significantly modified. In most cases neither superpower will be prepared to use such leverage if it comes at substantial risk or cost to itself. Therefore we are talking about leverage that can be applied either because it is so intrin-

sic to the relationship with third states that something of a patron-client interaction occurs or because the asymmetry in the interaction with third states is so great in power terms that the cost of exercising leverage is minimal.

This assessment of the importance of leverage is not ignorant of the limits of leverage. Nor does the assessment suggest that leadership, negotiating skill, knowledge of the issues, and finesse are less significant. What is highlighted here is that many of the truly difficult disputes cannot be mediated, to say little of being actually resolved, unless substantial leverage, both positive and negative, is brought to bear. For example, does anyone doubt that the Camp David Accords would have failed had the United States not been prepared to contribute what is now about $1.2 billion a year to Israel and about $1.0 billion to Egypt, plus additional side payments from interested allies such as Saudi Arabia? Conflict resolution is not solely based on superior wisdom or moral rectitude.

The question of leverage—"callables" in the arcane language of the U.S. Congress—also suggests that the superpowers must choose carefully the disputes to which they feel they might have some contribution to make.[15] To some extent, the selection will be dependent not only upon how far apart the antagonists are in political terms. The choice of dispute regarding joint participation by the superpowers will depend in part upon how much is expected of each super-

14. Joseph S. Nye, Jr., ed., *The Making of America's Soviet Policy* (New Haven, CT: Yale University Press, 1984), pp. 339-49.

15. Richard Rosecrance, *America's Economic Resurgence: A Bold New Strategy* (New York: Harper & Row, 1990), pp. 176-77.

power and what the nature of the political coinage will be.

Third, an approach that has already provided dividends in conflict resolution involves paired but separate conflicts where quid pro quos can be established by the superpowers. The nature of the cooperation is based on the well-known observation that each superpower has been the source of some difficulty for the other in terms of the latter's relation to its clients. By withdrawing support from, or merely signaling the need to negotiate to, clients in a dispute that is locally problematic for the superpower adjacent to the dispute, the superpower in effect makes the opposition elements or governing elite in such a dispute better disposed to bargain in good faith with the party favored by the adjacent superpower.

The reason this approach is so successful is severalfold. Parallel action by the superpowers is sufficient here. No elaborate coordination of policy is necessary. The normal routes of communication are used. The normal channels of negotiation between the affected local parties to the dispute remain those employed, although the local participants may innovate new routes or strategies if they desire. But the principal reason progress occurs is that implicit or explicit intervention by the opposite superpower is what has been catalyzing the dispute all along. When that support, either military or merely diplomatic, is removed, the local disputants on each side recognize that the time is ripe for a new, more serious phase of negotiations to reduce or perhaps resolve the dispute. The side favored by the opposite superpower can no

longer count on its assistance, or at least on its unqualified assistance. The side favored by the adjacent superpower recognizes that the moment is ripe for its best offer, since a better opportunity to end the dispute is not likely to arise. Sudden, rather spectacular progress can occur in terms of the cessation of military hostilities and even toward the formation of new coalition governments.

Actual experience with such an exchange of quid pro quos involved policy on Afghanistan and Nicaragua recently. Scarcely a secret, U.S. military and diplomatic support to various of the *mujahidin* groups via Pakistan was responsible for much of the success of the guerrilla groups fighting against the Soviet-backed Kabul government.[16] Likewise scarcely concealed was the Soviet support for the Sandinistas through military supplies from Eastern Europe as well as from Moscow, some economic support, and, primarily, ideological encouragement.[17] When the United States changed its policy toward the Kabul government by acknowledging that perhaps that government could remain in power as an interim solution, it acknowledged both that the guerrilla groups could not find agreement between themselves on an adequate coalition and that they had become bogged down on the battlefield in the aftermath of the Soviet with-

16. Joseph Collins, "Soviet Policy toward Afghanistan," in *Soviet Foreign Policy*, ed. Robbin F. Laird (New York: Academy of Political Science, 1987).

17. Peter Sherman, in *Soviet Foreign Policy*, ed. Laird, pp. 211-22; Alfred Stepan, "The U.S. and Latin America: Vital Interests and Instruments of Power," *Foreign Affairs*, 58(3): 659-81 (1980).

drawal of troops accompanied by equipment resupply. When the Soviet Union allowed *perestroika* to proceed in Eastern Europe, indicating that the model that the Sandinistas had implicitly been attempting roughly to emulate was bankrupt, and when Moscow ceased to supply assistance of the same type and level to the Sandinista government, a sudden change in the willingness to abide by democratic solutions to government led to the election of the Chamorro government. Neither of these changes is explained solely by the altered role of the opposite superpower. Neither outcome is necessarily the end of a political dispute that is deep and violent within each country locally. But the spectacular change of events in Afghanistan and in Nicaragua could not have occurred without the implicit cooperation of the superpowers at the top of the system.

Limits exist for this type of parallel action toward conflict management and perhaps resolution. The largest limit is that the opposite superpower must be a very significant factor in a dispute for its changed posture to count for so much. Also, each superpower must be willing to accept a compromise solution and even face down considerable local disenchantment by its clients regarding the outcome. Local clients will argue that they have been sold out by a deal at the top of the system regardless of how hopeless their own strategy of continued fighting may be. The superpowers must also be able to find such a paired set of disputes where implicit coordination of diplomatic action, albeit carried out unilaterally, is feasible. Most disputes may not fall

into such equivalent categories. Many disputes will not involve participants who are well positioned to take advantage of a new atmosphere externally in order to make progress toward immediate betterment of the political environment internally.

Finally, regional and Third World conflicts can perhaps be ameliorated jointly by the United States and the Soviet Union when the disputants are willing to submit their quarrels to multilateral forums in which the superpowers have some influence. These include not only the United Nations Security Council and the World Court but also lesser multilateral agencies and organizations not always recognized as stages for conflict resolution.

A principal advantage of the organizational approach to conflict resolution is that it distances the involvement of the superpowers from the belligerents somewhat, much as multilateral economic assistance distances the donor from the recipient. The belligerents may feel less impinged upon, less subject to imperial influence, when an international organization is the mediator or intermediate negotiator. An international organization can provide a very useful source of legitimation for dispute settlement even though the principal stimulus to that settlement may remain with the largest members of the organization.

International organizations, both governmental and nongovernmental—an example of a nongovernmental organization is the International Chamber of Commerce—have panels and experts who are available for just such exercises in conflict resolution.

Perhaps pieces or aspects of larger disputes can be delegated to such institutions for auxiliary bargaining and discussion even if the central problems can most usefully remain in the bilateral or trilateral context. Likewise, international organizations may find utility in the implementation of a peace process through the deployment of a multilateral peacekeeping force, for example, after a dispute has otherwise and elsewhere been dismantled. The international organizational approach does not need to be the sole focus or even the centerpiece of a complex process of dispute resolution.

Regularization of dispute settlement is one of the chief attractions of international organizations as a route to a more stable regional environment. Insofar as the level of East-West tensions has declined and diffused, the organizational route in terms of both universal and regional organizations—examples of the latter include the Organization of African Unity or the Arab League—may become more effective instruments of conflict resolution.[18] But because of third-party economic and security involvement outside this organizational membership, the superpowers

18. Adda Bozeman, *Conflict in Africa* (Princeton, NJ: Princeton University Press, 1976).

will always be likely participants, if not at the core of negotiations, at least on the sidelines as cheerleaders and referees. This is as it should be and is not an inglorious or trivial role for great states to play.

In short, pragmatism and flexibility will serve the superpowers well in their quest to generate a more stable and secure Third World political environment in their own and in the system's interest. Those conflicts that lend themselves most to joint U.S.-Soviet involvement on behalf of conflict regulation or resolution may be conflicts outside local spheres of influence, conflicts where the leverage available to Washington and Moscow with respect to one or both disputants is greatest, disputes that can be paired and are subject to workable quid pro quos, and conflict situations that can be submitted to international organizations within which the superpowers hold significant membership. Overall, the historical and structural setting, the situations in which the United States and the Soviet Union find that their own respective interests are converging, and Third World regional conflicts and conflict issues that, for reasons outlined, are most susceptible to resolution are the types and areas of dispute management most attractive for further analysis and policy prescription.

ANNALS, *AAPSS*, **518**, November 1991

The Concept of Balance of Interests and U.S.-Soviet Interaction

By VADIM V. UDALOV

ABSTRACT: Effective and continuous Soviet-American cooperation in handling regional problems is hardly possible without a shared understanding of conflict in general and optimum ways for affecting its dynamics. Most American schools of conflict research proceed from the concept of balance of power. Soviet political thinking has suggested a competing approach based on the concept of balance of interests. This conceptual deadlock can be overcome through an elaboration of what precisely is meant by balance of interests. Such an analysis shows that balance of interests is virtually an external manifestation of balance of power, and its character typically depends on the latter's transformation. In broader terms, balance of interests means an equilibrium between elements of confrontation and cooperation. The concept of balance of interests proves to be a lot richer in its implications than reliance on power fluctuations, since it justifies a possibility not only of a settlement, but also of resolution of some conflicts by reconsidering and drawing apart interests that seemed to be mutually denying. This concept is a promising tool for conflict analysis and diplomacy.

Vadim Udalov is a career diplomat at the Ministry of Foreign Affairs of the USSR. Since 1987 he has been a staff member of the Research Coordination Center of this ministry. In 1991 he was a visiting fellow at the United States Institute of Peace.

NOTE: The views expressed in this article are the author's own and not necessarily those of the Soviet Ministry of Foreign Affairs or the United States Institute of Peace.

UNLIKE the détente of the 1970s, when Soviet-American contradictions, being relaxed in the central sphere, were partially transferred to the periphery, current changes in the world seem to be of a genuinely global nature. This time the conflict between the First and the Second Worlds is not just modified but is, to a great extent, exhausted, including its Third World dimension.

This development, however, not only fails to eliminate the knots of contradictions but, on the contrary, lays bare many of them. The spread of weapons technology creates a favorable environment for militarizing these contradictions. The South becomes the principal source of potential threats to international stability. All these factors prompt an active Soviet-U.S. cooperation to neutralize the emerging menace.

Soviet-American interaction in settling a number of regional conflicts has become a reality. Now that both sides are overcoming the syndrome of ideological irreconcilability, they have discovered that they are interested in each other's positive involvement in Third World conflicts.

But there is a danger that if these efforts are concentrated mainly on a pragmatic search for specific diplomatic solutions, as happens now, they will only have a temporary effect and will reach their limits, as the existing major conflicts rooted in the aftermath of the Cold War have been localized. In order to institutionalize this cooperation and make it embrace future preventive tasks, it will be necessary to find a broader conceptual basis for it by developing a vision, shared by both sides, of the nature of conflict as a phenomenon of international life and of optimum ways for affecting its dynamics.

To what extent is this realistic? It may seem that there is a lot of reason to doubt that this goal can be achieved.

First and foremost, it is extremely difficult, if possible at all, to bridge the unavoidable gap between theoretical research into conflict resolution and the practice of dealing with real conflicts. The reason for this is not that scholars lack insight or that decision makers are narrow-minded; it would be unfair to claim either, although sometimes both might be the case. What creates the problem is an inherent impossibility for theory to take care of the whole range of political realities affecting practical policymaking.

In addition, there is an obvious disparity between the development of conflict research in the United States and its development in the USSR, with Americans having a distinct lead. But even more important in this case are the substantial differences in general approach. With all the diversity of American concepts, they generally proceed from the premise that conflicts are manageable through the balance of power in a conflict system, by expertly manipulating the components of this balance. Soviet foreign policy thinking is mainly oriented toward achieving comprehensive solutions and thus eliminating the very reasons for conflict.

Not so long ago this general Soviet approach was somewhat developed by putting forward the concept of balance of interests as a methodological basis for such comprehensive solutions. Later on, this concept was elaborated in a number of political documents as well as in Soviet academic writings.[1] But in both cases the main emphasis was still on the difference and even the antagonism between balance of interests and balance of power. It seems, however, that this perceived difference is caused by the Soviet concept's not being sufficiently developed. To prove that this is so, let us try to clarify what is—or should be—the specific meaning of balance of interests compared to balance of power.

POWER AND INTEREST

First of all, it must be pointed out that it is incorrect to counterpose the initial notions of interest and power. Such an opposition in the Soviet literature seems to have its roots in the predominantly negative attitude that Soviet authors have toward the theory of political realism. Ideologized labels, beyond which even the most serious of those authors could not venture, prevented them from, among other things, giving due credit to certain ideas derived from this theory. In condemning it for its obsession with power, its Soviet critics noted only in passing that its exponents saw a state's power as the sum total not only of material factors intended to be used directly as a means of physical violence but also of ideological, cultural, ethical, psychological, and

numerous other factors. Such a distortion gave ample theoretical ground for denouncing the "aggressive bigstick policy of imperialism."

It should be admitted, however, that there is also one purely intrinsic phenomenon involved here. It has to do with the psycholinguistic fact that the term "power" and the Russian word "sila," which is generally used to translate it, have different sets of connotations. "Sila" designates not only power but also strength, force, and even violence. Thus the whole concept based on this notion, in its Russian interpretation, was bound to be perceived as predominantly coercive.

In any case, if the relationship between power and interest is considered in the strict terms of the theory of international relations, it is easy to discover an inherent connection between the two notions. On one hand, the fundamental, all-pervasive foreign policy interest of any state is to build up, diversify, and create favorable conditions for employing its power. On the other hand, the power of a state can be defined as "its ability to defend its interests and attain its goals on the international scene."[2]

What we have here is not shortcomings of a system of concepts that breed tautologies but a real intertwining of power and interest. After all, interests are ultimately conditioned by objective requirements and are a product of realizing them. But requirements themselves shape up largely in accordance with the ability

1. See, for example, S. M. Rogov, *The Soviet Union and the USA: Search for a Balance of Interests* (in Russian) (Moscow: Mezhdunarodniye Otnoshenia, 1989), pp. 11, 321.

2. E. A. Pozdnyakov, *Foreign Policy Activity and State-to-State Relations* (in Russian) (Moscow: Nauka, 1986), p. 135.

to meet them—here we have a vivid example of the dialectics of direct links and feedback—and ability, in our case, is power.

It follows that interest has a sort of power filling, for it is formed according to a state's power, and at the same time it stimulates and determines the specific character of the further growth of this power. Discounting accidental deviations, we may assume that, as a general rule, foreign policy interests develop when and where their emergence is conditioned by the power of the state concerned in a given period of history.

Thus we may say, putting it in a somewhat simplified manner, that by genesis a state's interest is derivative of its power, and by function it is aimed at ensuring a buildup of this power. Hence the correlation of interests of different states is virtually a kind of external manifestation and political projection of the correlation of their power.

ACHIEVING A BALANCE OF INTERESTS

To arrive at a balance of interests, it is essential not only to specify what is to be balanced but to have a clear idea of how the balancing can be done.

This analysis can be based on classifying interests according to the nature of their interrelation. Scholars have already attempted it.[3] Proceeding from their endeavors, we would

3. See *Détente and Confrontation: Two Trends in Contemporary International Relations* (in Russian) (Moscow: Nauka, 1987), pp. 237-43; Rogov, *Soviet Union and the USA*, pp. 303-24.

divide interests into coinciding, mutually exclusive, and nonintersecting. Each of these types, taken in isolation from the others, would correspond to a definite model of relations: coinciding interests in their pure form would give rise to an ideal cooperation model; mutually exclusive interests, a strictly confrontational model; and nonintersecting interests, a neutral one. In reality, all three types of interests almost always combine and work simultaneously, their proportion predetermining the prevailing mode of overall relationship between the states concerned. Next, it should be pointed out that what is meant by "balance of interests" is in essence a balance of satisfied interests, that is, of interests met in parallel, without detriment to any side.

Obviously, satisfaction is not a problem in the case of coinciding interests, for they can be met in equal measure merely because they are practically identical. The coinciding interests of the overwhelming majority of countries include, for instance, their desire to see a well-functioning international communication system, growing international trade, respect for certain international standards and traditions, and so on.

A special case is the emergence of coinciding interests when a common threat has to be taken care of. One of the most well known examples of this is the joint efforts of the anti-Hitler coalition during World War II. It is important to note, however, that that was not a common interest; rather, individual interests of the cooperating sides coincided in the given situation. The reason why the United

States helped the Soviet Union fight Germany was not solidarity, as one can gather from most political writings meant for the broad public, but a global calculation, namely, the conviction that the domination of Eurasia by a power or coalition hostile to the United States would be contrary to long-term American interests. With this danger removed, as a result of the victory over fascism, U.S. interests came naturally to diverge from Soviet interests, for now it was the USSR that was perceived in Washington as the main source of a similar geopolitical danger.

Paradoxically, from the point of view of results, the third type of interest, nonintersecting, is similar to the coinciding type. But, for nonintersecting interests, what produces these results is the very difference between parties holding these interests, for it allows the interests of one side to be met without any particular detriment to the other. For instance, Central American countries can solve their problems practically without prejudice to the major interests of, say, Indochina, and vice versa.

The number of such insular interests is dwindling as the world becomes more interdependent, and they give way to still divergent, but interconnected and mutually complementary interests. Their interlocking may produce rather sharp international collisions. For instance, Greece, which has no particular stake, unlike the United States, in the latter's military presence on its soil, is in need, however, of increased U.S. military and economic aid. In this case, meeting one interest is linked to meeting another, and the problem of balancing the interests acquires a real substance. Even so, its solution encounters no insurmountable obstacles, for the interests themselves essentially do not contradict each other, which means that they can be harmonized by political and diplomatic means.

It is revealing in this respect that students of the theory and methodology of negotiations see one of the prerequisites for a successful negotiation process in the asymmetry of interests. "A satisfactory agreement is made possible because each side wants different things," write R. Fisher and W. Ury, "Differences in interest and belief make it possible for an item to be of high benefit to you, yet of low cost to the other side."[4]

The situation becomes entirely different if interests are mutually exclusive. Their very substance raises an insurmountable barrier to equally meeting them on both sides. This clash of interests imposes the rules of a zero-sum game, when what is gained by one side means an equal loss to the other. Moreover, the gain can be achieved only through confrontation, sometimes a truly violent one.

Until recently, the incompatibility of interests that their exponents saw as vital was the source of the global conflict between the two sociopolitical camps. Currently it remains the core of persisting regional conflicts.

In the Middle East, for instance, the formula of peace in exchange for land might work if Israel were to

4. R. Fisher and W. Ury with B. Patton, ed., *Getting to Yes: Negotiating Agreement without Giving In* (New York: Penguin Books, 1983), p. 76.

need only peace but not territory. But even though the Palestine Liberation Organization has expressed its readiness to recognize Israel and build peaceful relations with it, Israel is defending its own territorial interests, flowing from Zionist doctrine, which preclude satisfaction of the opposing interests of the Palestinian Arabs. Under these circumstances, Israel can be prompted to agree to some kind of compromise only if the power pervading its interests is eroded, that is, on the basis of balance of power and as a result of a shift in it.

It follows that the whole question comes down to how the concept of balance of interests can be applied to the clashes of mutually exclusive interests governed from the outset by the laws of balance of power. The following are suggested solutions, based on the reconsideration of interests, the generation of new coinciding interests, and positive interdependence.

Reconsideration of interests

As is known, the formation of interests depends both on the objective determinants mentioned earlier and on numerous subjective factors, which occasionally cause the operational interests of a state to deviate considerably from its real requirements. Selecting concrete objectives and the means to be used for attaining them is a still more complex process, providing a great variety of options. Decisions made against such a background, many of them far from ideal, in an atmosphere of severe confrontation generally turn into positions of principle and become self-serving.

An attempt can be made to untie knots of this kind by ascertaining, preferably with all the sides concerned participating, the true interests or, even better, requirements interacting in the given situation. The purpose of this process should be to identify differences in the interests that seemed to be mutually exclusive and switch them to different traffic lanes—in other words, to transform them into nonintersecting interests, which, as was shown previously, can be balanced by negotiation.

International experience provides a lot of examples of such a revision. One of the latest and probably the most striking of them is the deideologization of state-to-state relations. Indeed, from the moment the state that proclaimed socialism its aim came into existence, relations between it and the capitalist world always involved a globalized conflict of mutually exclusive ideological ambitions, the final establishment of one system of values being declared conditional on the abolition of the antipodal system. From time to time, developments in the world wrapped this core conflict in a covering of cooperation, as happened in the years of World War II and then in the period of détente. Nevertheless, the conflict remained unresolved. It went on developing underneath and in the end erupted again in still more menacing proportions, as it did during the Cold War and the spasm of confrontation in the early 1980s.

The deideologization of Soviet foreign policy, prompted by the realization of the futility of this antagonism, removed its very source. Under new conditions, it turns out that many of the military, geopolitical, economic, and other interests of East and West, formerly distorted under the impact of ideology and represented as mutually exclusive, are in reality nonintersecting and in some cases even coinciding.

Another example, now regarded as a classical one, confirming the possibility of balancing interests on the basis of reappraising them and pulling them apart, is the solution of the Cuban missile crisis of October 1962. After the Soviet leadership had realized and made it clear to the American side that the purpose of stationing Soviet missiles in Cuba, under the circumstances, was not to pose an additional threat to U.S. security but to defend the Cuban revolution, and after the U.S. leadership, for its part, had explicitly confirmed that it did not intend at that juncture to intervene directly in Cuban affairs, the problem was settled in a fairly short time by peaceful, diplomatic means.

There is a difficulty, however, in that such a mode of balancing interests requires of politicians extraordinary—and mutual—foresight, competence, flexibility, and courage. These qualities, which both sides displayed in 1962 and demonstrate today, helped reverse the destructive logic of the crisis at that time and make it possible to end confrontation today. Unfortunately, there are no guarantees that this will be the case always and everywhere. This is particularly unlikely where the sides have long been locked in a deep con-

flict that has in effect got out of their control.

Generating new coinciding interests

In situations where the chances of finding a reasonable way out have been missed or where no such possibilities have been found, there remains a solution that is more painful and bound to take longer but that exists nonetheless. Even in a protracted clash of mutually exclusive interests when balance of power remains decisive, the state of this very balance may undergo qualitative changes that would generate on both sides new coinciding interests prompting them to limit the conflict or even to seek a settlement.

This may come when the parties to the conflict have exhausted their strength and thus are interested more and more in scaling down confrontation so as to avoid any further weakening. Such a situation developed in the final phase of the Iran-Iraq war, when Baghdad and then Tehran realized that it was in their interest at least to freeze the conflict, and this new factor added elements of cooperation that outweighed confrontational factors.

Another variant of qualitative transformation in the balance of power may develop due to the growth of power to proportions making it destructive for its very possessors. This has begun at long last to be the case between the Soviet Union and the United States now that these leading nuclear powers have come to realize the disastrous effects of a continued military rivalry. They now show a distinct interest in arms cuts.

The initial mutually exclusive interests causing conflict were not met in either case. Directly balancing them against each other would be still problematic, to put it mildly. But a different type of balance of interests emerged, one between mutually exclusive, or confrontational, interests, on one hand, and coinciding, or cooperative, interests, on the other hand, the former being balanced by the latter.

The chief problem arising in these circumstances is that it takes the parties to the conflict too much time and effort to realize the trends developing in the balance of power and to formulate corresponding cooperative interests. In the case of the Iran-Iraq war, this process took at least five years, and in the case of the Soviet-U.S. nuclear arms race, nearly thirty years, from the Russell-Einstein Manifesto, which revealed the threat of universal annihilation, to the Geneva statement in 1985 that nuclear war must not be fought because it cannot be won.

In a sense, this delay is understandable. For a new interest arising from the requirement for self-preservation to take shape and be seen as crucial for the state and not imposed from outside, it is essential that the threat giving rise to this requirement present itself as an immediate mortal danger and not as an abstraction or something likely to happen only in the distant future. Truly, "the possibility of positive development becomes real only when all possibilities for negative development have been exhausted."[5] In situations of this nature, the only objective catalyst is the dynamics of the balance of power, and hence a game according to its rules becomes the only promising means of convincing the sides of the need to revise their policies.

Tactics based on such a game are often used for stirring up a deadlocked conflict. For instance, the 1973 Arab-Israeli war was intended by the Egyptian leadership supported by the United States to shift the balance of power in the region, to demonstrate to Israel the increased potentialities of its adversaries and thus create further incentives for unfreezing confrontational attitudes. It should be admitted that this particular goal was achieved at the time; how this achievement was used afterward is another matter. A similar role was expected to be played, in the end, by the Palestinian uprising in the occupied territories. The *intifada* was universally expected to provide a chance to start a conflict settlement process. Experience has shown, however, that such active manipulation of the balance of power may touch off a new chain reaction of crises, with unpredictable consequences.

Also possible is a passive alternative of using the balance of power by carefully keeping it in a state of rough parity in the hope that sooner or later the sides will realize the futility of attempts to upset it and will engage in a search for different, nonviolent

5. E. Pozdnyakov and I. Shadrina, "Humanizing and Democratizing International Relations," *Mirovaya ekonomika i mezhdunarodniye otnoshenia* (in Russian), 1989, no. 4, p. 18.

means of solving their problems. This is the purpose of negative symmetry, a principle gradually taking root in international relations. It implies a coordinated refusal to supply arms to parties directly involved in a conflict. The same logic evidently underlies the proposals for stabilizing the regional balances of power in Central America, in the Middle East, and in other conflict-ridden zones, along with a considerable reduction of the general level of these balances.

A similar approach was actually taken with respect to the Iran-Iraq war when third parties cautiously put military aid in one or the other pan of the scales. In that contingency, the distribution mechanism functioned well enough, thanks to the coinciding interests of its operators, who did not wish either side to win. But this process may take an entirely different course under a different set of geopolitical circumstances. Besides, it is very difficult to predict whether such tactics will lead to an early stalemate, if any at all.

There is one more alternative— that of building up the balance of power until it reaches potentially suicidal proportions. Indeed, this is the current trend of many conflicts, such as the one between India and Pakistan, which is already being fitted out with nuclear missiles; or the Middle East conflict, oversaturated with up-to-date weapons and likewise showing a trend toward nuclearization. The experience of Soviet-U.S. relations may seem to suggest that, in the end, this road must lead the sides to the realization of the inapplicability of force and thus prompt them to re-verse the course. By following an abstract line of reasoning, one can even go so far as to conclude that since the objective trend of development points in this direction, we ought to deliberately urge it on in order to help raise the level of regional balances of power, their nuclear component included, merely seeing to it that no marked fluctuations occur.

Yet the same Soviet-American experience has shown how very dangerous this road is not only for those directly involved in a conflict but for all of humanity. This is why its pioneers must do everything in their power to prevent others from repeating experiments that may prove fatal to all.

Positive interdependence

There is a further model that holds increasing promise for an end to the deadlock over a clash of mutually exclusive interests. This model, too, is structured on counterbalancing mutually exclusive interests with coinciding cooperative interests, which emerge, however, outside the conflict. Such coinciding interests are present nearly always, even in relations between belligerents, and may have to do with, say, an exchange of prisoners of war. When the coinciding interests gain in number and, above all, in share, they begin pushing mutually exclusive interests into the background and damping them down or, in other words, balancing them.

This model is essentially a modification of the previous one, the only difference being that in the former case the driving force is coinciding interests arising from negative interdependence—a real danger of mutual annihilation or an unacceptable weakening—while in the latter case coinciding interests are likewise at work, but they are a result of realizing the existence of positive interdependence, namely, the possibility of mutually strengthening both sides by joint efforts.

An example of how seemingly inherent hostility gives way to cooperation geared to serving the interests of both sides is clearly furnished by postwar French-West German relations. The new situation in Europe and the world naturally prompted the two countries to renounce their perpetual rivalry and to set out to develop a durable and ramified system of the most diverse ties, including those in the military sphere. The stabilizing role of this interdependence can be fully appreciated now that the unification of Germany could unfreeze the conflict potential in French-German relations.

Qualitative changes of a similar nature are maturing, it is hoped, in Soviet-U.S. relations today. While both sides have sufficient reason to differ over a number of issues, including very important ones, the new realities confronting them today create more and more incentives for their joint efforts in solving shared problems. As the American analyst C. Morris writes, "It is entirely conceivable . . . that mutual American-Soviet interests could increase to the point where normal intercourse would not include implicit threats of nuclear missile attacks. Gradually,

indeed, such threats might begin to sound silly."[6]

Of course, this model, attractive as it is, also has weak points. The very possibility of cooperation, even where it is quite real, often becomes a hostage of the conflict. The parties involved in it always try to compare which is more important for them—a probable benefit of such cooperation or the goals that constitute the objective of the struggle but that are likely to be given up in this case, at least temporarily. Under normal conditions, as a rule, parties tend to favor the latter. Besides, it is next to impossible to arrange for an environment to generate positive interdependence and hence coinciding interests when it is urgently necessary to find something to offset a conflict that has already broken out. However, a balance of interests so designed, with its solidity and stability, is actually expected to perform not so much the role of a fire extinguisher but the function of a strategic safeguard against the impact of a possible crisis.

With regard to Soviet-U.S. relations, this implies that as the more painful military and political problems are eliminated and the two sides reach a limit beyond which they cannot afford further concessions because of real mutually exclusive interests, growing attention will have to be devoted to another area of their relationship in which coinciding cooperative interests could begin to in-

6. C. Morris, *Iron Destinies, Lost Opportunities: The Arms Race between the USA and the USSR, 1945-1987* (New York: Carroll & Graf, 1988), p. 441.

teract. One indication of incipient progress in this direction is the fact that transnational problems have occupied one of the highest places on the typical agenda of Soviet-U.S. meetings.

This also applies to regional problems that do not lend themselves to settlement. Rather than working out more and more new complex and cumbersome designs for reconciling all the contradictory interests of the numerous parties, it might be worth trying to accentuate the search for still-vacant niches of positive interdependence so as to ensure that subsequently the evolving structure of cooperation will impose itself on the structure of the conflict and gradually modify the whole system of relations. Effort to this end is all the more promising since objective developments in the world are preparing the ground for it.

CONCLUSION

It follows from these deliberations that balance of interests is not just a version of compromise. Its interpretation in this way would considerably dilute the concept and in some cases even make it lose contact with reality altogether. The ideas underlying the concept, provided they are sufficiently elaborated, make it possible to turn it into an instrument suitable for both analyzing international relations and producing a practical impact on them.

In a preliminary way, the vision of balance of interests can be formulated as follows. In the narrow sense, it is a balance between nonintersect-

ing interests. In the broad sense, it is a combined balance of the whole system of interests at work on both sides, with mutually exclusive and coinciding interests balancing each other along with nonintersecting interests.

In general terms, the attainment of a balance of interests comes down to neutralizing mutually exclusive interests. This can be done either by revising mutually exclusive interests and transferring them to the category of nonintersecting ones or by offsetting them with additional coinciding interests. Such countervailing interests can arise on the basis of the balance of power in the course of confrontation or independently from it.

This approach makes balance of power not an antipode but an integral part of balance of interests. Moreover, in one of the previously mentioned models, balance of power plays the main role in generating balance of interests.

As could be noticed from what was said about this model, variants of transition from balance of power to balance of interests proceed very much along the same lines as the concept of conflict management. Indeed, what is meant here is actually taking control of the forms and intensity of confrontation by regulating the power potentials of those involved. But in contrast to the tactics of management, which, as seen from the Soviet perspective, implies possible actions aimed at a deliberate escalation of a conflict as well as its settlement, the same mechanics, but subordinated to the ideology of balance of interests, acquires a definitely constructive character. Besides, it should be specially emphasized that the concept of balance of interests as it is suggested here does not, and should not in any other modification, include an option of direct armed interference in the basic conflict from outside, whereas the concept of management accepts and justifies such a military action.

In addition, the broad interpretation of balance of interests substantiates one more method of scaling down the conflict reaction, namely, placing it into a cooperative environment. Of major importance is also the fact that such an interpretation, while urging a renunciation of a somewhat idealistic view on the opportunities in directly balancing mutually exclusive interests, provides a real basis for coping with the clash of these interests through accentuating their asymmetrical aspects. Thus it opens up a more promising prospect for not only conflict settlement but also conflict resolution.

In sum, the concept of balance of interests does not negate but considerably complements the theories structured on the principle of balance of power, including the concept of conflict management. Of course, the correlation between the two concepts will require a more thorough examination. But even now it seems appropriate to claim that the idea of balance of interests is apt to constitute a common intellectual basis for Soviet-American interaction on regional problems in an interdependent world.

ANNALS, *AAPSS,* **518,** November 1991

Superpower Conflict Resolution:
Lessons for the Future

By MARK N. KATZ

ABSTRACT: Despite the significant progress that the United States and the USSR have made in cooperating to resolve regional conflicts, many of these conflicts continue. One reason for this is that the Soviet and American governments have had differing expectations regarding what the outcome of superpower conflict resolution efforts should be. Yet even when Soviet and American aims are similar, there are other obstacles to conflict resolution. Among these are the lack of commitment to democracy on the part of one or more of the local antagonists in regional conflicts, and involvement by other external parties in the conflicts. There is no guarantee that the superpowers can successfully resolve regional conflicts even if they adopt a common approach to conflict resolution, but adopting a common approach may at least allow Washington and Moscow to unlink their overall relations from those conflicts that cannot be resolved.

Mark N. Katz received a Ph.D. in political science from the Massachusetts Institute of Technology in 1982. He is currently an assistant professor of government and politics at George Mason University in Fairfax, Virginia.

THE present era of Soviet-American relations is unique in that, unlike the Cold War period, both superpowers now see their interests as being better served through disengaging from and resolving regional conflicts. Yet, despite dramatic agreements to resolve some regional conflicts, fighting rages on in several parts of the Third World.

Can any lessons for the future be drawn from recent superpower efforts to resolve regional conflicts? Attempting to draw generalizable lessons from different cases is a difficult task. Each conflict is unique in terms of its causes and evolution. Each conflict is also unique in terms of the nature, strength, and motivations of both the local antagonists and their external supporters.

Since such a high degree of variability exists between different regional conflicts, the most obvious generalization that can be made about them is that there is no generalizable resolution formula applicable to them all. Another generalization that can be made is that a mutual desire on the part of the superpowers to resolve regional conflicts is not a sufficient condition to bring about their peaceful conclusion.

These two generalizations do not provide a hopeful basis for drawing lessons about superpower conflict resolution in the future. To assume that no lessons at all can be drawn from disparate cases, however, may lead us to overlook genuinely useful experience and to commit avoidable errors in the future.

One way to examine whether generalizable lessons for the future of superpower conflict resolution exist is to analyze the applicability of superpower expectations or models regarding conflict resolution as well as the applicability of successful instances of conflict resolution to other conflicts. For whether generalizable models of conflict resolution actually exist, it is clear that Soviet and American leaders have expectations—which, of course, are evolving—regarding what the outcome of superpower conflict resolution efforts should be. In addition, the successful or partially successful experience of conflict resolution efforts in one country or region raises the question of whether a similar solution is applicable more generally. What these expectations and experiences are, as well as their realism and general applicability, will be examined here.

BEFORE GORBACHEV: UNILATERALIST MODELS

Until the Gorbachev era, neither Soviet nor American leaders seriously envisioned superpower cooperation as a means of resolving Third World conflicts, especially insurgencies. Instead, each viewed these conflicts in zero-sum terms; a loss for one superpower was a gain for the other. The maximum goal was to help one's own allies achieve victory over the other's allies. The minimum goal was to prevent the other's allies from defeating one's own.

From the late 1940s, the model guiding American foreign policy was one of containment. This worked well with regard to strategic nuclear weapons and Europe. The variant of containment envisioned for the Third World was successful counterinsurgency warfare. By the early 1970s however, the American public, Congress, and the executive branch had reached the conclusion that large-scale American counterinsurgency efforts were too unpopular within the United States to be sustained after the Vietnam experience. In other words, this model was seen by the American public to have failed in Vietnam and to have no applicability elsewhere. Hence the United States did little to prevent pro-Soviet Marxist guerrillas from seizing power in several Third World countries during the 1970s.

In the 1980s, when it became clear that pro-Soviet Marxist regimes were vulnerable, the United States supported anti-Soviet rebels in many countries, a practice known as the Reagan Doctrine. This policy was generally effective: although no Third World Marxist regimes were overthrown, none completely defeated their opponents, and no Marxist regime came to power in the 1980s.

The Soviet approach to Third World conflict was virtually the mirror image of the American approach in the years before Gorbachev. Moscow supported a series of so-called national liberation wars after the end of World War II through the Brezhnev era. This policy was especially successful in bringing Marxist regimes to power in the 1970s. When anti-Soviet insurgent activity increased in a number of them, Moscow adopted a counterinsurgency policy. Moscow was not successful in suppressing rebel forces, however, despite costly, long-term efforts to do so.

Just as American leaders did in the early 1970s, the Gorbachev lead-

ership in the mid-1980s concluded that counterinsurgency was an unproductive and costly means of preserving one's influence. As early as 1987, it became clear that Gorbachev sought to disengage the USSR from several Third World conflicts. Prospects arose for genuine Soviet-American cooperation to resolve a number of Third World disputes. Nevertheless, each side at first had very different expectations concerning the outcome of these conflict resolution efforts.

AMERICAN EXPECTATIONS: THE SOUTH VIETNAM MODEL

The USSR, Cuba, and Vietnam had sent large numbers of troops to protect weak Marxist regimes in Afghanistan, Angola, and Cambodia. Because of the expense and the fruitlessness of their efforts, all three intervening states decided to withdraw their troops as part of a settlement process in these three countries.

In the United States, foreign policymakers expected that Communist troop withdrawals would lead to certain consequences. In its most optimistic form, the expectation of American policymakers was that the withdrawals would lead to the collapse of the Marxist regimes that these soldiers had previously defended. This expectation was based on the American experience in Indochina, where U.S. troop withdrawal was followed shortly by the overthrow of the regimes that Washington had previously supported in South Vietnam, Laos, and Cambodia. This expectation was widely held with regard to the future of the Najibullah regime immediately after the complete withdrawal of Soviet troops from Afghanistan in February 1989.

These optimistic—from the American point of view—expectations have not been met so far. Are they likely to be? In other words, is the South Vietnam model a generalizable expectation with regard to conflict resolution now? The answer to both questions is, probably not.

There are three reasons why the South Vietnam model is probably not applicable now. First, with regard to Afghanistan, the opposition forces are not unified and their factional infighting has increased following the departure of Soviet troops—a phenomenon that only helps the Kabul regime.

Second, the Marxist regimes in all these countries enjoy some degree of internal support, partly because significant sectors of the population view the opposition groups as less desirable than the existing government. In Afghanistan, many fear that the overthrow of the Kabul regime will mean that the most extreme Islamic fundamentalist *mujahidin* groups will come to power. In Cambodia, the most powerful opposition group is the murderous Khmer Rouge, compared to which the Hun Sen regime's rule is far more benevolent. In Angola, the Popular Movement for the Liberation of Angola (MPLA) is led by mesticoes and Mbundus; these groups prefer it to the National Union for the Total Independence of Angola (UNITA), which is dominated by the Ovimbundu.

Third, the withdrawal of American forces form Indochina in 1973 was followed by the congressional cutoff of arms transfers to U.S. allies there in 1974. It was shortly after this, in 1975, that these regimes collapsed. Despite the withdrawal of Communist armed forces from Third World countries recently, however, the Soviet Union continued to provide arms to its allies.[1] Unlike in America in the 1970s, domestic pressure to end arms transfers to Third World clients is still ineffective in the Soviet Union. Nor is cost a deterrent to continued Soviet arms transfers: with the drawdown of Soviet armed forces in both the USSR and Eastern Europe, Moscow has a huge excess of weapons that it can provide to others.

A dramatic regime change clearly took place in Nicaragua, but this is hardly an example of the applicability of the South Vietnam model. The regime change took place only after American funding to the contra rebels had been ended and the contras had virtually been driven out of the country. Further, the Sandinistas defeated the rebels without large numbers of foreign Communist troops participating in combat operations as in Afghanistan, Angola, and Cambodia. If there is any lesson that can be drawn from Nicaragua, it may be that dramatic regime change is more likely to occur only after external as-

1. Soviet arms transfers to certain Marxist Third World regimes have continued at least through 1990. Holman Jenkin, Jr., "Oil, Two Armies and Time," *Insight*, 1 Oct. 1990, p. 14; Sheila Taft, "As Arms Supply Winds Down, Afghan Rebels Close Ranks," *Christian Science Monitor*, 15 Nov. 1990. See also U.S., Department of Defense, *Soviet Military Power, 1990* (Washington, DC: Government Printing Office, 1990), pp. 17-19, 101.

sistance to the rebels and the rebel insurgency itself have effectively ended; this is a proposition that will be examined later.

If the South Vietnam model is to work, it would do so only if the United States and its allies beefed up their military support for rebel groups to the point where the latter could seize power. Such an achievement, however, seems highly unlikely. While a certain amount of aid is needed to assist a rebel group to avoid defeat, a much greater amount is probably necessary to enable it to seize power from a government still enjoying substantial external support. At present, it is doubtful that current levels of American support will be maintained, much less increased, to rebel groups in Afghanistan, Angola, and Cambodia. In Cambodia, the United States ended its minimal support to the two non-Communist opposition groups for fear that this aid would ultimately serve to benefit only the Chinese-backed Khmer Rouge.[2]

Earlier American expectations that the South Vietnam model could serve as a pattern of conflict resolution, then, appear unrealistic. The one country, Cambodia, where this model has a better chance of being implemented than anywhere else is also the one case in which the success of this model would be least desirable, considering which group is most likely to come to power there.

2. Despite Chinese government assurances that it had halted military aid to the Khmer Rouge in September 1990, the Khmer Rouge continue to receive Chinese arms. Steven Erlanger, "Khmer Rouge Get More China Arms," New York Times, 1 Jan. 1991.

SOVIET EXPECTATIONS:
THE NORTH YEMEN MODEL

Soviet statements during the 1986-89 period reveal that Moscow's notion of the outcome of conflict resolution agreements was very different from Washington's. The Soviets seemed to think that the withdrawal of Soviet, Cuban, and Vietnamese troops would not result in the fall of Marxist regimes in Afghanistan, Angola, and Cambodia. Instead, they expected opposition rebel groups to collapse. This would occur for two reasons: (1) in return for the withdrawal of Communist armed forces, the United States and its allies would end military assistance to the rebel groups; and (2) in some countries, rebel forces would begin fighting among themselves once foreign armed forces had departed. The type of internal settlement that Moscow envisioned for these countries and others was essentially a cease-fire, and amnesty for rebel forces—except the top rebel leadership—and permission for the former rebels to become part of the existing regime.[3] Soviet relations with these regimes would remain close, and Soviet arms supplies would continue.

Moscow experienced a similar situation once before, in North Yemen. For five years in the 1960s, Soviet combat pilots and advisers helped 60,000 Egyptian troops try to defend a republican regime against Saudi-backed royalist rebels. The war proceeded miserably, and Egypt finally decided to withdraw in 1967. To encourage Egypt's withdrawal, Saudi

3. Mark N. Katz, Gorbachev's Military Policy in the Third World (New York: Praeger, 1989), chap. 4.

Arabia agreed to end its aid to the royalists. Even so, the republican regime seemed on the point of defeat and was barely being kept alive by a last-ditch Soviet airlift when the royalist opposition literally fell apart. Two years later, an agreement was reached whereby the royalists, minus their top leadership, were granted amnesty and allowed to hold office in the existing republican regime.[4]

Is this North Yemen model generally applicable now? Probably not. For while Soviet arms transfers can prevent Marxist Third World regimes from being overthrown, opposition forces are unlikely to be defeated so long as they continue to receive military assistance themselves.

So long as external support to anti-Soviet rebel groups continues, the internal aspects of insurgencies are unlikely to be settled along the lines of the North Yemen model. Thus earlier Soviet expectations that the North Yemen model could serve as a pattern of conflict resolution also appear unrealistic.

EAST EUROPEAN MODEL

Of course, superpower expectations at the outset of or during negotiations are not the only models of conflict resolution. As Soviet officials used to say, "life itself" suggests other models. Particularly noteworthy among these are examples of successful political transformation, especially when they occur peacefully

and even though they may have taken place without much advance planning. The peaceful transfer of power from Communist to non-Communist governments in Poland, Hungary, East Germany, Czechoslovakia, and Bulgaria during 1989-90 appears to be an especially desirable model. Is it applicable to the Third World?

Again, the answer is, probably not. The peaceful transfer of power in these five East European nations occurred under special circumstances. In 1989, Gorbachev signaled that the Soviet Union would not use force to ensure the continuation of orthodox Communist rule in Eastern Europe as the USSR had done in the past. The orthodox Communist leaderships in each of these five countries also concluded that the use of force against the opposition was no longer permissible. Indeed, these orthodox Communists basically lost confidence in both their ability and their right to continue ruling. In all of these countries, opposition forces enjoyed enormous popular support, while the Communist regimes had almost none. In addition, the opposition forces in each of these countries were committed to democratization —they did not seek to install their own dictatorships. As part of this democratization process, opposition forces were willing to allow the former Communist rulers to retain their parties and compete in elections. For the Communists, losing power did not mean losing their lives as well. In fact, they retained the right to participate in politics.

Most of these conditions are not present in the Marxist nations of the Third World. In Afghanistan, Cambo-

4. Mark N. Katz, *Russia and Arabia: Soviet Foreign Policy toward the Arabian Peninsula* (Baltimore, MD: Johns Hopkins University Press, 1986), pp. 24-32.

dia, and Ethiopia, the Marxist regimes are still prepared to use force against the opposition. In none of these countries is the opposition committed to democratization. For the Marxists in these countries, then, losing power could well mean losing their lives in addition to any meaningful right to participate in politics.

Perhaps the most fundamental obstacle to applying the East European model of peaceful transformation in the Third World is that democracy is highly valued generally in the former Marxist countries of Eastern Europe while it is not in the Marxist countries of the Third World. As long as this remains true, peaceful political change via elections is highly unlikely in the Third World. An obvious exception, though, is Nicaragua, where a Marxist regime did allow itself to be voted out of office. If this could occur in Nicaragua, could it occur elsewhere?

THE NICARAGUAN MODEL

It is not clear why the Sandinistas agreed to hold free elections in February 1990 after ruling in an undemocratic manner since they came to power in 1979. Perhaps they thought they would win. To the surprise of most observers, the elections were fair and the Sandinistas lost. What is perhaps most remarkable is that the Sandinistas acknowledged that they had lost and agreed to transfer power to the victorious United Nicaraguan Opposition (UNO) party, led by Violeta Chamorro. Part of their grace in defeat may have been due to the fact that Mos-

cow had cut its direct supply of arms to the Sandinistas. The Sandinistas probably realized that had they tried to remain in power despite the results of the election, domestic opposition would have arisen, the United States would have supported it, but Moscow would not have supported them.

In addition, the Sandinistas understood that, as in Eastern Europe, losing power did not mean that they would lose their lives or be eliminated from politics. Indeed, the Sandinistas remain the largest single party in the National Assembly. If the UNO coalition of 14 parties breaks up, the Sandinistas will play a key role in the assembly. In addition, unlike the Communist parties of Eastern Europe, the Sandinistas appear to enjoy a credible chance of being reelected to power in the future.

One of the underlying prerequisites for the peaceful resolution of the conflict in Nicaragua was that each side in the election agreed to respect the election results even if the other side won. They did not agree to this simply through idealism but because both sides understood that the electorate demanded it. This should not be surprising, though, considering that, unlike some other parts of the Third World, Latin America has increasingly valued republican democracy. With the exception of Cuba and Guyana, Latin American states either are democracies or are making significant progress toward democracy. Indeed, Latin America has had greater experience with democracy than Eastern Europe.

Can the Nicaraguan model be applied to other conflicts? As with the East European model, it probably cannot be in countries or regions where governments, opposition forces, and populations generally do not value democracy. Indeed, free elections would be difficult to conduct if any one of these groups did not agree to respect the results. Conflicts where a consensus to respect election results appears doubtful include Afghanistan, Cambodia, the Horn of Africa, and the Middle East.

THE GULF MODEL

An unprecedented level of Soviet-American cooperation occurred in response to the August 1990 Iraqi invasion of Kuwait. Most notably, this cooperation involved Soviet support for 12 American-sponsored U.N. Security Council resolutions directed against Baghdad, including one allowing the use of force against Iraq if it did not fully withdraw from Kuwait by 15 January 1991.

It is highly doubtful, though, that Soviet-American cooperation in the gulf crisis can serve as a model for superpower collaboration in similarly extreme cases involving the complete conquest of one country by another. While the United States and the USSR would both oppose such conquest or attempted conquest, it is highly unlikely that the Soviet or the American government would consider its interests outside the gulf to be so threatened that either of them would be willing to commit its own armed forces to the task of liberating the conquered nation. Nor is it likely that Soviet or American public opinion would now tolerate protracted military intervention in any other part of the Third World. Probably the most that the two countries would be able to do in such a situation is to jointly isolate an aggressor and work to contain it from further expansion.

CONCLUSION

Can any lessons for the future be drawn from recent superpower efforts to resolve regional conflicts? The preceding analysis suggests that there may be relatively few. Nevertheless, there are some.

One lesson is that despite the progress in superpower conflict resolution that has been made so far, superpower diplomacy is unlikely to fully resolve conflicts if Washington and Moscow adhere to differing models of what the outcome of their conflict resolution efforts should be. It must be remembered that differences over the Third World played a large role in contributing to the breakdown of détente in the 1970s. Important differences over the outcome of conflict resolution could lead to both superpowers' remaining militarily involved in regional conflicts, the breakdown of their efforts to resolve conflicts, and negative consequences for détente.

Can these negative consequences of differing superpower expectations be avoided? They might be if the superpowers modified their expectations so that the other's interests were not threatened, or at least agreed on a common approach to conflict resolution. U.S. Secretary of State James Baker and Soviet Foreign Minister Eduard Shevardnadze made considerable progress toward such a common approach in 1990 with regard to Nicaragua, Afghanistan, Cambodia, and Angola.

But even if the superpowers could agree on a common approach to conflict resolution, could they hope to devise and implement an effective one? A second lesson that can be drawn from the preceding analysis is that even successful examples of conflict resolution have, at best, limited applicability to other conflicts. To be successful, then, any joint superpower approach to conflict resolution would have to be flexible enough to encompass a wide variety of conflicts as well as accommodate each other's interests.

Such an approach would need to include four elements. The first is the reduction or elimination of superpower arms transfers. The experiences of Afghanistan, Angola, and Cambodia have demonstrated that the withdrawal of interventionary forces alone is not sufficient either to resolve conflict or to end superpower involvement in it. A serious obstacle to the achievement of both these goals is the continuation of arms supplies by the superpowers to the warring parties in regional conflicts. It is the continuation of these arms transfers that allows the warring parties to avoid negotiations and seek military victory over their opponents. A mutual superpower arms cutoff—or at least reduction—might convince them that military victory is not possible and therefore they must negotiate a peaceful settlement.

There are, of course, problems with an across-the-board formula for a superpower arms cutoff to the pro-

tagonists in all regional conflicts. The United States and the USSR are not the only arms suppliers. Each has allies that might for their own reasons continue arms transfers to the local antagonists. Each superpower, however, might well interpret this as proxy activity carried out at the behest of the other superpower. Both Washington and Moscow must be willing to reduce their support to any ally in order to reassure each other that neither is attempting to subvert an arms cutoff agreement. In some cases, a government over which Washington and Moscow have little influence may heavily arm one side in a regional conflict. Under these circumstances, the United States and the USSR may have little choice but to jointly arm the other side in order to create a stalemate that may in turn induce all parties concerned to seek a peaceful solution to the conflict.

The second element to an effective approach to conflict resolution is sustained diplomatic initiative. A cutoff or reduction of superpower arms supplies to the warring parties in a regional conflict is important for signaling to them that the superpowers will not back their military efforts indefinitely. This action by itself, however, will not serve to end the conflict. What is needed in addition is a sustained diplomatic effort to convince the warring parties and their backers that their interests would benefit from conflict resolution, while they would be harmed if the conflict continued.

This diplomatic initiative might occur in any number of ways. The two superpowers might work on it jointly, or the initiative might be taken by one. The warring parties might talk to each other directly or through a superpower intermediary. Each unique conflict will require its own unique diplomacy to resolve it. What is important is that some form of sustained superpower diplomatic effort be undertaken.

The third element is neutralization. Since each superpower fears that conflict resolution efforts will result in the other one's gaining an ally, a way to avoid this—and hence avoid obstruction of conflict resolution—is for both superpowers to agree that neither will be closely allied to whatever government emerges from a conflict resolution process. In other words, even if the government emerging from a conflict resolution process seeks close military relations with one of the superpowers, both superpowers should eschew such relationships in order to avoid misunderstandings with the other superpower that could threaten their efforts at conflict resolution generally.

Finally, an effective joint superpower approach needs the promotion of free elections. With Gorbachev's encouragement of genuinely free elections in Eastern Europe and increasingly free ones in the Soviet Union, it is doubtful that Moscow would seek to block elections in the Third World. Indeed, Gorbachev's acceptance of elections and renunciation of the Soviet Communist Party's monopoly on power in the USSR is having a profound effect on Third World Marxists who based their political structures on the Soviet model.[5] Thus there may now be a greater

acceptance of the concept of free elections in countries that have never had them before. The recent elections in Namibia and Nicaragua are proof that this can happen.

For such elections to be regarded as legitimate, it is important that no party be excluded from them. The people themselves should decide the extent to which Najibullah of Afghanistan, Jonas Savimbi of Angola, or even the Khmer Rouge in Cambodia should be represented in government. Attempting to exclude any leader or group from an election only gives those excluded an incentive to fight on. The superpowers, however, must undertake special efforts to isolate parties—such as the Khmer Rouge—that make clear that they will not respect the outcome of elections. The superpowers need to impress upon the warring parties that conflict is unlikely to end in any given country unless regularly held free elections are a fixture of its political life.

There can be no standard formula for how the initial elections should be conducted in each case. In Namibia, they were held under the auspices of the United Nations, though South African administration continued. In Nicaragua, the existing Marxist government carried them out. Other solutions have been suggested for other conflicts, including temporary coalition governments and full-scale United Nations control. As with diplomatic initiatives, the appropriate format for conducting free elections must be determined to fit the needs

5. For example, Joe Slovo, head of the South African Communist Party, recently de-

nounced the concept of a one-party state. Christopher S. Wren, "In Pretoria, Last Throes of Marxism?" *New York Times,* 19 Feb. 1990.

of the particular case. What is important is that free elections be held.

There is no guarantee that the superpowers can successfully resolve regional conflicts even if they adopt a common approach to conflict resolution. Adopting a common approach, however, may at least allow the superpowers to unlink their overall relations from those conflicts that cannot be resolved. This alone would be a great benefit to them, one that will be far less likely to occur if the superpowers continue arming opposing sides in regional conflicts.

Book Department

INTERNATIONAL RELATIONS AND POLITICS

BECKSTROM, JOHN H. *Evolutionary Jurisprudence: Prospects and Limitations on the Use of Modern Darwinism throughout the Legal Process.* Pp. 142. Champaign: University of Illinois Press, 1989. $24.95.

TYLER, TOM R. *Why People Obey the Law.* Pp. vii, 273. New Haven, CT: Yale University Press, 1990. $30.00.

These two books are part of a burgeoning literature that addresses the legal process in modern society, including the formation of laws, compliance with them, and the judicial disposition of offenders. Each book adopts a quite different perspective, and together they reflect the variety of approaches that continues to enrich our understanding of the operation of the legal process and how it might be changed.

John Beckstrom's *Evolutionary Jurisprudence* is a challenging attempt to apply sociobiology to the law. Sociobiology proposes that human behavior results from the interaction of individuals' ge-
netic makeup with their environment and culture. It thus represents an attempt to impose some precision in the often murky debate over the relative importance of nature and nurture in explaining human behavior. As Beckstrom says, it is logical that sociobiology and the law should quickly find common ground, but as it emerges from this book, the ground is anything but firm. It is one of the strengths of *Evolutionary Jurisprudence* that no dogmatic claims are made for sociobiology. For example, Beckstrom discusses the notion that genetic affinity predisposes individuals to aid close relatives more readily than strangers, but he recognizes that other variables intervene. The problem is that it is virtually impossible to separate the genetic from the social factors at play.

Tom Tyler's *Why People Obey the Law* tackles the legal process from a quite different angle. This book is based on a survey, carried out in Chicago, on attitudes toward many aspects of the law, from calling the police to being dealt with by the courts. There are many fascinating insights here, and a short review cannot possibly do justice to the complexity of the study. What is important, though, is Tyler's conclusion that the predominant reason people obey the law is that they perceive it to be fair and legitimate. Tyler ends by rejecting the notion that it is self-interest—through fear of punishment, for example—that produces a law-abiding citizenry; instead, he feels that this citizenry develops from the sense that the legal process is unbiased and allows individuals an opportunity to present their cases. Again, the study raises important questions. Why do people not obey the law? Does the emphasis upon the legal process not obscure the importance of the substance of the law?

Neither of these books sits particularly comfortably with the other. For example, Tyler eschews self-interest, but Beckstrom argues for a kind of genetic self-interest in which there is a general predisposition on the part of individuals to favor those of a similar genetic make-up. Nonetheless, each book demonstrates that the legal process continues to be a fascinating field of empirical research and lively speculation.

RODERICK PHILLIPS

Carleton University
Ottawa
Ontario
Canada

HAASS, RICHARD N. *Conflicts Unending: The United States and Regional Disputes*. Pp. xiv, 172. New Haven, CT: Yale University Press, 1990. $22.50.

ROSENAU, JAMES N. *Turbulence in World Politics: A Theory of Change and Continuity*. Pp. xviii, 480. Princeton, NJ: Princeton University Press, 1990. $55.00. Paperbound, $14.50.

At first comparison, these two books appear unconnected. Richard Haass offers a single theory to explain a series of case studies, while James Rosenau presents alternative theoretical perspectives without much application. Both, however, advance the study of international politics through some rethinking of old paradigms, although the emphasis differs.

Haass focuses his attention on conflicts that have continued for decades without resolution. The key, he argues, is "ripeness," a condition resulting from a shared leadership preference for negotiations over fighting and from leadership's ability to persuade followers that national interests can be protected during negotiation.

The absence of ripeness characterizes the five cases that form the core of the book: the Middle East, Cyprus, India-Pakistan, South Africa, and Northern Ireland. Each conflict, however, entails different circumstances preventing ripeness. A complete lack of trust between sides in the Arab-Israeli conflict and mutual unacceptability of compromise positions undermined the prospects for negotiation. The Cyprus and India-Pakistan conflict solution is limited by weak leaders and is complicated further by the nuclear issue in the latter case. Several problems limit resolution in South Africa, including highly polarized white and black populations. Polarization also has stymied solutions to Northern Ireland's tragedies.

What, then, can the United States do? In most cases, not much, according to Haass. Perhaps the most important response is to avoid mediation efforts until ripeness forms. Premature efforts can often worsen matters, as did the Carter nuclear restrictions on Pakistan and Shultz's peace efforts in the Israeli-Palestinian crisis. The United States can, though, encourage the development of ripeness. Confidence-building measures, for example, might prove effective in the India-Pakistan dispute, as might efforts at supplying the technical means of verification for possible arms control measures.

Rosenau's latest book is an ambitious effort to explain the "turbulence" seen as responsible for the rapid political changes of the 1980s. Rosenau suggests a new search for relevant theory that can replace the focus on continuity and state-centered paradigms that may mask turbulence. He also suggests that the nature of turbulence needs to be better understood. Is it cyclical, self-sustaining, episodic? What parameters are involved, and what is the relationship between them? Rosenau identifies three such parameters, the macro, or structure and rules; micro, or people in relationship to authority; and a relational parameter to connect the two. What do they show us? According to Rosenau, the rules are changing at the structural level, individuals are more significant—partly because of decentralized authority—and there are new and important relational parameters, especially nonstate actors. As states become more rigid, individuals break habits and adapt to new environments, thus increasing turbulence.

Structural change, for Rosenau, can be found in the relationship between the "state-centered world" and the "multi-centered world." The growing limits of the state-centered world lead to more influence by the Polish Solidarity movement or the Organization of Petroleum Exporting Countries, while state-centered products like treaties and alliances fade away. Nonstate elites become more important, as do global television and computers, which allow more global interaction between elites.

As for the future, Rosenau proposes four scenarios, ranging from "global society," with much clearer norms, to the restoration of the state-centered system.

Both books are thought-provoking challenges to some established means of thinking about international politics.

Some readers may demand more evidence, and more confirmation is needed before either argument can be fully accepted. Both authors, however, have advanced the conceptualization of these issues.

DAVID S. SORENSON

Denison University
Granville
Ohio

HULL, ELIZABETH. *Taking Liberties: National Barriers to the Free Flow of Ideas.* Pp. 172. New York: Praeger, 1991. $38.95.

This monograph considers domestic policies that inhibit American citizens from obtaining international information. Elizabeth Hull is not addressing formal wartime censorship, sedition laws, or grievous secrecy incorporated in laws like the atomic energy statute that makes it a crime even to imagine anything about nuclear energy. Instead, she focuses on restrictions on passports, travel, and exchanges of documentary films. The violations cited are few and seldom recent. They are more like annoyances than restrictions. Hull insists aliens are entitled to the same protections as citizens. Would she place no limits on passports? She calls for wiser bureaucrats and bolder judges, hardly imaginative correctives.

Hull, a political science professor at Rutgers University, wants judges to expand protections. She is correct in criticizing judicial reluctance to supervise administrative agencies, but does experience show that courts can do this very effectively?

The text totals only 80 pages; law journals run longer articles. The rest is documentation. Some individual footnotes run to two pages. In addition, while Hull certainly cannot be blamed for the manufacture of her book, the conclusion to this expensive volume is misbound, appearing after the notes.

JOHN D. STEVENS

University of Michigan
Ann Arbor

AFRICA, ASIA, AND
LATIN AMERICA

EVANS, GRANT. *Lao Peasants under Socialism*. Pp. xv, 268. New Haven, CT: Yale University Press, 1990. $30.00.

As if further evidence were needed of the disastrous consequences of the application of Marxist-Leninist principles to the agrarian economies of underdeveloped countries during this century, Grant Evans, a senior lecturer in anthropology at the University of Hong Kong, traces what he terms the "rapid learning curve" of the government of the Lao People's Democratic Republic (LPDR) since 1975 in trying to develop a "socialist agriculture." Research for the book was carried out in Laos itself between 1979 and 1987 during biannual or annual visits to "many villages and cooperatives in various parts of the country."

This is an important volume, which Evans rightly calls "the first major study" of Laotian rural society. Thoroughly annotated, enlivened by many photographs of Laotian peasant life, and rich in statistical detail, its pages systematically take up the initially dogmatic approach toward socialist collectivization taken by LPDR leaders and Communist party cadres, the important party self-critique of 1979 that "command collectivization" just was not working, followed by the general "thrust" of policy since then toward what Evans calls "market socialism." The latter appears to be a much more flexible policy, giving greater scope to private initiative, to kinship-based authority over land use, and to traditional patterns of cultivation, plus, of course, state supervision. But in an illuminating chapter on this modified Lao version of what Lenin already had called a "system of civilized cooperators" in agrarian economic relationships, Evans concludes after examining some case studies that this new modification also did not have much success in developing an effective cooperative system of Lao peasant producers. For example, in many instances peasants rejected the distribution mechanisms of the farming cooperative as "an act of rational self-interest, not a symptom of class conflict." Evans notes that grouping landowning and landless peasants together in a single cooperative "ruined the incentives of the former," destroying their incentives toward greater productivity, while the poorer peasants who remained in the cooperative "became dependent on state inputs to remain viable." To those who remember the fate that befell the Communist cooperative experience in Marxist-Leninist states with an identical problem, from the USSR to China and from Vietnam to Cuba, these observations will evoke familiar echoes.

It is in his close observation of actual Lao agrarian life that Evans makes a particularly valuable contribution. Over and over he documents the details of why socialist collectivization, even if in the relatively benign form of Marxist-Leninist-inspired initial "cooperatives," can keep running up against persistent peasant traditions of production organization. Carefully preserved and demonstrably practical balances between the food production requirements and consumption needs of a Lao peasant household performing as a unit, balances that shift with the maturing of the generations, clashed with the inflexible system of quotas and of allocation of "labor points" imposed by LPDR cooperative administrations. Thus older farmers, for example, began fearing "that they would not be able to work as fast as the younger workers and therefore would not be able to earn as much" in the state-promoted peasant cooperative system. At the same time, lumping disparate groups of unrelated people and strangers together in a collectivization experiment inevitably aroused resentment among those who felt that the state program was permitting "lazy people to live off us."

In a somewhat confusing concluding chapter, Evans tries to survey the limits of Marxist dogma when applied to peasant rural economies generally. He takes to task the approaches of what he calls "radical or Marxist anthropologists." Among the latter, Evans notes—*rara avis!*— that somehow "the image of socialism as being the opposite of capitalism persists" and that "radical anthropologists" still criticize capitalism "from the perspective of precapitalist culture." But Evans's own attempt to delineate, on the basis of his Laotian examples, the dynamics of a hybrid system of "market socialism" as a model raises interesting questions and speculation. Included in the latter is whether anthropologists anywhere ever could bring themselves in the future to use the term "Adam Smith-oriented anthropologists" or "Milton Friedman-oriented anthropologists," now that the practice of the Marxist-Leninist model — whatever its hybrid form—seems to have been demonstrated to be such a spectacular failure.

JUSTUS M. VAN DER KROEF
University of Bridgeport
Connecticut

FOX, RICHARD G. *Gandhian Utopia: Experiments with Culture.* Pp. x, 330. Boston: Beacon Press, 1989. $27.50.

Richard Fox, professor of anthropology at Duke University, battles two rising forces: postmodernist anthropology in the West and militant Hindu nationalism in India. Fox enlists the faith, courage, and activism of the great Indian reformer Mahatma Gandhi as he girds himself for his own struggles in encouraging a more socially relevant academy and a more egalitarian and compassionate society.

Fox minces no words. He denounces the self-indulgent nihilism of postmodernist anthropological scholarship, "the reflexive accounts that start anywhere and go nowhere, the unwillingness to venture beyond the statement that all intellectual ventures are fictional and methodologically problematic, the unwillingness to take intellectual responsibility under the guise of destroying scholarly authority." As to militant Hindu nationalism, "it is intolerant of all social identities other than Hindian [*sic*]"; "violence seems wedded to the movement"; and it perpetuates inequalities. "It actually covers up current class differences in India." "From confrontations with the backward castes, forward-caste Hindus seem to move easily to pogroms against Untouchables and Muslims."

Fox's anthropological concern with culture is in its sanction of social inequalities. The cultural change he spotlights is redress of those inequalities, and Gandhi is an excellent protagonist. The Mahatma fought against both British imperial hegemony and Indian caste and religious inequalities. Early chapters situate Gandhi's reformist cultural synthesis within a continuum of earlier nationalists. Later ones follow his legacy downhill in the post-independence period as it was hijacked by the voluntaristic daydream of Vinoba Bhave, the centralizing political vision of the Congress Party, and finally, painfully, the militant, sometimes violent Hindu nationalism of the Rashtriya Swayamsewak Sangh and its political party ancillaries, now the Bharatiya Janata Parishad.

Fox characterizes his own study of Gandhi—a mature native informant of great acuity and an activist of great power—as a new form of cultural anthropology, a study of the individual in his society, mediated by the anthropologist's insights. At the same time, it provides an opportunity to examine a truly humane utopian vision. Gandhi formulated a working theory of his own culture at risk in the face of British cultural and political hegemony and indigenous social cruelty. Through his old-new methods of *ahimsa* (nonviolence), *satyagraha* (truth force, nonviolent resistance), and *swadeshi* (use of indigenous materials and concepts), he fought to sustain and enhance that culture and bring it to individual and national *swaraj* (self-rule).

Gandhi anticipated the corrosiveness of organized politics. At independence he urged his followers to abandon electoral politics in favor of social service. Today's corrupt, undisciplined, violent political parties reveal only the wreckage of Gandhian utopia. There are voluntary movements, not examined by Fox, which do, however, stress a Gandhian vision with some success, such as the Chipko environmental movement in the north and several working-class women's organizations, especially the Self-Employed Women's Association in Ahmadabad, a latter-day spin-off of Gandhi's own textile labor union. But, in general, Fox is unfortunately correct in lamenting the passing of Gandhian utopia. His presentation of Gandhi's commitment to active experimentation in reforming society and politics, based on one's best available truth, challenges us to do better, both as scholars and as citizens.

HOWARD SPODEK

Temple University
Philadelphia
Pennsylvania

FRANKEL, FRANCINE R. and M.S.A. RAO, eds. *Dominance and State Power in Modern India: Decline of a Social Order.* Vol. 1. Pp. xv, 443. Delhi: Oxford University Press, 1989. $19.95.

In this collection of eight essays, edited by Francine Frankel and M.S.A. Rao, the relationship between power and dominance in India is examined, particularly their role in effecting social change. The focus is identified in the introductory essay by Frankel as the "articulation of changing relationships between social dominance and political power." It is a theme echoed by Rao in the second essay, "Some Conceptual Issues in the Study of Caste, Class, Ethnicity and Dominance."

The empirical essays that follow explore the proposition that old power elites—in the six states examined here—are giving way to "new social formations" and that these are gradually seizing the reins of government and the instruments of dominance wielded by traditional elites. All but two of the authors have found that new elites are emerging as the old ones increasingly lose legitimacy.

The exceptions are in Tamil Nadu and Bihar, examined by, respectively, D. A. Washbrook and Frankel. In both, the Brahmans' community, for long dominant, lost the legitimacy it once enjoyed. No other castes emerged to fill the void, however. The consequences of this have been far more distressing for Bihar, as Frankel's essay demonstrates, than for Tamil Nadu, where the multiplicity of castes, along with the statewide appeal of anti-Brahman Dravidianism and Tamil nationalism, have curbed destablilizing trends. In Bihar, however, the breakdown of the Brahmanic social order resulted in chaos and violence.

In Uttar Pradesh, Karnataka, and Andhra Pradesh, on the other hand, where new castes have emerged as dominant, stability has been maintained but at the price of a very slow pace of change. Land reforms, though modest, have tended to dissipate—but not necessarily to neutralize—the forces of instability. As Zoya Hassan's essay on Uttar Pradesh shows, the patterns of dominance over the traditionally disadvantaged groups remain the same.

In Karnataka and Andhra Pradesh, other features account for the greater stability that characterizes the political process. James Manor, for example, stresses the greater cohesiveness of Karnataka's people, compared to most other states. He suggests further that the more or less equitable distribution of land and other "key resources" may explain why social and political divisions are not as deep and wide as in other states.

In Andhra Pradesh, more than in most other states, the change in patterns of dominance has resulted in far more equitable political conditions for the most disadvantaged elements of society—at the local level, at any rate. Here, says G. Ram Reddy, the increased representation of lower castes, untouchables, and tribals in local governmental and political institutions has compelled the upper castes increasingly to share power. At the state level, says Reddy, there has been no "qualitative change" except perhaps for the shift of domination away from the Brahmans toward other upper castes.

The fastest pace of change has undoubtedly been experienced in Kerala. K. C. Alexander attributes this to the impact of Christianity and communism on Kerala's old social order, which was thoroughly shaken by such egalitarian ideologies and organizations.

We turn now to the conceptual contributions of the editors, starting with Rao's essay, wherein he ponders on the many theorists who have analyzed the dramatic changes in India, while almost as many disagreed about their causes and the process of change. He limits his discussion to the "controversial views" of Marx and Weber, whose models of change

have emerged as dominant. While Marx asserts that power and dominance depend on class relations, Weber argues that "classes, status and parties" are dependent on the distribution of power in a community.

Rao departs from both approaches, viewing concepts like caste and class as "heuristically distinct domains," meaning, presumably, that while such constructs may have a particular meaning in Marxist or Weberian theory, Rao chooses to treat them as independent of any theoretical scheme. He does, however, differentiate dominance as a form of power characteristic of society from political power, which entails a monopoly over the legitimate use of force and is distinctive of the state.

Since independence, as noted elsewhere, "new social formations" are increasingly involved in the maintenance of social and political order, as well as in the process of social and political change. Frankel tries to explain these changing patterns of dominance and power through a "new logic of reasoning," offered to help us understand "the historical processes of social change under Indian conditions." This "new logic" rests on Frankel's analytical distinction between dominance and power. The need for this arises, says Frankel, because of the inadequacies of the "old" logics. One of these underpins the "developmentalist" model of social change, first adopted by Almond and Coleman in their 1960 study on political development. A major inadequacy of this is its ethnocentric tendencies, which persist despite efforts to exorcise them.

The other "old" logic of social change is encompassed in the Marxist model—which, incidentally, is incorrectly equated with "dependency theory" on page 15. This model is also found lacking because Marxist analysts of Indian society have yet to agree on basics like the mode of production in India or on the identity of the class with the most revolutionary potential.

Finally, Frankel departs from both the developmentalist and the Marxist models by dispensing with any "theory of history, whether linear and evolutionary, or dialectical and revolutionary." She and the contributing authors, says Frankel, "agreed on the tactical and strategic utility" of excluding such worldviews "from the common approach."

While a welcome and useful study of an important topic, Frankel and Rao's analysis has some weaknesses, which blemish an otherwise fine work. Principal among these is a lack of clarity in the crucial distinction between dominance and power. Both terms are defined by Frankel as an "exercise" or "exertion" of authority (page 2), which in turn is defined by Rao as "legitimized power" (page 40). Further, dominance in society means in essence the "power of command," while political power is equated with a monopoly by the state in the use of force. Upon reflection, it becomes clear that such distinctions are equivalent to those made between influence and power, a path which, though well traveled, has yet to bring us to its final destination. Second, it seems inappropriate to dispense with a worldview, or at least to remain silent about it, simply in order to avoid arguments for the sake of a more "fruitful intellectual collaboration on other major issues of substantive importance." Finally, a concluding chapter to round out the analysis is sorely needed. A second volume is referred to in this work, but it was not in print at the time of this writing. Presumably, all conclusions will be found there, but their absence from volume 1 has introduced some uncertainty and perhaps unfairness in the assessment of the present work.

Given these weaknesses, it must be stressed that ambitious tasks undertaken by a scholar are worth their salt only if they stimulate further thought and questions. This volume has been immensely successful in that respect.

MARY C. CARRAS

Rutgers University
Camden
New Jersey

MARTIN, DAVID. *Tongues of Fire: The Explosion of Protestantism in Latin America.* Pp. xiii, 352. Cambridge, MA: Basil Blackwell, 1990. $29.95.

Tongues of Fire is an awe-inspiring work. It is an extraordinary accomplishment of scholarship, both in scope and depth, on an increasingly relevant albeit poorly studied topic. David Martin examines the spread of Evangelical Protestantism throughout Latin America in a way that no other author has, in spite of the number of studies on religion, society, and politics produced in the recent past.

The book is divided into five parts. Part 1 covers the historical and theoretical foundations from the comparative perspective of Anglo and Latin cultural patterns. Part 2 focuses on the past and present of Evangelical Protestantism in the region, including case studies of Brazil—the most dramatic instance of the mushrooming of Protestantism—Chile, Argentina, Ecuador, El Salvador, Guatemala, and Mexico, among others. Part 3 presents comparative case studies within and without the region, including examples from Africa and Asia. Part 4 tackles analytical issues at the heart of the sociology of religion, such as the impact of Protestantism on economic and political culture. Finally, part 5 offers conclusions.

Martin argues that Pentecostalism "shifts religion away from the core structures of society, necessarily rooted in hierarchy, power and violence, towards the cultural realm." He adds that "Methodism and Pentecostalism alike construct models of equality, fraternity and peace-ability in the religious enclaves of *culture*, but do not generalize from these in terms of coherent world views." The central research question revolves around what, if any, economic and political repercussions the conservative worldview generates. To answer it, Martin resorts to a variety of data and methods, ranging from historical comparisons to biographical testimonies.

Based on these approaches and sources, Martin reaches several insightful conclusions. First, Pentecostal reproduction in Latin America differs from country to country, for indigenous societies do not merely copy but translate imported cultural patterns. Therefore, Latin America is not falling victim to "Americanization"—even if this is a misnomer—via Pentecostalism, a fiery controversy in the literature. On the contrary, Martin claims that Evangelical religions in the region are going native. Second, Pentecostalism "has provided a vehicle of autonomy and advancement for some sections of the middle class."

Tongues of Fire could be strengthened by fleshing out some of the case studies and extending the footnotes, but these are minor suggestions for an already ambitious and fulfilling work. Martin's book will set trends, inspire informed debate, and provoke thought for a long time to come, perhaps the true marks of great scholarship.

DAMIAN J. FERNANDEZ

Florida International University
Miami

EUROPE

CAMPBELL, JOAN. *Joy in Work, German Work: The National Debate, 1800-1945*. Pp. xi, 431. Princeton, NJ: Princeton University Press, 1989. $37.50.

Joan Campbell has written what she terms "a social history of ideas"—in particular, of the ideas of German intellectuals about work as these have developed over the past two centuries. The theme is a fascinating and important one. Certainly, questions of how modern conditions of work transform the worker and shape political community have been at the center of major traditions of theoretical and political inquiry in Germany and elsewhere. These problems appeared earliest in the writings of socialists—Marx and less well-known German radicals—who were, well before the era of industrial capitalism, developing a critique of the logic of capitalism that centered on its impact on the work life and very personality of the worker. Campbell reminds us, however, that theorists emerging from other, very different theoretical perspectives also took on the problem of work in the nineteenth century. For example, the conservative sociologist Wilhelm Heinrich von Riehl, best known for his studies of family and German folk traditions, also established himself as a pioneer in the study of work.

In the socialist tradition, the early theory had already established what would remain a persistent tension for leftist intellectuals and organizers: whether their ultimate task was "to humanize labor or to abolish it." Campbell argues that, in effect, socialists concentrated mainly on the latter route, through, for example, tactics that emphasized cutting the workday. The ideological result was that the terrain of the discussion of the character of work itself, and of methods for reforming it, was dominated by bourgeois opponents of socialism.

The chapters on the history of the science of work from the turn of the century through the Weimar era are really the core and richest contribution of the study. A whole range of theories and organizations come under discussion: the *Kathedersozialisten* who formed so distinctive an element in the German ideological spectrum of the turn of the century, German "Fordists" and "Taylorites" who drew on an international currency of the 1920s, the German entrepreneurs of the Weimar era who engaged in an ideological battle for the hearts and minds of German workers even while they made determined efforts to combat the free—socialist—unions, as well as the advocates of industrial democracy who hoped to offer an alternative to class conflict. Campbell also documents the efforts of these various camps to develop techniques for empirical research—by the 1920s, surveys of workers' attitudes toward their work were becoming commonplace. Even if, as Campbell suggests, these surveys were heavily structured by the preconceived notions of the responses, they differed from their predecessors in the willingness of their creators to depart from the realm of abstract speculation and attempt to connect their notions with the experience of work as articulated by workers.

The study also documents the clear connections between these ideas about work and Nazi efforts to alter the situation and consciousness of German workers in the Third Reich. That some of the earlier movements and ideas fed into Nazi programs such as "Strength through Joy" is logical, but the comparative question of how much this was a peculiarly German tradition remains open. Campbell also pushes her data too far in her attempt here to infer workers' attitudes from scattered biographical data, whereas in the preceding analysis she was consistently more careful in attributing ideas and agendas concerning work to particular individuals and institutions and skeptical of drawing any connections between her evidence and actual workers' views. Certainly workers' attitudes toward the Nazi state, and that state's effort to de-

fuse political arguments phrased in class terms, need study. But Campbell's departure from her analysis of intellectuals and organizations to draw far-reaching conclusions about broad classes of German society—for example, that the "German 'workers' seem to have adhered to an ethic of work hardly distinguishable from that of their 'bourgeois' compatriots"—is debatable and quite beyond the range of the data at hand.

As a foray into the social history of ideas, this is an engaging and promising study, even if it might have pushed harder against the limits of the genre of the history of ideas. Campbell explores the writings and activities of a broad range of individuals, thus avoiding the limitations of studying only the great thinkers who used to be the mainstay of intellectual history. The complexity of the ideological landscape she sketches is a strength, even though it is confusing to follow its contours. The use of biography is effective, but more sustained treatment of representative individuals, as well as more serious efforts to examine workers' attitudes—the subject of study of an increasing number of labor historians—would help to clarify the argument and root particular attitudes about work in locations in the social structure as well as in the political spectrum. The growing literature on intersections between work and family history would also have much to offer such an analysis. In the era of preindustrial capitalism with its incipient proletarianization, before Marx and Riehl, changes in the work force were bound up with changes in family organization. Campbell's observation of the intellectuals' lack of concern with women workers raises the related question of how work itself was defined and bounded to exclude virtually all work done in the household. Attention to social context would push Campbell to think in more analytic terms, to actually place her multitude of individual stories and perspectives into a social landscape—indeed, to create what would be even more emphatically a social history of ideas.

MARY JO MAYNES
University of Minnesota
Minneapolis

FORREST, ALAN. *Conscripts and Deserters: The Army and French Society during the Revolution and Empire.* Pp. viii, 294. New York: Oxford University Press, 1989. No price.

This splendid book, published during the year of the bicentennial of the endlessly controversial French Revolution, exemplifies the influence of the more recent French historiographical revolution in such conventional areas of research as military history. Investigating new questions and new sources, French, English, and American social historians have rewritten much of early modern European history in recent decades. Looking at the epic of the making of the modern world from a different perspective, from below, they have asked what the Reformation or Absolutism or the Revolution meant to ordinary people rather than to jurists or intellectuals. They have worked their way through the archives of provincial villages as well as capital cities in order to determine how these developments both reshaped and were shaped by traditional structures of life and death, belief, community, and conflict.

Revolutionary legislatures in Paris, of course, did demolish many of the building blocks of the political, social, and religious order of the Old Regime, from the monarchy to the calendar. They did not, however, manage to transform the mentality of the French people overnight or reorganize the country without massive difficulties. In principle, they sanctified liberty and glorified unity. In reality, they struggled with dissension and resorted to

coercion. Many historians have discussed the more spectacular episodes of opposition to Revolutionary changes emanating from the capital, most notably the popular uprisings in the Vendée. Alan Forrest has studied the less dramatic and less ideological but more pervasive resistance to military recruitment in more than a dozen of the 83 departments.

Devoted to unknown conscripts and deserters rather than to celebrated generals and heroes, this book deals not with battles abroad for the exportation of Revolutionary ideals but with battles back home for the consolidation of Parisian authority over the French population. With admirable attention to local circumstances and regional variations, Forrest explains how and why peasants and townspeople, like their ancestors and their descendants, resisted the efforts of the central government to mobilize the human resources of the country. In fascinating detail, he describes, for example, how men mutilated themselves or purchased replacements in order to avoid conscription and how communities made it difficult for outside authorities to apprehend and punish men who deserted the army. Forrest cites dozens of arresting flesh-and-blood cases, and he synthesizes all of them into the larger context of the modernization of the French state.

JEFFREY MERRICK
University of Wisconsin
Milwaukee

JARAUSCH, KONRAD H. *The Unfree Professions: German Lawyers, Teachers, and Engineers, 1900-1950.* Pp. xiv, 352. New York: Oxford University Press, 1990. No price.

This pioneering volume focuses on the status and attitudes of members of three selected professions—lawyers, *Gymnasium* (academic high school) teachers, and engineers—in the half century from the late German empire through the Weimar and Nazi to the early postwar West German eras.

Konrad H. Jarausch, a leading historian of modern Germany and professor at the University of North Carolina, is interested not only in writing a history of three important professions within the context of changing German political systems but also in examining within the parameters of society, culture, and polity the reasons why so many professionals assisted the Nazi cause. Thus half of the chapters are devoted to the breakdown of liberal professionalism in the Weimar period, the rise of Nazi professionalism, and its "Germanizing" and deprofessionalization process. The role of professionals in the pre-Nazi and post-Nazi periods receives comparatively less attention.

Most lawyers, teachers, and engineers were intent, partly through their professional associations, on increasing their income or status, on establishing their own identity, and on maintaining autonomy from the state. Jarausch notes that the outlook of the politically conservative professionals was hardly "cosmopolitan, egalitarian, or progressive." For instance, in early Weimar the association of lawyers considered women "not suited to becoming attorneys or judges." It took a legislative act in 1922 for women to enter the profession. Continuing prejudice meant that one decade later only 79 of them had become attorneys.

Jarausch notes that, even though the professionals were conservative in outlook, the majority during the late Weimar era did not endorse the concepts of Nazism; indeed, only 3-5 percent had become Nazi party members prior to 1933. Yet because many professionals had a nationalist outlook, the Nazis, once in power, had little difficulty in co-opting them with respect to their cause and in purging Jews and other "undesirables" from the professions. Soon most lawyers, teachers,

and engineers embraced Nazism and did not attempt to stop the Nazis from "purifying" the professions. As a consequence, the professionals helped to support the Nazi dictatorship in its domestic and foreign policies. In the aftermath of the Nazi catastrophe, most of them were able to continue in their careers. For pragmatic reasons, they had accepted the democratic system even though their commitment to it was far from complete.

Jarausch's valuable and original study, based on an array of source materials, hardly makes references to the role and attitudes of professionals in other countries. A comparative study by a team of scholars would be welcome.

GERARD BRAUNTHAL

University of Massachusetts
Amherst

MLYNAR, ZDENEK. *Can Gorbachev Change the Soviet Union? International Dimensions of Political Reform.* Translated by Marian Sling and Ruth Tosek. Pp. viii, 184. Boulder, CO: Westview Press, in cooperation with the Austrian Institute for International Affairs, 1990. $28.50.

HAZAN, BARUCH A. *Gorbachev and His Enemies: The Struggle for Perestroika.* Pp. vi, 335. Boulder, CO: Westview Press, 1990. $49.50.

The original purpose of Mlynar's book "was to analyze the specifically Soviet historical and ideological conditions for a change of the system that could take place without dangerous disruption." In chapter 1 Mlynar analyzes the influence of Russian and Soviet historical experience on the process of current reform. Chapter 2 is devoted to the discussion of the role of the Communist Party in the reform of the Soviet system and to the question of how political institutions are to be changed in order to establish in the country a democratic process of decision making. In chapter 3 Mlynar deals with the international aspect of the Soviet reform program, pointing out that the main impact of Gorbachev's New Thinking is primarily evident in foreign relations.

Mlynar's analysis is sound and logical, but his conclusions exemplify the simple truth that predicting the future is a thankless task. The book was written in the summer of 1988, and by the time it was translated and published, in 1990, most of its conclusions had become irrelevant. Mlynar is correct in asserting that reform is inevitable and that real change in the Soviet Union will take many years, but he deludes himself by believing that, instead of replacing the existing institutions with a new democratically elected system of political and economic management, the Soviet Union can be changed by reforming an old compromised and corrupt system of government. Mlynar underestimates the danger of national strife in the USSR; he does not anticipate the abolition of one-party rule, nor does he expect the breakup of the Soviet-East European bloc.

A college classmate of Mikhail Gorbachev and a leading Communist bureaucrat in Czechoslovakia in the 1960s, Mlynar, currently residing in Vienna, is still under the influence of his Soviet education. He is unable to foresee the appearance of new anti-Communist forces in Soviet society, nor can he envision the disintegration of the USSR. Furthermore, he overestimates the power of Communist ideology to hold together the Soviet state. He claims that one "cannot expect official Soviet ideology to abandon either its declared objectives (the building of communism) or its traditional sources (especially Lenin's ideas). The idea that this is what can be expected from the reform movement is among the unrealistic notions accepted in the West." It is paradoxical that Mlynar expects democratic change from the very people who stifle reform and sabotage *perestroika*.

Hazan's book, *Gorbachev and His Enemies*, convincingly illustrates the opposition to reform. It attempts to assess Gorbachev's style and methods of pursuing his domestic and international goals, and it gives a day-by-day detailed account, from 1985 to 1989, of the political infighting and the struggle for power in the Soviet leadership. According to Hazan, Gorbachev is the great reformer who is opposed by party conservatives, state bureaucrats, Russian nationalists, and democratic radicals, as well as by the army and the KGB. Special attention is devoted to the relationship of Gorbachev with Ligachev and Yeltsin. Hazan suggests that *perestroika* is hampered by a silent coalition of conservative ideologists and the bureaucratic apparatus, but there is no open anti-Gorbachev defiance, because there is no alternative to reform. Gorbachev's enemies represent different interest groups fighting for the preservation of the status quo and for their own narrow group interests. Hazan provides the reader with a wealth of information useful to the future historian, and yet he fails to give us a definite notion of the objectives and goals of Gorbachev's policies, nor does he clarify the actual meaning of the term *perestroika*. It is commonly accepted that *glasnost* is one of the great achievements of *perestroika*, but it is also obvious that much of Gorbachev's *perestroika* is a spontaneous reaction to current political, economic, and social factors rather than a well-designed and well-administered plan for economic and democratic reform.

The pace of political change in the Soviet Union is so rapid that most books about the current situation in the USSR are outdated before they are published. This notwithstanding, the books under review offer a number of interesting and useful insights and provide the future historian with a wealth of information and ideas that will be assessed by future scholars from new and different perspectives.

N. N. SHNEIDMAN

University of Toronto
Ontario
Canada

UNITED STATES

ALLEN, MICHAEL. *Western Rivermen, 1763-1861: Ohio and Mississippi Boatmen and the Myth of the Alligator Horse.* Pp. xii, 261. Baton Rouge: Louisiana State University Press, 1990. $25.00.

Ohio and Mississippi flatboatmen played a substantial role in American cultural mythology during the nineteenth century, symbolizing virtually superhuman capacities in shooting, fighting, and general hell-raising. They also played a major role in opening up the Middle West and Great Plains economically, from their pioneering days in the late eighteenth century, when up to 3000 rivermen plied the trade, to the heyday of the flatboat during the early industrial revolution, when as many as 200,000 boatmen between 1823 and 1861 carried a growing array of raw materials, foodstuffs, immigrants, and outright tourists.

This meticulously researched book provides the first extensive study of the boatmen, and it will surely become a standard account. Michael Allen consulted a wide variety of archives, turning up an impressive array of firsthand statements by boatmen and, for the industrial period, by some of their passengers and other observers. A host of topics flesh out the account: we learn the dangers of river travel, the relationship between the boatmen and riverbank cities from Pittsburgh to New Orleans, the cargoes the boats carried, the kind of people who served the boats, and the recreations they enjoyed.

This is, furthermore, a labor of love by an author not only tireless in inquiry but also directly and deliberately experienced through three years as a riverboat deckhand; the enthusiasm for the subject sparks the writing and adds to its impact.

Two analytical issues set the framework for the account. First, Allen plays with the tension between cultural myths about the vulgar prowess of the riverboatmen, current particularly toward the middle of the nineteenth century but surviving in Disney versions even to the present day, and the more prosaic realities of their actual working lives. There is some ambiguity here, as Allen vacillates between a myth-reality contrast and an admission that important facets of the myth corresponded to common behaviors. The second interpretive pole, on the whole more successful in execution, involves a clear periodization between the initial riverboat phase, to the 1820s, and the industrial heyday, when boat transport so greatly expanded and behaviors became more subdued, family involvements more common. During this second period, interestingly, the riverboat myth helped boatmen themselves define their identity, perhaps explaining—though here Allen does not tread—the absence of class consciousness in a more conventional sense even as commercial organization expanded and technological competition from the steamboats mounted. An epilogue deals with a third period, of outright decline, but in briefer compass.

The study has its weaknesses. What riverboatmen did in later life is not very clear, though some used their labor to supplement an agricultural youth while a few committed to merchant status. Explanations of the currency of riverboat mythology, referring to early-industrial Americans unhappy with their own lives, are mere assertions. Perhaps most disappointing is the absence of comparison with other labor groups, including merchant seamen who have been extensively studied for the same period. Allen makes little effort to situate his study in labor history more generally.

In the end, the study offers most to readers interested in regional development patterns, from Pittsburgh's early entrepreneurial bustle to Natchez's lead in riverine vice. Allen's careful romance with worlds we have lost comes through as well and sustains the book even in the absence of consistently ambitious analysis.

PETER N. STEARNS

Carnegie Mellon University
Pittsburgh
Pennsylvania

ARKES, HADLEY. *Beyond the Constitution.* Pp. 278. Princeton, NJ: Princeton University Press, 1990. $24.95.

Arkes is willin'. Writing in an engaging style and with considerable earnestness, he surveys a broad range of constitutional issues, under the beamish—Arkes' favorite word—conviction that all difficulties will dissolve if only we will look to the "universal" and "eternal" moral principles that guided the constitutional framers.

Along the way, Arkes generates some worthy insights, especially into the contemporary relevance of the Federalists' objections to the Bill of Rights and into the futility of debates on and off the Supreme Court regarding which constitutional clauses ought to govern various controversies, when the decisive questions often turn out to be the same. Arkes' main point, however, is to establish his methodology of constitutional decision making by moral reasoning, and here his book fails.

If we assume that any moral principles merit the ontological status of universal truths, to nominate principles of federalism for that honor is almost bizarre. Yet Arkes' most persistent contention is that a priori moral reasoning will establish that there are no powers proper to any legitimate government that are not constitutionally available to our federal government.

Moral reasoning cannot determine the division of powers between the tiers of a federal system, and, despite his rhetoric, Arkes never attempts to show otherwise. He relies mainly on a naive essentialism—if the federal government lacked any legitimate powers, the Constitution would not have created a "nation"—bolstered by intentionalism that actually contradicts his universalist methodology. The force underlying Arkes' conclusion about federal powers derives not from a priori reasoning but from the empirical findings of Morton Grodzins that the tiers of government in our federal system share rather than divide their functions.

Arkes contends that the constitutional reference to "all Cases, in Law and Equity," empowers the federal judiciary to apply not only technical rules of law but the "reasoning spirit" of equity. Perhaps he is unaware that the separate courts of equity were nearly as swamped in technicalities as the law courts. Arkes should read *Bleak House.*

Elsewhere, Arkes enlists the great Chief Justice John Marshall as a soldier in the crusade against legal positivism. He does not mention Marshall's opinion in *Johnson* v. *M'Intosh,* as hardheaded a piece of legal positivism as one could ask for.

Arkes' basic problem, however, is that even if there are moral truths capable of resolving constitutional conflicts, he admits in his conclusion that there is no agreement on what those truths are. If Arkes and I agree on a principle to govern a particular case, it will make no difference whether that principle is "universal" or "true." If we disagree, we shall be brought no closer to resolution of the case by a shared belief that whichever of us is right is "universally," "eternally," and "truly" right.

Ockham's razor, applied to *Beyond the Constitution*, would leave some worthy ideas in this book but would cut out the core.

DANIEL HAYS LOWENSTEIN

University of California
Los Angeles

BEAN, LEE L., GERALDINE P. MINEAU, and DOUGLAS L. ANDERTON. *Fertility Change on the American Frontier: Adaptation and Innovation.* Pp. xiii, 295. Berkeley: University of California Press, 1990. No price.

This volume represents over 15 years of work by the authors and others in creating and analyzing a large, complex, microlevel data base for the study of the fertility transition of a segment of the American population. During the 1970s, Lee Bean conceived the idea of the Mormon Historical Demography Project. Since then, he and his colleagues—among others, his present coauthors, Geraldine Mineau and Douglas Anderton, who were both his doctoral students—have used the resources of the Genealogical Society of the Church of Jesus Christ of Latter Day Saints (the Mormon Church) to construct a genealogical data base with over 185,000 families, representing approximately 1.2 million individuals. The study centers on the nearly 200,000 females born between 1800 and 1899 who participated in the migration from Europe, New England, and the Midwest to settle and develop Utah. Most of these women and their descendants were associated with the Mormon Church, and this association provided, via a theological imperative of the church, the rich genealogies for the data base.

While the use of genealogy to study historical demographic phenomena is not unique—as is seen in the recent book by John Knodel on a sample of German villages in the eighteenth and nineteenth centuries and also Robert Fogel's work on nineteenth-century American mortality—the work is difficult, time consuming, and resource intensive. Although the Mormon Historical Demography Project's data base contains more than just the records of individuals linked by family ties—dates of birth, death, marriage, birth and death of children, and so on—the primary focus here is overall fertility, marital fertility, and nuptiality. The authors analyze structure, secular change, and differentials in these demographic behaviors.

The demographic transition, and even the basic demographic conditions, in the nineteenth-century United States were unusual. Fertility was quite high in the late eighteenth and early nineteenth centuries—for example, there were total fertility rates of 7-8—especially at the frontier. Fertility declined from around 1800 continuously, considerably before the decline in northern and western Europe, whose fertility transition—with the notable exception of France—dated from about 1870 or later. Although the American fertility decline was due largely to adjustment of marital fertility, as it was in Europe, there were also changes in nuptiality. The age at first marriage for females rose from a relatively young 18-19 years in 1800 to moderate levels—about 23-24 years—in 1900. Western and northern Europe already, by the early nineteenth century, had developed the so-called European marriage pattern of late female age at marriage and significant proportions of women who never married. This pattern limited potential adjustment of overall fertility through nuptiality. The demographic transition in the

United States also did not follow the standard pattern. Fertility fell prior to mortality, the mortality decline dating from only about the 1870s. The American fertility transition began when the United States was still largely rural and agrarian, and fertility in both rural and urban places declined in parallel. The standard explanations do not easily account for this.

Considerable attention has been paid to the nineteenth-century American fertility transition with the use of published census data to create child-woman ratios; it should be remembered that the United States was not fully covered by vital statistics until 1933. Micro data from census manuscripts and some local records have also been brought to bear, providing estimates of age-specific overall and marital fertility rates and of nuptiality. But genealogical data have not, as yet—with the exceptions of the work of Wahl and of Kasakoff and Adams—shed much light on the process. The present work does much to fill that gap. Unfortunately, it deals with a peculiar, though very interesting, subpopulation in a peculiar region in a nation that experienced a peculiar demographic transition. Beyond the problem of how much one can learn from the United States in general, there remains the issue of whether families in Utah tell us enough about the general American experience. Overall, I believe that a good deal can be learned with the appropriate degree of caution.

One of the principal themes of the book involves whether fertility decline can be described as a behavioral innovation, with accompanying diffusion, or as an adaptation to changed socioeconomic circumstances. Related to this debate are the questions of whether pre-decline fertility was natural fertility—that is, where progression from one parity to another is independent of family size—and whether fertility decline involved only stopping, or termination, behavior—ter-

minating childbearing when the desired number of births has been achieved—or a combination of stopping and spacing behavior. The authors come down in favor of the adaptation view and produce evidence of considerable resort to the spacing of births as well as early termination of childbearing. Actually, early cohorts of women on the Utah frontier experienced an increase in fertility—both from a rise in age-specific marital fertility and a decline in marriage age—which the authors call the "frontier effect." Later, for the cohorts of women born after about 1850, fertility decline set in as the region became more urban, more commercialized, and more integrated into the national economy.

One of the interesting findings in this volume is that for the cohorts practicing family limitation, residence was more important than religion in determining the extent of control, but there was a significant interaction between them. Nonetheless, fertility declined among all religious categories and in both rural and urban areas. A significant part of the transition can be explained as a shift in the behavior of women to birth-spacing patterns already existing in the population. That is, it was a compositional shift to existing behavior, not diffusion of innovative birth-spacing behavior. Indeed, one of the most fascinating things about the results is the consistency of spacing patterns across time within parity groups, that is, women grouped by levels of children ever born. There is evidence, using Bongaarts's model of the proximate determinants of fertility, that there were voluntary—as opposed to involuntary and biological—reductions in fertility; that major population subgroups shared in the decline; that lengthened interbirth intervals accompanied a decline in parity; that there was no geographically bounded or diffused reliance on truncation; that there was considerable heterogeneity in the combinations of marriage

age, spacing, timing, and termination of childbearing, suggesting a multiphasic response in fertility decline; and that an explanation based on adjustment to changed socioeconomic circumstances fits the data better than does an explanation based on behavioral innovation spreading through the population.

Overall, this book is a must for those with interests in historical demography in general and the American experience in particular. It is dense and filled with data and tables, and some of the more abstract sections make heavy going. But it represents an enormously detailed study of a particular population that suggests the complexity of the fertility transition, especially in the United States, where the frontier experience and longtime period of decline may have conditioned particular forms of adaptive demographic behavior.

MICHAEL R. HAINES
Colgate University
Hamilton
New York

GINZBERG, LORI D. *Women and the Work of Benevolence: Morality, Politics, and Class in the Nineteenth-Century United States*. Pp. xii, 230. New Haven, CT: Yale University Press, 1990. $25.00.

In this lucid and important book, Lori Ginzberg argues that in the middle decades of the nineteenth century, the "ideology of benevolent femininity" evolved synchronously with other changes in American reform ideology and political culture. In the 1830s and 1840s an ideology of female roles in charity and reform offered what she calls a "conflation of femaleness and morality," a rhetoric of women's superiority and solidarity, even across classes, based on common natures and gendered experiences. Cultural and political developments in the 1850s and 1860s, however, led to a post-Civil War consensus that the work of philanthropy was essentially a class-based, not gender-based, activity that properly reflected the techniques and philosophy of the business culture it sprang from.

Ginzberg effectively synthesizes the arguments of other historians while proposing her own vigorous thesis. She agrees with George Fredrickson that the Civil War saw the emergence of the efficiency ideal in charity work, but she finds its roots in the 1850s, a time of decreased optimism about the degree of change achievable through social action. Parallel with the absorption and truncation of antislavery by mainstream American politics, the culture of benevolence retreated from reform to institutionalism and statism. Among women reformers and women's rights activists, the rhetoric of female exceptionalism shifted crucially: "They demanded ... that women's status be 'raised' to a level of equality with men rather than that men should aspire to the standard supposedly set by women." From here on, Ginzberg argues, women's work in philanthropy and reform would strive to be complementary to rather than exemplary for that of men.

Ginzberg emphasizes the generational component of the ideological shift of the 1850s and 1860s. Those reformers' children not alienated from the work of benevolence or reform either took a reform commitment for granted or, more poignantly, felt themselves unworthy of the heroism of the previous generation. Too young for the conversion experiences of their elders, they found a locus for their passions in the war itself and threw themselves into the work of the Sanitary Commission and local soldiers' aid societies. And the volunteer ideology of the wartime culture, as Fredrickson pointed out, was corporate efficiency and discipline, not sentimental humanitarianism. For Josephine Shaw Lowell and others, the war became the central experience shaping their lives and careers.

The major amendment I would offer to Ginzberg's argument would be to complicate its postwar sector. There were middle-class rebels against the cold efficiency of the charity organization movement even before the Progressive decades, and within the Gilded Age Protestantism that Ginzberg sees as defensively conservative were theologians and pastors absorbing from transatlantic sources the social Christianity that would form a counterrhetoric to middle-class reactionism after the Civil War. Overall, Ginzberg has done an excellent piece of work, intelligent, gracefully written, and creatively cognizant of its historiographical context.

MINA CARSON

Oregon State University
Corvallis

GOODSTEIN, ANITA SHAFER. *Nashville, 1780-1860: From Frontier to City.* Pp. xv, 278. Gainesville: University of Florida Press, 1989. $29.95.

The years between the American Revolution and the Civil War witnessed the remarkable growth and expansion of the United States. A rising population and a dynamic economy accompanied the dramatic westward push of the nation. Anita Shafer Goodstein's history of early nineteenth-century Nashville, "a city emerging from the wilderness," provides a microcosmic view of that process of growth and change.

An isolated frontier fort in 1780, Nashville had emerged as a major economic center on the trans-Appalachian urban frontier by 1860. Goodstein emphasizes the degree to which the antebellum history of this rising western city was shaped by large economic and political forces. Three major themes run through the book, providing an interpretive

framework. First, Goodstein clearly demonstrates the powerful links between economic development and political power, between entrepreneurship and political leadership. Land speculation in the early years, and trade and banking later on, motivated Nashville's "expectant capitalists," who also tended to control political office. As Goodstein puts it, in early Nashville, it was "assumed that leadership belonged to the economically successful." Changing perceptions of community provide a second important theme, as family networks, voluntary associations, and a broadly inclusive Whig Party mediated social, economic, and political divisions in the growing city. Nashville's strong sense of community, however, ultimately foundered on the question of slavery and race, which provides Goodstein's third major organizing theme. Indeed, the sections on Nashville's free black and slave communities are among the strongest contributions of the book. Despite the travails of slavery and persistent white hostility, and lacking any political or economic power, Nashville's antebellum blacks built strong family networks and community institutions, especially churches and schools.

Goodstein's book remains mostly a local case study of western urban growth and change. Nevertheless, she has sought, with moderate success, to provide a broader interpretive context for understanding the growth of Nashville. She has demonstrated an awareness of contemporary historiographical currents in urban and social history, and she has incorporated some of the new research methodology of social history. She has made effective use, for instance, of manuscript census materials, tax lists, court records and wills, and land-grant records, as well as more traditional sources such as newspapers, political and church materials, and manuscript collections. This book, in short, adds importantly to our understanding of urban development on the western frontier in early nineteenth-century America.

RAYMOND A. MOHL

Florida Atlantic University
Boca Raton

HATCHER, PATRICK LLOYD. *The Suicide of an Elite: American Internationalists and Vietnam.* Pp. ix, 429. Stanford, CA: Stanford University Press, 1990. $35.00.

The Vietnam war was a tragedy of enormous proportions. More than 50,000 U.S. troops were killed and the United States lost the conflict. Patrick Lloyd Hatcher offers an explanation for the reasons underlying this debacle. His argument is that American national security planners made deliberate military, political, and economic errors that were largely avoidable.

Hatcher rejects Daniel Ellsberg's argument that Vietnam was a quagmire where one erroneous decision led to another. Instead, he argues that Vietnam policy represented an internal conflict between policy conservatives and liberals. American national security policymakers, in his view, were consciously aware of their goals and objectives. Unfortunately, they were wrong in their assumptions and knowledge of Southeast Asia.

Militarily, the conflict was never confined to Vietnam. Instead, U.S. forces were also required to contain Communist threats in Laos and Cambodia. The concept of limited war prevented an all-out assault on North Vietnam due to the fear of a Chinese intervention.

Politically, the war was a battle between Ngo Dinh Diem in the south and Ho Chi Minh in the north. When the Kennedy administration did nothing to stop the coup against Diem in 1963, South Vietnam was left with a very weak and ungovernable military coalition.

Hatcher is especially critical of the misperceptions of Presidents Kennedy and Johnson. Kennedy is blamed for the early escalation as part of the containment policy against Soviet expansionism. Johnson is portrayed as being overly aggressive, too involved in details, and highly deceptive in explaining war objectives to the American public.

None of Hatcher's arguments are new. His conclusions can be challenged in at least two respects. First, he is not at all convincing that American national security policymakers were cohesive. The title of the book is misleading. The elites did not commit suicide. Instead, their policies were suicidal. Second, Vietnam had a peculiarly regional rather than international character. While containment policy failed in Vietnam, it continued to work in Europe. Neither the Soviets nor the Chinese intervened directly with troops, even after the United States mined North Vietnam's harbors.

Hatcher's thesis is that American international elites competed rationally but ineffectively in their military, political, and economic strategies regarding Southeast Asia. Others have argued that policy goals concerning Vietnam were so inconsistent and confusing that they can be more effectively explained by flawed approaches to decision making. Hatcher's book could have been improved by considering Irving Janis's groupthink explanation, Barbara Tuchman's *March of Folly*, and Richard Gabriel's *Military Incompetence*.

ALAN SHANK

State University of New York
Geneseo

LANZA, MICHAEL L. *Agrarianism and Reconstruction Politics: The Southern Homestead Act.* Pp. x, 153. Baton Rouge: Louisiana State University Press, 1990. $22.50.

The tragedy of the Reconstruction, Michael Lanza suggests, is encapsulated in the history of the Southern Homestead Act of 1866. The act, in his view,

was a grand visionary attempt to legislatively right old wrongs, reorient the South's economy to bring it more into conformity with the rest of the country, and to inaugurate a massive social reform by providing a newly freed citizenry with an economic base for their future advancement (p. 4).

In opening up 46 million acres of federal lands in Alabama, Arkansas, Florida, Louisiana, and Mississippi to homesteading and in restricting speculation, this legislation provided the best hope for freedmen and poor whites in the South to gain land. The Southern Homestead Act failed to live up to its promise, however, and Lanza examines the host of contributing factors that explain why, including poor land quality, bureaucratic failures in the General Land Office, poor administration on the local level, concerted opposition from Southern landowners, and limited Republican commitment to equal rights.

Lanza's brief study is based on primary research in congressional records, the papers of the General Land Office, contemporary newspapers, and quantitative analysis of land records. Unfortunately, missing data made it impossible for him to draw "far-reaching conclusions" about who settled homesteads, although it is clear that only 6 percent of all the public land was proved up. Lanza highlights the perseverance of homesteaders, especially freedmen and freedwomen, who settled and worked the land in the face of seemingly insurmountable obstacles.

Working from the papers of George Julien, chair of the House Committee on Public Land, Lanza demonstrates that the Indiana congressman clearly desired to reshape Southern society, help the freedmen, and punish the South. This does not mean, however, that the Southern Homestead Act of 1866, which he shepherded through Congress, was a "massive social reform." On the contrary, the weight of the evidence presented by Lanza belies this claim. Indeed, Lanza concludes his book with the admission that "the program failed because the act was only a mere gesture in the right direction." Perhaps contemporary press and political leaders, who paid "scant" attention to the act, were right. Its significance should not be overestimated. That has been the judgment also of previous Reconstruction historians, whose sparse comments on the act remain largely unchallenged by this study.

MARK LAWRENCE KORNBLUH

Washington University
St. Louis
Missouri

RUSSELL, GREG. *Hans J. Morgenthau and the Ethics of American Statecraft.* Pp. 258. Baton Rouge: Louisiana State University Press, 1990. $27.50.

In his preface, Greg Russell writes that "the objective of this study is to differentiate Morgenthau's theory and philosophy of American realism from the normative roots and political concepts associated with the European heritage of *raison d'état*." This is indeed a theme that runs throughout the book. It is developed in some detail in the first chapter, with concise summaries of the contributions of Thucydides, Machiavelli, Richelieu, Hobbes, and Bismarck. If this were the central focus of the book, however, it would be of interest mainly to students of political philosophy. But, fortunately, most of the volume deals with the much more interesting subject of the views of Hans J. Morgenthau on diplomacy and statecraft, with emphasis on the national interest, power, and morality and with particular reference to U.S. foreign policy and diplomacy since World War II.

As is well known, Morgenthau was a leading exponent of political realism. His contention that the basis of foreign policy should be the national interest conceived in terms of power became one of the most frequently quoted aphorisms in the study of international relations. But many failed to perceive that this approach was deeply rooted in political philosophy and moral values. Russell's careful analysis helps to refute "the popular misconception that his [Morgenthau's] political thought is concerned exclusively with power to the neglect of purpose and morality." Frequent comparisons and contrasts of Morgenthau's realism with that of three other leading American exponents—George F. Kennan, Reinhold Niebuhr, and Walter Lippmann—add to the value of Russell's exposition.

Morgenthau was not only a profound scholar; he was also a political activist. He was a persistent critic of many aspects of post-World War II American foreign policy. As Russell observes, "Perhaps the central tenet of Morgenthau's criticism of United States foreign policy ... was that American responses abroad dissolved 'into a series of stereotyped reactions, organically connected neither with each other through an overall design nor with the interests of the nation.' " He believed, in Russell's words, that "American statesmen have persistently misunderstood the nature of foreign policy and its moral significance. They have often failed to perceive the real national interest, and the limits of military power."

A strong critic of the U.S. involvement in Vietnam, Morgenthau argued that the national interest could not be served by a war that was "politically aimless, militarily unpromising, and morally dubious." Because of such views, he incurred the wrath of many U.S. political leaders who were supporting and directing the war in Vietnam. I once heard him say that he had made Richard Nixon's hate list and that he regarded this as a distinction!

In the field of international relations, Hans J. Morgenthau was one of the few real giants. He was, as Russell points out, "perhaps the first American realist to develop a systematic and broad-gauge theory of international politics." His influence on the development of this field of inquiry has been tremendous. Those who were privileged to know him personally, including this reviewer, will remember him with affection as well as with deep respect.

NORMAN D. PALMER

University of Pennsylvania
Philadelphia

SCHMIDT, DAVID D. *Citizen Lawmakers: The Ballot Initiative Revolution.* Pp. xi, 345. Philadelphia: Temple University Press, 1989. $32.95.

Over the past two decades, the American political system has witnessed a marked increase in the use of the initiative and referendum to address important public concerns. Whether it be the case of setting limits on local property taxes or encouraging the inclusion of a nuclear freeze as a feature of national foreign policy, a growing number of American citizens have chosen the path of "legislating for themselves" with respect to these important political issues. In *Citizen Lawmakers: The Ballot Initiative Revolution*, David Schmidt endeavors to account for this sudden upsurge in the use of this basic form of direct democracy. He also seeks to provide some guidance for those who might try their own hand at this type of political participation.

In the first section of his book, Schmidt provides a broad overview of the origins of the initiative and referendum. He writes that the practice of direct legislation has its historical roots on both sides of the Atlantic, embracing, as it does, the spirit of the Swiss *Landsgemeinde* and the New England town meeting. Schmidt notes, however, that it was not until the latter part of the nineteenth century that the practices of initiative and referendum became widespread features of the American political landscape. He attributes their eventual emergence to the Populist and Progressive movements and stresses that their appeal has always been strongest where these two political movements had their largest impact—in the West and Midwest.

In addition to chronicling the subsequent decline of the initiative and referendum during the middle portion of the twentieth century, Schmidt provides a discussion of the arguments that have been traditionally advanced both in support of and in opposition to these methods of direct legislation. He notes the continuing reluctance of Americans to surrender all decision-making authority to their legislators and the suspicions harbored by the average voter that the common citizen's voice carries only limited influence in any legislative hall. Smith suggests that the initiative and referendum processes tend to counteract these feelings of political alienation. Furthermore, he maintains that they tend to instill a modicum of political interest and efficacy in an electorate that frequently feels excluded from the policy debate.

In the second section of the book, Schmidt presents several case studies of citizen political participation via the referendum and initiative. Here he recounts the struggles of tax cappers, nuclear freezers, and environmental activists. Each case study provides an excellent profile of the heartbreaks and successes to be found in any initiative campaign. His portrayals of the tax-revolt and nuclear-freeze campaigns of the early 1980s are particularly well drawn. They illustrate not only the effectiveness of citizen

participation but that the initiative and referendum are not destined to be the exclusive tools of the political Right or Left.

The final section of Schmidt's book is an extended discussion of the nuts and bolts of organizing an initiative campaign. He gives advice on such varied topics as publicity, fund-raising, securing media coverage, complying with state and local regulations, amassing sufficient signatures, and combating opponents' tactics. The clear message is that the average citizen need not be put off by the supposed political complexity of such a campaign. There are a number of successful models that can be copied and adapted to the needs of a given situation. The book concludes with two useful appendices. The first gives a state-by-state capsule history of the use of the initiative and referendum processes. The second provides voting results for the various propositions that went before the voters in the November 1988 election.

On the whole, *Citizen Lawmakers* is a worthy addition to the growing body of literature on citizen activism. Schmidt presents his views in a clear style and argues his points on behalf of citizen participation with considerable skill. The text is carefully documented and the footnotes, appendices, and bibliography are likely to be of considerable use to both the scholar and the activist. Those interested in the process of political change will derive much from this book.

DOUGLAS C. NORD

University of Minnesota
Duluth

ZUNZ, OLIVIER. *Making America Corporate, 1870-1920*. Pp. x, 267. Chicago: University of Chicago Press, 1990. $24.95.

The author of this elegant and instructive study is concerned with the rise of a white-collar, corporate class in the late nineteenth and early twentieth centuries. Moving beyond Alfred D. Chandler's brilliant analysis of corporate management, Olivier Zunz re-creates the social milieu and culture of middle-level managers and engineers, salesmen, and clerks during this period. He is intent upon explaining "why so many ordinary Americans were involved in the creation of the modern work culture and why their lives were historically significant." In the process, he gives greater substance to the new middle class adumbrated by Robert H. Wiebe in *The Search for Order, 1877-1920* (1967). Zunz concentrates on the old industrial belt that stretched from the eastern seaports to the Great Lakes. He has done extensive archival research and has exploited the personnel records of five large corporations: the Chicago, Burlington, & Quincy Railroad; the E. I. Du Pont de Nemours Powder Company; the Ford Motor Company; the McCormick—later International Harvester—Company; and the Metropolitan Life Insurance Company. He has identified and built career profiles for hundreds of these corporations' employees. The resulting case studies make use of collective biography and insights derived from social history.

The diverse white-collar workers described in this work did more than react to the new corporate world; they also did much to design it. As Zunz observes, "corporate goals were simultaneously adopted and devised by an aspiring new salaried class that grew with the corporations themselves and that helped transform the larger middle-class." This study illuminates many features of the emerging corporate culture: the growth of a working bureaucracy; the transformation of the urban landscape; the extension of the middle class to include office workers and clerks; the feminization of office work; the

increasingly active role of white-collar employees in the larger society, including their commitment to social betterment; and the efforts of the new class to reconcile its multiple loyalties to employers, independent professional organizations, and community associations. On occasion, the reader may suspect that Zunz has exaggerated the independence and influence of these middle-level managers and white-collar employees. Nevertheless, he has painted a convincing portrait of a previously indistinct but vital part of the emerging corporate world in the United States.

DEWEY W. GRANTHAM

Vanderbilt University
Nashville
Tennessee

SOCIOLOGY

ABEL, RICHARD L. *American Lawyers*. Pp. xv, 406. New York: Oxford University Press, 1989. $29.95.

In *American Lawyers*, Richard L. Abel synthesizes more than 100 years of empirical research on the nature of the American legal profession and its relationship with American society. Abel is explicit about the book's purpose as well as its limitations: his objective was to produce a quantitative, historical sociology of the profession as a whole rather than an ethnographic or psychological portrait of its individual members. He also chose to focus primarily on the economic aspects of the practice of law because of his justifiable belief that "for most lawyers law is a means of earning a living before it is anything else." Accordingly, his major topics include the historical demographics of the profession, controls on the supply of lawyers, controls on the production and marketing of legal services, demand creation and other innovative economic strategies, and the problems engendered by the stunning economic and status disparities within the profession.

Abel identifies three major theoretical perspectives from which sociologists have analyzed the professions. The first, which he associates with Weber, views a profession as an organized effort to control the market for its members' services by limiting both entry and production. From the Marxist perspective, according to Abel, the critical issue has always been where to locate the professions in the class hierarchy: are professionals a subclass of capital, an elite "black-coated" group of workers, or a new class destined for independence in the ongoing class struggle? Finally, the "structural functionalists," whom Abel traces to Durkheim, take a more sanguine view of the professions, seeing them as disinterested communities that help to maintain social order by counterbalancing both the power of the state and the atomizing forces of capitalism. Although he is attracted to many questions posed by class analysis, Abel concludes that the Weberian framework provides the most meaningful insights into the dilemmas faced by lawyers, who, as private practitioners, are primarily concerned with marketing their services.

Abel is identified with the critical legal studies (CLS) movement. Sympathetic readers will applaud Abel's unyielding skepticism and, in particular, his unwillingness to accept at face value even the most appealing of the legal profession's self-justifications. But even those who are hostile to CLS should find Abel's thorough and dispassionate empiricism beyond reproach. His political views make a significant appearance only in the last few pages of the book, when he makes a frankly personal plea for reform of the profession along egalitarian lines. Moreover, his writing is devoid of the inflated rhetoric and gratuitous jargon that characterize so much of the CLS literature. Indeed, Abel's straightforward prose style is one of the book's great strengths. As a lawyer with little formal training in sociology, I was entirely comfortable with the presentation, and I expect that other nonspecialists will have similar reactions.

Although the book has few significant intellectual shortcomings, one recurrent question concerns the relative reliability of Abel's sources. Virtually every assertion is supported by a citation, but there is little critical commentary on the validity of the studies cited, some of which are very old. Readers who lack Abel's familiarity with the original sources—and this group will include almost everyone—are left to rely on the author's judgment and on the mutually corroborating effect of the huge number of sources cited. An additional minor problem is that the publisher has done Abel a disservice by reproducing all of his tables en masse at the end of the book, in a typescript format that is unattractive and sometimes difficult to read.

These small criticisms aside, Abel has been remarkably successful in achieving the objective he set for himself. While some readers might wish that he had undertaken one or more of the tasks that he disclaimed, he has produced a sociology of the legal profession that is both comprehensive and provocative. Curiously, the dust jacket understates its worth by describing it as "a valuable reference work." On the contrary, it is a good story that can be read from cover to cover, and a book that will be of value and interest to social scientists, open-minded lawyers, and others concerned with the law and its practitioners or, more generally, with the sociology of American institutions.

JOHN M. CONLEY

University of North Carolina
Chapel Hill

BRETON, RAYMOND, WSEVOLOD W. ISAJIW, WARREN E. KALBACH, and JEFFREY G. REITZ. *Ethnic Identity and Equality: Varieties of Experience in a Canadian City.* Pp. viii, 342. Toronto: University of Toronto Press, 1990. $50.00. Paperbound, $22.50.

This collaborative effort by four sociologists at the University of Toronto targeted their city to test the thesis that Canada's ethnic "cultural mosaic"—in contrast to the melting-pot concept—persists because it sustains an entrenched class system. Utilizing a 167-item, closed-end questionnaire but also relying on government statistics, they focused on three issues: (1) the extent of the duration of ethnicity over time and the processual dynamics involved; (2) the processes of the incorporation of "members of ethnic collectivities in society as a whole" relative, say, to issues of inequality or the variability in integration in social, economic, and political structures; and (3) the extent to which ethnic organization is negative, positive, or neutral relative to incorporation.

Their sample, totaling 2338 completed interviews, focused on "majority Canadians"—persons of English, Irish, or Scottish background whose families had been in Canada for three generations or more—and eight "minority groups"—first- and second-generation English, Germans, Ukrainians, Italians, Jews, Portuguese, Chinese, and West Indians. The sample was defined "to include only persons who are in the labor force and between the ages of 18 and 65." The data are summarized in numerous tables throughout the text. There are two helpful appendices, "Technical Notes on the Survey Research Design" and "The Interview Schedule."

Between an apparently collaborative introduction and conclusion, particular chapters contributed by the authors address various aspects of the research findings. Isajiw's chapter "Ethnic Identity Retention" explores the nature of ethnic identity, especially in terms of transgenerational retention, rebellion, and the search by later generations for their roots. Kalbach reviews the issue of "ethnic residential segregation and its significance for the individual in an urban setting," emphasizing the importance of the finding that "evidence of sociocultural assimilation reflected in declining residential segregation through successive generations can be found only in a few populations of British and other western and northern European origins." "Ethnic concentrations in labor markets and their implications for ethnic inequality" is the focus for Reitz's contribution. Breton, despite the title of his chapter, "The Ethnic Group as a Political Resource in Relation to Problems of Incorporation: Perceptions and Attitudes," also puts a major emphasis on job discrimination.

In the summary of their findings, the authors include the following. While certain ethnic groups do become fully incorporated into Canadian society, some groups, such as the Chinese, West Indians, and Jews, do not. Ethnic retention and societal incorporation must be viewed as distinct phenomena. Retention can but need not have an effect on the degree and pattern of incorporation in the larger society; moreover, it is capable of facilitating and impeding the process. Finally, incorporation and retention do not evolve in the same way across generations for all the ethnic groups considered.

The study is useful but must be read cautiously. Among other things, it relies too heavily on official government data and ignores such real-world considerations as (1) a housing market that, around 1960, became super-inflated, which, when coupled with the requirement that home buyers take short-term mortgages, renegotiated at ever-rising interest rates, heavily influenced residential stability; and

(2) the degree to which interviews were skewed by a significant number—perhaps as much as 20 percent of Toronto's population—of undocumented immigrants.

M. ESTELLIE SMITH

State University of New York
Oswego

MEIER, KENNETH J., JOSEPH STEWART, Jr., and ROBERT E. ENGLAND. *Race, Class, and Education: The Politics of Second-Generation Discrimination*. Pp. xiv, 194. Madison: University of Wisconsin Press, 1990. $37.50. Paperbound, $14.95.

CHALL, JEANNE S., VICKI A. JACOBS, and LUKE E. BALDWIN. *The Reading Crisis: Why Poor Children Fall Behind*. Pp. xv, 191. Cambridge, MA: Harvard University Press, 1990. $25.00.

These excellent studies—the one, *Race, Class, and Education*, concerned with the politics of equal access to integrated education for African Americans; the other, *The Reading Crisis*, with the development of literacy among children from low-income families—share a concern for the student at risk and an emphasis on the school and the teacher for the education of that student.

The research for *Race, Class, and Education* was based on 174 school districts in the United States, involving 15,000 or more students and a 1 percent black enrollment. The Office of Civil Rights was the major source of data for the study.

The analysis stresses the political forces that affect black education. The approach to providing equal educational opportunity has been through school desegregation, taken to mean the largely mechanical mixing of black and white students. It has not resulted in integration—the interaction of students in a multiracial learning environment where students are status equals and have equal opportunity to achieve. Rather, desegregation has resulted in a new form of separate but unequal second-generation discrimination. Here discrimination appears in the guise of ability grouping, curriculum tracking, discipline, and special education that constitutes a pattern generally involving a disproportionate number of black students. School districts with a politically developed black population, a large population of lower-class whites, and a large percentage of black teachers exhibit less second-generation discrimination, however. The black teacher is the most important factor. Not only does the teacher have the strongest influence on a student's overall learning environment; the teacher is the most important among those who make the decisions that affect equal access to education.

To counter second-generation discrimination in general and to increase the number of black teachers demand political action. Thus the increase in the number of black school-board members can be expected to result in an increase in the number of black administrators and, in turn, an increase in the number of black teachers.

The Reading Crisis is a study of a group of 30 children, both white and black, from low-income families living in a small industrial city in the northeast. Interviews and questionnaires involving home, family, and teachers provided data, as did classroom observations and extensive testing of the children. The children were in grades 2, 4, and 6 and were retested in grades 3, 5, and 7 a year later. Although it was assumed that both school and home would affect literacy and language, the concern was mainly with the school.

The study confirms the long-established proposition that the gap in literacy achievement among low-income children actually becomes greater with increased schooling. The approach in *The Reading Crisis* is one that views reading as involving abilities and skills that change as children develop. In pursuing this developmental approach, it became clear that in the primary grades the children differed hardly at all from the norm. At grade 4 and beyond, however, their scores decelerated in comparison with mainstream children. For an explanation and a basis for change, Chall and her associates looked to the school and home rather than to culture or politics.

Among much else, it was found that there are indeed classroom measures more successful than others in fostering literacy and language development. The research confirmed that literacy has separate aspects. What promotes growth in one may not in the other. Thus, of the four classroom variables selected, word recognition seems most responsive to classroom structure and the challenge of difficult reading.

As for the influence of the home, those where a strong literacy environment existed were not unlike those classrooms where children made significant gains in that they offered a stimulating and challenging context for reading and vocabulary development. When children in the fourth grade and beyond began to decelerate, however, fewer of the families were sufficiently educated and literate to help the children, and the role of the school became more important.

Together these studies implicitly reject the notion that the educational shortcomings of students at risk are related to innate cognitive disabilities. In as much as the needs of these children are essentially the same as those of most children, both studies find separate programs unacceptable. Moreover, having equal access to and being a part of the larger educational experience benefits the individual and the society. Each study concludes with the emphasis on the classroom teacher, whose teaching can foster achievement by all students, including those at risk.

ARNOLD A. SIO

Colgate University
Hamilton
New York

SCOTT, JAMES C. *Domination and the Arts of Resistance: Hidden Transcripts.* Pp. xviii, 251. New Haven, CT: Yale University Press, 1990. $29.95.

Five years ago James Scott published a book on the forms of resistance in the everyday life of poor peasants in Malaysia, *Weapons of the Weak.* This book, focusing on a small community, moved away from the common emphasis on organized movements and revolt to a perceptive analysis of more hidden forms of resistance, such as foot-dragging, dissimulation, desertion, and slander. In the last chapter of that book, Scott attempted a generalization of his argument to all subordinate classes and to a criticism of Gramsci's concept of hegemony. In the book under review, he continues the generalizing to the extent that he leaves out all ethnographic or historical considerations.

His basic argument is that one should look not only at the open interaction between subordinates and those who dominate—what he calls "public transcript"— but also at discourse that takes place beyond direct observation of powerholders, which he calls "hidden transcript." While it seems obvious that interaction always has hidden and public aspects, Scott only examines them from the angle of a simple dichotomy of powerfulness and powerlessness. Although Scott realizes the role of fantasy and wish fulfill-ment in the hidden transcript, he entirely ignores psychoanalytic arguments about what is hidden in human action. More generally, we do not find much of a critical review of other relevant writings on the subject, such as the contribution of Goffman.

I do not think that this book has much to offer beyond what Scott has already said in *Weapons of the Weak*. On the con-trary, the decontextualization of his argu-ment shows more clearly its theoretical weakness. Caste hierarchy in India is lumped in one category with North Amer-ican slavery, because in both cases there are "hidden transcripts" of resistance. I do not think that this furthers our under-standing. For example, in the Indian case one may find an open discourse on the hidden, occult powers that subordinate castes may control, which is directly re-lated to concepts of impurity and inaus-piciousness. These powers are hidden but at the same time openly celebrated. They certainly are part of resistance, while nevertheless reproducing a hierarchical system. The relation between open and hidden as well as that between domi-nance and resistance is much more com-plex than Scott wishes to acknowledge. Another example is Scott's interpretation of the power of jokes. He argues that the power of an ascetic priestly class is pro-foundly damaged if the class is shown to be promiscuous and gluttonous. It seems to me that the power of a priestly class depends on a complex set of social rela-tions that forms the context in which jokes are interpreted and have their ef-fect. All this is not to say that cross-cultural comparisons cannot be made but to argue that comparison becomes use-less when one generalizes about human action under the unproblematized ru-brics of power and resistance.

Finally, there is an important method-ological difficulty in Scott's enterprise due to the simple fact that the hidden is indeed hidden. Although Scott is clearly aware of the problem, he does not show us a way out of it.

PETER VAN DER VEER

University of Pennsylvania
Philadelphia

ECONOMICS

COWELL, FRANK A. *Cheating the Gov-ernment: The Economics of Evasion.* Pp. xii, 267. Cambridge: MIT Press, 1990. $19.95.

Soviet documents acknowledge that nearly 40 percent of all garden sheds in the Soviet Union were constructed by il-legal business enterprises. For Frank Cowell, reader in economics at the Lon-don School of Economics, this is an exam-ple of "cheating the government." To the probable surprise of people caught by the title of this book, unauthorized produc-tion of garden sheds is viewed by Cowell not as an economic problem or a symptom of an economic problem. It is taken to be merely a law enforcement problem.

The economic aspect cries out for dis-cussion, but this book ignores it. Who suffers because these garden sheds are produced? No doubt there are govern-ment employees whose job it is to produce legal garden sheds, but perhaps they charge too much or their work is shoddy or they have a long waiting list. Other government output of consumer goods—neckties, for example—may go unsold be-cause money is spent in the illegal sector. The presumption today is that in the So-viet Union the legal sector is inefficient and that private production of garden sheds and other commodities should be legalized. This could be argued, and that argument would be economics. Cowell's book does not raise the question.

Indeed, after the first two paragraphs there is no further mention of garden sheds or even the Soviet Union. The book explicitly addresses income tax evasion, entrepreneurs' taking cash payments that are not declared as taxable income. The scene shifts abruptly to the United States.

Here, we might expect, is an opportunity for a better case to be made that underground production is socially harmful. The market economy is presumably hard at work allocating resources on the basis of prices that reflect not only consumer preferences but social overhead costs, too. Selling cocaine is socially harmful, but tax evasion is not the motive. We get back to something like a garden shed, built by a workman who does not pay taxes on the cash income he receives. Whom does this hurt, and how?

Cowell simply assumes that taxes are necessary in order to provide public goods. Implicitly he assumes that the menu and distribution of public goods is optimal and that all prices for goods and resources correctly reflect the need for public goods. In reality, taxes merely make one group of people pay for what another group enjoys. To demonstrate that the end result is best for all, in a particular case or in general, would be daunting for an economist. Perhaps tax evasion is good for what ails us. The title and, to an important degree, the tone of Cowell's book suggest that useful ideas on this subject are being explored in the book. They are not.

This is a treatise on law enforcement for its own sake. Cowell writes, "Nothing should be allowed that will undermine the effectiveness of those who have the authority to coerce." So much for unauthorized garden sheds; the Evil Empire strikes back!

We might expect from this book, then, at least some helpful insights on law enforcement by tax collectors. When the question is raised whether it is better to prevent tax evasion or to penalize evaders, our analytical spirits stir. But disappointment is in store. Cowell presents a set of theoretical formulations, employing more type fonts than seems prudent. What these come down to is that, as punishment and/or interrogation increases, the extent of tax evasion will fall. This is not counterintuitive; it is obvious. Deterrence deters. The simplistic canon for tax collectors is to "instill a wholesome horror."

Cowell does ask us to think whether the cost of enforcement can exceed the gain. He explains that enforcement is primarily a matter of obtaining information. Since the information problem depends on the particular nature of the tax, it seems to follow that different varieties of taxes—sales, value-added, income, customs—should be compared as to data costs for tax collectors. We would also want to consider new technology—computer applications, for example. These aspects are not mentioned.

Despite its title, the book's explicit objectives are modest and so is its value. It does illustrate that economics is useful only when it reveals counterintuitive relationships.

WALLACE F. SMITH

University of California
Berkeley

FLOUD, RODERICK, KENNETH WACHTER, and ANNABEL GREGORY. *Height, Health, and History: Nutritional Status in the United Kingdom, 1750-1980.* Pp. xxi, 354. New York: Cambridge University Press, 1990. No price.

KOMLOS, JOHN. *Nutrition and Economic Development in the Eighteenth-Century Habsburg Monarchy: An Anthropometric History.* Pp. xvii, 325.

Princeton, NJ: Princeton University Press, 1990. $39.95.

Each of the books reviewed here uses anthropometric data collected primarily from military recruitment data to assess changes in the levels and distribution of welfare in the early stages of industrialization in Europe. Because measures of the heights of army recruits are available in each study over an extended period of time, and because body size is thought to reflect key components of population welfare including levels of nutrition and exposure to death, the basic premise of the books seems reasonable.

As both books clearly recognize, analysis of military recruitment data is also subject to many pitfalls. Of principal importance is the fact that the population measured may not be a representative sample of the population in the corresponding region or country. Except in the case of true lottery systems, certain groups may be overrepresented in the recruitment population. Moreover, a common feature of recruitment data is that individuals below a certain height are excluded from the sample entirely.

Similar methods are used to surmount these difficulties. First, statistical corrections for the absence of short recruits are introduced. Second, the authors focus on long-term trends in height rather than short-term fluctuations that are unlikely to be a result of changes in the nutritional status of the underlying population. Finally, care is taken to compare observed patterns in height in military groups with other anthropometric, economic, and demographic data. While questions remain about the selectivity of those who are recruited, the results are robust enough in both studies to suggest that the authors have uncovered meaningful trends in height in working-class populations as a whole.

In addition to differences in the regions and time periods considered, the books differ in terms of the attention that is given to measuring and interpreting anthropometric patterns. *Height, Health, and History*, which focuses on the United Kingdom during the period of 1750-1980, puts the anthropometric measures on center stage. It is a pleasure to read. Particular strengths include a lucid discussion of the difference between within- and across-population variation in height—a key question is whether Sherlock Holmes would have been justified in using height as a criterion for distinguishing suspects from different regions and occupational groups—a careful statistical analysis that uses both simple and sophisticated techniques and is described in a way that is accessible to those with little statistical training; and a good summary of the recent literature on health and nutrition in low-income countries.

Given the energy that has obviously gone into the analysis of trends in anthropometric status, it would be disappointing to find that the authors could do little more than confirm results inferred from other types of data. We are not disappointed, however; resulting patterns contrast sharply with the general impression that has emerged from studies of wage and price series from the first half of the nineteenth century. The proposed resolution of this difference is intriguing: despite rises in real income during the early stages of the industrial revolution, an accompanying deterioration in living conditions, especially in urban areas, could have led to a decline in body size among working-class men.

While anthropometric measures are central to the argument presented by Floud, Wachter, and Gregory, they play more of a supporting role in Komlos's discussion of the eighteenth-century Hapsburg monarchy. In particular, anthropometric measures are used to show that there was an increase and subsequent Malthusian decline in welfare during the period of 1730-90. It is then argued that concern on the part of the monarchy about declines in the health and welfare of its population led to changes in institutional constraints that, in turn, provided a solid foundation for industrialization in the subsequent century. This Boserupian argument, that population growth and consequent economic adversity can lead in the long run to welfare-improving technological and institutional changes, is then synthesized into a more general model of economic change.

A standard problem with this sort of argument is that it is impossible to know whether this institutional change would have taken place if not for the deterioration in nutritional status. The best argument presented is the suggestion that the monarchy had a direct interest in the health and strength of its soldiers and thus would have been greatly concerned about declines in the body sizes of recruits.

While this book is worth reading because of the insight it provides into economic change in Austria-Hungary during the eighteenth century, a number of the interpretations of variation in nutritional status are not convincing. The observed relative decline in nutritional status in rural areas that Komlos attributes to decreases in transactions costs could easily have resulted from increased exposure to illness in rural areas. He also emphasizes the direct biological mechanisms relating nutrition, marriage, and fertility at the expense of equally plausible mechanisms driven by economic or social factors that might underlie both anthropometric and demographic change. While neither of these problems is fatal to the general

model presented, they detract from an otherwise interesting argument.

ANDREW D. FOSTER

University of Pennsylvania
Philadelphia

LIBECAP, GARY D. *Contracting for Property Rights*. Pp. ix, 132. New York: Cambridge University Press, 1990. No price.

Social institutions are the stuff of social science: why they are what they are, how they work and change over time and from place to place. Since Adam Smith, economists have been particularly concerned with the working of free and unfettered markets as an institution to foster the welfare of persons and the wealth of nations. But markets can be expensive to organize. In practice, moreover, they are not complete and competitive, and the resulting distributions of income and wealth are not necessarily consistent with political stability. Nor, one might add, are the resulting patterns of resource use consistent with the sustainability of modern economic endeavor.

These observations lead political economists to think outside the rigid framework of neoclassical market economies—which include, if at all, market failure as an aberration—and study economies where politicians, bureaucrats, and ordinary citizens interact and bargain with one another, each having the objective of enhancing self-interest. In *Contracting for Property Rights*, Gary Libecap mixes contract theory and economic history to illuminate the institutional development of natural resource use in the United States. He presents four case studies: underground mining; federal land policies—the alienation of farm, timber, and grazing lands; fisheries; and oil extraction, focusing on the consolidation of oil fields.

Property rights are particularly useful as a central concept because it is the institution of these rights that is critically exogenous in neoclassical economies. These rights enable the markets that drive the system to perform efficiently. To Libecap, rights are critically endogenous, generated by ongoing contracting. For this, history—initial conditions—matters, and the ultimate outcome is path dependent and is not unique: property rights may or may not develop in more or less attenuated forms. The optimistic view that property rights will evolve in a timely way to support efficient resource allocation is rejected as a general proposition.

The exploitation of oil fields is a notable example in American economic history. Diverse holders of surface rights, which include rights to drill and extract, compete in a rush to extract the black gold from a common pool. Because of the rush, extraction is premature, capitalization is excessive, and the natural pressure underground is dissipated. Unitization of the field at an early stage of development, as a sole owner would do, is needed to avoid gross inefficiency and dissipation of economic rent. But unitization is rare and is more likely to come near the final stages of economic extraction.

In a similar way, common-pool problems dominate fisheries so that diverse user groups engage in competition to preempt others from capturing the same fish first. Overcapitalization of fleets, wasted labor, and depleted stocks combine to dissipate rents. Fishers generally appreciate both the causes and the effects of their rush to capture, but they have been notably ineffective in contracting for fishing rights to ameloriate common-pool inefficiencies.

Economic homesteading of federal lands best suited for extensive grazing or forestry would have been on parcels larger than the traditional 160 acres. But interested parties failed to contract for the larger allocations through regular channels. By contrast, federal law came to define and protect private mineral rights in conformity with informal rules devised by miners to support efficient extraction.

Since much of the material in this book has already been published by Libecap (with others), the volume is an opportunity to review, compare, and analyze the different histories of "contracting for property rights."

PHILIP A. NEHER
University of British Columbia
Vancouver
Canada

WHITE, JOSEPH and AARON WILDAVSKY. *The Deficit and the Public Interest.* Pp. xxiv, 691. Berkeley: University of California Press; New York: Russell Sage Foundation, 1989. No price.

Joseph White and Aaron Wildavsky have provided their readers with the most detailed, exhaustive, and reliable source of information regarding the political struggles over taxes and the federal domestic budget during the decade of the 1980s. Drawing upon thorough and balanced utilization of documentary material, they have added to the extensive print record by means of numerous interviews with most of the major congressional figures and members of the executive branch who were involved in constructing those budgets. The reader can gain an intimate, detailed view of what went on in public and behind closed doors during the 1980 tax and budget controversies. Untainted by technical jargon, the book provides an intense survey of one of the most important series of events of the Reagan presidency, and those who want to know what happened and who said what to whom will be satisfied by this chronicle. The Reagan revolution has received one of its most important, and sympathetic, descriptions.

The book gives a blow-by-blow account of the major tax and budgetary issues of the Reagan years, largely from the vantage point of insider analysts revisiting the trenches of politics. Reagan's tax reform, which White and Wildavsky seem to admire, is given a full treatment, as are the origins and significance of the Gramm-Rudman-Hollings Act. The tax-reform story is well told, with many juicy quotations from key players. White and Wildavsky's verdict on tax reform gives President Reagan high marks for "transferring taxes from individuals to business," thus showing a willingness to impose costs on his own followers. There are many other such benign judgments about the events of the Reagan years.

Curiously, White and Wildavsky are rather optimistic about the prospects for resolving the problem of reducing the national deficit. In fact, they seem to view the deficit as a minor issue, largely symbolic in form, and lacking the attributes of a genuine crisis, in spite of the posturing of many politicians, including Ronald Reagan. The authors are less optimistic about the prospects of breaking the political stalemate between the president and Congress over control of the budgetary process. The long stalemate over the deficit seems to be a symptom of more serious flaws in domestic policymaking.

With the wisdom of hindsight, I cannot avoid noting that the "moderate proposals on the deficit" made by the authors for dealing with the federal budget deficit were far too modest and missed the eventual 1990 deficit-reduction law by a wide margin. The deal struck by President Bush and the Congress could not have been predicted by the theory provided in this book. In 1990 a law was passed that was supposed to reduce the budget deficit by nearly $500 billion, and in the process a Republican president accepted a series of tax increases without securing a cut in federal spending. In view of the still unwinding savings and loan costs and the remilitarization caused by the Persian Gulf crisis, there is a strong probability that the views of budgetary politics that the authors express in their book will be even less a guide to the future.

Ultimately, then, the book succeeds as a description of the tax and budget politics of the Reagan years, but it does not construct a convincing theoretical framework for the analysis of budgetary politics. In spite of the prodigious labor spent on preparing this book and the careful attention to detail given on virtually every page, White and Wildavsky simply cannot provide a powerful explanation of what is really going on in budgetary politics. It is not that anyone else has given us a better theory; it is just that political history, however well done, has not been able to provide sufficient insight into the process to really grasp what is going on beyond the deals patched together by politicians. Nor is the reader shown how national budgetary politics differ from state or local processes

Economic theory, which White and Wildavsky largely discount, has done little better. The authors relegate economics to a single chapter, where it is treated as mere ideology parading as profound insight. Amateur economists like Senator Bill Bradley and Jack Kemp are taken as seriously as professionals. White and Wildavsky understand the superficiality of Reaganomics, but they seem to applaud its results more than those more liberal economists and scholars who feel that the poor and the weak have been greatly harmed by the economic redistributions that Reagan championed.

White and Wildavsky refuse to portray any of the players of this domestic drama as heroes or villains. In fact, politicians come out rather better and more enlightened than most journalists or most ordinary citizens would believe. If we understand the significance of White and Wildavsky's tales, it seems that organized public opinion eventually prevailed, while the politicians in some dim way served the public interest, as they understood it and heard it expressed. Whatever happened may have been inevitable, urged on by Ronald Reagan's popularity.

JAY A. SIGLER

Rutgers University
Camden
New Jersey

OTHER BOOKS

ADELMAN, JONATHAN R. *Prelude to the Cold War: The Tsarist, Soviet, and U.S. Armies in the Two World Wars.* Pp. viii, 287. Boulder, CO: Lynne Rienner, 1988. $30.00.

ANDERSON, MARGO J. *The American Census: A Social History.* Pp. xiii, 257. New Haven, CT: Yale University Press, 1988. $30.00.

ANDREWS, PAT. *Government in Action.* Pp. 230. Lanham, MD: University Press of America, 1990. Paperbound, $14.75.

ARGYRIS, CHRIS. *Integrating the Individual and the Organization.* Pp. 330. New Brunswick, NJ: Transaction, 1990. Paperbound, $19.95.

BAKER, TOD A. et al., eds. *Political Parties in the Southern States: Party Activists in Partisan Coalitions.* Pp. 264. New York: Praeger, 1990. $42.95.

BALDWIN, PETER, ed. *Reworking the Past: Hitler, the Holocaust, and the Historians' Debate.* Pp. 308. Boston: Beacon Press, 1990. $29.95.

BARBER, BERNARD. *Social Studies of Science.* Pp. 278. New Brunswick, NJ: Transaction, 1990. $34.95.

BARBER, PAUL. *Vampires, Burial, and Death: Folklore and Reality.* Pp. viii, 236. New Haven, CT: Yale University Press, 1990. Paperbound, $9.95.

BARKER, LUCIUS J., ed. *Black Electoral Politics: Participation, Performance, Promise.* Pp. 250. New Brunswick, NJ: Transaction, 1990. Paperbound, $19.95.

BELL, CORAL. *The Reagan Paradox: U.S. Foreign Policy in the 1980s.* Pp. 182. New Brunswick, NJ: Rutgers University Press, 1990. $30.00. Paperbound, $11.95.

BIBERAJ, ELEZ. *Albania: A Socialist Maverick.* Pp. vii, 147. Boulder, CO: Westview Press, 1990. $35.00.

BILLINGS-YUN, MELANIE. *Decision against War: Eisenhower and Dien Bien Phu, 1954.* Pp. xiv, 199. New York: Columbia University Press, 1988. $25.00.

BINDER, GUYORA. *Treaty Conflict and Political Contradiction: The Dialectic of Duplicity.* Pp. 240. New York: Praeger, 1988. $39.95.

BIRENBAUM, ARNOLD. *In the Shadow of Medicine: Remaking the Division of Labor in Health Care.* Pp. 184. Dix Hills, NY: General Hall, 1990. $34.95. Paperbound, $18.95.

BISSELL, RICHARD E. and CURT GASTEYGER, eds. *The Missing Link: West European Neutrals and Regional Security.* Pp. vii, 203. Durham, NC: Duke University Press, 1990. $34.50.

BONANNO, ALESSANDRO, ed. *Agrarian Policies and Agricultural Systems.* Pp. xi, 331. Boulder, CO: Westview Press, 1990. Paperbound, $32.50.

BOTTOMORE, TOM. *The Socialist Economy: Theory and Practice.* Pp. 149. New York: Guilford Press, 1990. $35.00. Paperbound, $14.95.

BUCKLEY, JOHN. *Statute of Limitations.* Pp. 365. New York: Simon & Schuster, 1990. $19.95.

CENTRE FOR DEVELOPMENT OF INSTRUCTIONAL TECHNOLOGY. *Indian Social and Economic Development, 1989: An Index to the Literature.* Pp. 208. Newbury Park, CA: Sage, 1990. $25.00.

CLARK, WILLIAM A. *Soviet Regional Elite Mobility after Khrushchev.* Pp. xi, 206. New York: Praeger, 1989. $42.95.

COCKS, GEOFFREY and KONRAD H. JARAUSCH, eds. *German Professions, 1800-1950.* Pp. viii, 340. New York: Oxford University Press, 1990. $45.00.

CONRAD, ROBERT EDGAR, ed. and translator. *Sandino: The Testimony of a Nicaraguan Patriot, 1921-1934.* Pp. xxii, 516. Princeton, NJ: Princeton University Press, 1990. $55.00. Paperbound, $17.95.

DANFORD, JOHN W. *David Hume and the Problem of Reason: Recovering the Human Sciences*. Pp. xii, 228. New Haven, CT: Yale University Press, 1990. $25.00.

DECALO, SAMUEL. *Coups and Army Rule in Africa*. 2d ed. Pp. xvii, 366. New Haven, CT: Yale University Press, 1990. $37.50. Paperbound, $17.95.

DIMAND, ROBERT W. *The Origins of the Keynesian Revolution: The Development of Keynes's Theory of Employment and Output*. Pp. vii, 213. Stanford, CA: Stanford University Press, 1988. $32.50.

EGGERTSSON, THRAINN. *Economic Behavior and Institutions*. Pp. xv, 385. New York: Cambridge University Press, 1990. No price.

FOERSTER, SCHUYLER and EDWARD N. WRIGHT, eds. *American Defense Policy*. 6th ed. Pp. xi, 654. Baltimore, MD: Johns Hopkins University Press, 1990. $65.00. Paperbound, $24.50.

FRIEDENBERG, ROBERT V., ed. *Rhetorical Studies of National Political Debates 1960-1988*. Pp. xiii, 223. New York: Praeger, 1990. $42.95.

GOLDSTEIN, MELVYN C. and CYNTHIA M. BEALL. *Nomads of Western Tibet: The Survival of a Way of Life*. Pp. 192. Berkeley: University of California Press, 1990. $45.00. Paperbound, $17.95.

GOLDWIN, ROBERT A., ART KAUFMAN, and WILLIAM A. SCHAMBRA, eds. *Forging Unity out of Diversity: The Approaches of Eight Nations*. Pp. 468. Lanham, MD: American Enterprise Institute, 1989. $32.50. Paperbound, $18.75.

GOLDWIN, ROBERT A. and ROBERT A. LICHT, eds. *Foreign Policy and the Constitution*. Pp. 152. Lanham, MD: AEI Press, 1990. $26.50. Paperbound, $13.95.

GOLDWIN, ROBERT A. and ROBERT A. LICHT, eds. *The Spirit of the Constitution: Five Conversations*. Pp. 120. Lanham, MD: AEI Press, 1990. $27.50. Paperbound, $14.95.

GRAUBARD, STEPHEN R., ed. *Living with AIDS*. Pp. 463. Cambridge: MIT Press, 1990. Paperbound, $14.95.

HABERMAS, JÜRGEN. *Moral Consciousness and Communicative Action*. Translated by Christian Lenhardt and Shierry Weber Nicholsen. Pp. 224. Cambridge: MIT Press, 1990. $19.95.

HAEBERLE, STEVEN H. *Planting the Grassroots: Structuring Citizen Participation*. Pp. x, 151. New York: Praeger, 1989. $38.00.

HARRIS, TIM, PAUL SEAWARD, and MARK GOLDIE, eds. *The Politics of Religion in Restoration England*. Pp. xii, 259. Cambridge, MA: Basil Blackwell, 1990. $39.95.

HASKINS, LOREN and KIRK JEFFREY. *Understanding Quantitative History*. Pp. xxv, 366. Cambridge, MA: MIT Press, 1990. $27.50.

HOIDAL, ODDVAR K. *Quisling: A Study in Treason*. Pp. 913. New York: Oxford University Press, 1989. $55.00.

HSÜ, IMMANUEL C. Y. *The Rise of Modern China*. 4th ed. Pp. xxxi, 971. New York: Oxford University Press, 1990. $35.00.

INGRAM, HELEN. *Water Politics: Continuity and Change*. Pp. viii, 158. Albuquerque: University of New Mexico Press, 1990. $29.95. Paperbound, $15.95.

INGRAO, BRUNA and GIORGIO ISRAEL. *The Invisible Hand: Economic Equilibrium in the History of Science*. Pp. 491. Cambridge: MIT Press, 1990. $47.50.

JAEGER, RICHARD M. *Statistics: A Spectator Report*. 2d ed. Pp. 402. Newbury Park, CA: Sage, 1990. $38.00. Paperbound, $18.95.

JAFFEE, DAVID. *Levels of Socio-economic Development Theory*. Pp. 232. New York: Praeger, 1990. $42.95. Paperbound, $16.95.

JÄNICKE, MARTIN. *State Failure: The Impotence of Politics in Industrial Society.* Translated by Alan Braley. Pp. xi, 171. University Park: Pennsylvania State University Press, 1990. $29.95.

JENKINS-SMITH, HANK C. *Democratic Politics and Policy Analysis.* Pp. vii, 248. Pacific Grove, CA: Brooks/Cole, 1990. Paperbound, $18.25.

JERNAZIAN, EPHRAIM K. *Judgment unto Truth: Witnessing the Armenian Genocide.* Translated by Alice Haig. Pp. 235. New Brunswick, NJ: Transaction, 1990. $24.95. Paperbound, $17.95.

JOYNER, CHRISTOPHER C., ed. *The Persian Gulf War: Lessons for Strategy, Law, and Diplomacy.* Pp. 272. Westport, CT: Greenwood Press, 1990. $45.00.

KAVANAGH, DENNIS. *Thatcherism and British Politics: The End of Consensus?* 2d ed. Pp. xii, 339. New York: Oxford University Press, 1990. Paperbound, $12.95.

KIVNICK, HELEN Q. *Where Is the Way: Song and Struggle in South Africa.* Pp. xv, 378. New York: Penguin, 1990. Paperbound, $9.95.

KREHBIEL, CARL C. *Confidence and Security-Building Measures in Europe: The Stockholm Conference.* Pp. xi, 388. New York: Praeger, 1989. $55.00.

KUKATHAS, CHANDRAN. *Hayek and Modern Liberalism.* Pp. xiv, 247. New York: Oxford University Press, 1989. $39.95.

KUMALO, ALF. *Mandela: Echoes of an Era.* Text by Es 'Kia Mphahlele. Pp. 161. New York: Penguin Books, 1990. Paperbound, $16.95.

LAMB, CHRISTOPHER JON. *Belief Systems and Decision Making in the Mayaguez Crisis.* Pp. xv, 304. Gainesville: University of Florida Press, 1989. $22.50.

LINDEN, CARL A. *Khrushchev and the Soviet Leadership: With an Epilogue on Gorbachev.* Updated ed. Pp. xi, 287. Baltimore, MD: Johns Hopkins University Press, 1990. $32.00. Paperbound, $12.95.

LOSS, RICHARD. *The Modern Theory of Presidential Power: Alexander Hamilton and the Corwin Thesis.* Pp. xv, 172. Westport, CT: Greenwood Press, 1990. No price.

LOWI, THEODORE J. and BENJAMIN GINSBERG. *Poliscide: Big Government, Big Science, Lilliputian Politics.* Pp. xxv, 306. Lanham, MD: University Press of America, 1990. Paperbound, $14.75.

LUARD, EVAN. *The Globalization of Politics: The Changed Focus of Political Action in the Modern World.* Pp. xii, 195. New York: New York University Press, 1990. $35.00.

LUK, MICHAEL Y. L. *The Origins of Chinese Bolshevism: An Ideology in the Making, 1920-1928.* Pp. viii, 366. New York: Oxford University Press, 1990. $32.50.

LYNN-JONES, SEAN M., STEVEN MILLER, and STEPHEN VAN EVERA, eds. *Soviet Military Policy.* Pp. xiii, 374. Cambridge: MIT Press, 1989. Paperbound, $14.95.

MacDONALD, CALLUM. *Britain and the Korean War.* Pp. vii, 112. Cambridge, MA: Basil Blackwell, 1990. $29.95.

MAIR, PETER, ed. *The West European Party System.* Pp. xi, 364. New York: Oxford University Press, 1990. Paperbound, $14.95.

MAJONE, GIANDOMENICO. *Evidence, Argument, and Persuasion in the Policy Process.* Pp. xiii, 190. New Haven, CT: Yale University Press, 1989. $22.50.

MARGULIES, HERBERT F. *The Mild Reservationists and the League of Nations Controversy in the Senate.* Pp. xiv, 300. Columbia: University of Missouri Press, 1989. No price.

MARSHALL, J. N., ed. *Services and Uneven Development.* Pp. xv, 307. New York: Oxford University Press, 1988. $66.00.

MARTIN, MALACHI. *The Keys of This Blood: The Struggle for World Dominion between Pope John Paul II, Mikhail Gorbachev, and the Capitalist West.* Pp. 734. New York: Simon & Schuster, 1990. $24.95.

McGHEE, GEORGE. *The US-Turkish-NATO Middle East Connection: How the Truman Doctrine and Turkey's NATO Entry Contained the Soviets.* Pp. xvii, 224. New York: St. Martin's Press, 1990. $35.00.

McLEAN, IAIN. *Democracy and New Technology.* Pp. viii, 204. Cambridge, MA: Basil Blackwell, 1990. $37.95.

MERKL, P. H., ed. *The Federal Republic of Germany.* Pp. xii, 505. New York: Columbia University Press, 1990. Paperbound, $20.00.

MORAN, MARY H. *Civilized Women: Gender and Prestige in Southeastern Liberia.* Pp. xv, 189. Ithaca, NY: Cornell University Press, 1990. $33.95. Paperbound, $11.95.

NAGEL, STUART S., ed. *Policy Theory and Policy Evaluation: Concepts, Knowledge, Causes, and Norms.* Pp. 256. Westport, CT: Greenwood Press, 1990. $45.00.

NAYAK, RADHAKANT. *Administrative Justice in India.* Pp. 248. Newbury Park, CA: Sage, 1989. $26.00.

PANKRATZ, DAVID B. and VALERIE B. MORRIS, eds. *The Future of the Arts: Public Policy and Arts Research.* Pp. 344. New York: Praeger, 1990. $45.00.

POPE, JACQUELINE. *Biting the Hand That Feeds Them: Organizing Women on Welfare at the Grass Roots Level.* Pp. 161. New York: Praeger, 1989. $39.95.

PUGH, MICHAEL and PHIL WILLIAMS, eds. *Superpower Politics: Change in the United States and the Soviet Union.* Pp. xi, 208. New York: Manchester University Press, 1990. $59.95. Paperbound, $12.95.

RADVANYI, JANOS, ed. *Psychological Operations and Political Warfare in Long-term Strategic Planning.* Pp. 168. New York: Praeger, 1990. $37.95.

RUMMEL, REINHARDT, ed. *The Evolution of an International Actor: Western Europe's New Assertiveness.* Pp. vi, 354. Boulder, CO: Westview Press, 1990. Paperbound, $35.00.

RUSCIANO, FRANK LOUIS. *Isolation and Paradox: Defining "The Public" in Modern Political Analysis.* Pp. 188. Westport, CT: Greenwood Press, 1989. $39.95.

SAATY, THOMAS L. and JOYCE M. ALEXANDER. *Conflict Resolution: The Analytic Hierarchy Approach.* Pp. xi, 252. New York: Praeger, 1989. $49.95.

SADARANANDA, DANA V. *Beyond Stalingrad: Manstein and the Operations of Army Group Don.* Pp. xi, 165. New York: Praeger, 1990. $42.95.

SANDHU, KERNIAL SINGH and PAUL WHEATLEY, eds. *Management of Success: The Moulding of Modern Singapore.* Pp. xxv, 1134. Boulder, CO: Westview Press, 1990. $125.00.

SCHWARTZ, NANCY L. *The Blue Guitar: Political Representation and Community.* Pp. xi, 181. Chicago: University of Chicago Press, 1988. $24.95.

SHAW, RONALD E. *Erie Water West: A History of the Erie Canal 1792-1854.* Pp. xii, 449. Lexington: University Press of Kentucky, 1990. $30.00. Paperbound, $15.00.

SHKLAR, JUDITH N. *The Faces of Justice.* Pp. 144. New Haven, CT: Yale University Press, 1990. $19.95.

SIDDLE, DAVID and KEN SWINDELL. *Rural Change in Tropical Africa: From Colonies to Nation-States.* Pp. 223. Cambridge, MA: Basil Blackwell, 1990. No price.

SINGER, J. DAVID. *Models, Methods, and Progress in World Politics: A Peace Research Odyssey.* Pp. vi, 314. Boulder, CO: Westview Press, 1990. $48.50. Paperbound, $21.95.

SMITH, ERIC R.A.N. *The Unchanging American Voter.* Pp. 283. Berkeley: University of California Press, 1989. $40.00. Paperbound, $13.95.

SNIPP, C. MATTHEW. *American Indians: The First of This Land*. Pp. 448. New York: Russell Sage Foundation, 1989. $49.95.

SOBEL, ROBERT, ed. *Biographical Directory of the United States, Executive Branch, 1774-1989*. Pp. 584. Westport, CT: Greenwood Press, 1990. $75.00.

STEIN, BURTON. *Thomas Munro: The Origins of the Colonial State and His Vision of Empire*. Pp. vi, 374. New York: Oxford University Press, 1990. $32.50.

STUCKEY, MARY E. *Getting into the Game: The Pre-Presidential Rhetoric of Ronald Reagan*. Pp. 216. New York: Praeger, 1989. $37.95.

SYPNOWICH, CHRISTINE. *The Concept of Socialist Law*. Pp. xv, 195. New York: Oxford University Press, 1990. $45.00.

TARAZONA-SEVILLANO, GABRIELA with John B. Reuter. *Sendero Luminoso and the Threat of Narcoterrorism*. Pp. 184. New York: Praeger, 1990. $35.00. Paperbound, $12.95.

TILLY, LOUISE A. and PATRICIA GURIN, eds. *Women, Politics, and Change*. Pp. 688. New York: Russell Sage Foundation, 1990. $45.00.

TIWARI, CHITRA K. *Security in South Asia: Internal and External Dimensions*. Pp. 330. Lanham, MD: University Press of America, 1989. $28.50.

VIGIL, MAURILIO E., MICHAEL OLSEN, and ROY LUJAN. *New Mexico Government and Politics*. Pp. 206. Lanham, MD: University Press of America, 1990. Paperbound, $14.75.

VITAS, ROBERT A. *The United States and Lithuania: The Stimson Doctrine of Nonrecognition*. Pp. vii, 175. New York: Praeger, 1990. $39.95.

WALLACE, WILLIAM. *The Transformation of Western Europe*. Pp. 122. New York: Council on Foreign Relations Press, 1990. Paperbound, $14.95.

WAMSLEY, GARY L. et al. *Refounding Public Administration*. Pp. 333. Newbury Park, CA: Sage, 1990. $39.95.

WHYTE, WILLIAM FOOTE and KATHLEEN KING WHYTE. *Making Mondragon: The Growth and Dynamics of the Worker Cooperative Complex*. Pp. 328. Ithaca, NY: ILR Press, 1988. $36.00. Paperbound, $14.95.

INDEX